To Terri, Steve, David &
Christie —

Best —

Dave Lieber
2004

The Dog of My Nightmares

Stories by Texas Columnist Dave Lieber

ALSO BY DAVE LIEBER

I Knew Rufe Snow Before He Was A Road
(with Tim Bedison)

Give Us A Big Hug
(with Tim Bedison)

THE DOG
of My Nightmares

Stories by
Texas
Columnist
Dave Lieber

 YANKEE COWBOY PUBLISHING

Published in cooperation with the *Fort Worth Star-Telegram*

FIRST EDITION

Yankee Cowboy Publishing
P. O. Box 123
Keller, Texas 76244-0123

For information on Yankee Cowboy Publishing,
contact publisher@yankeecowboy.com or write to the above address.
Phone: (817) 685-3830

Publisher's Note: These stories originally appeared in the *Fort Worth
Star-Telegram*. They are reprinted with permission. The final story in this
collection originally appeared in *The Philadelphia Inquirer.*

ISBN 0-9708530-3-3

Library of Congress Number: 2003104070
PRINTED IN CANADA.

This book is for
Karen Ann Pasciutti Lieber
The woman of my dreams

And for
Sadie Denise Lieber
The dog of my nightmares

A portion of the proceeds from this book will be donated to the Humane Society of North Texas to help pets like Sadie.

The Dog of My Nightmares

Stories by Texas Columnist Dave Lieber

Table of Contents

INTRODUCTION 13

CHAPTER ONE – *The Psycho Dog* 15
Dog's not all I need to fill hole in my life 17
Psycho Dog won't take it lying down 19
Beloved dog has one lesson left to teach 22
Bidding farewell to a 'doggone little dog' 24

CHAPTER TWO – *Karen, My Soul Mate* 27
Matchless act results in perfect match 29
Getting our kicks on old Route 66 31
Loosening the reins on my wife's dream 33
Gala with Bob is a hair-praising experience 36

CHAPTER THREE – *The Teen-agers* 39
Stepdaughter gives daddy a dance lesson 41
Heart of gold turns blue after birthday lapse 43
Greatest gift of all warms a dad's heart 45
Boy's baseball quest teaches important lesson 47
Teen-ager hits detour in effort to get license 50
Her shiny red convertible is a cut above 52
Sharp teen drives point home to dad 54
Columnist's stepson is a hit with his dad 57
In bottom of 9th, a prayer for victory 59
The Blessing is bestowed upon us all 62

CHAPTER FOUR – *Texas Edukation* 65
Education system is failing teachers 67
Keller first-graders educate teacher for a day 69

Zero tolerance means educators cannot practice what they preach . . 72

Educators should serve as examples to students 75

High schools are failing a key test 77

Tough love will be needed to fix our public schools 80

CHAPTER FIVE – *Intolerance, Texas Style* 85

For neighbors, hateful act has opposite effect 87

Maybe by waving hello, we can tell past goodbye 89

Bible Belt can sometimes feel too tight for comfort 92

Colleyville family reaches out to family hurt by bigot 94

CHAPTER SIX – *Austin James Lieber,*
**   *Native Texan*** 99

Fatherhood suddenly has new meaning 101

Little Lieber proud to be born a Texan 103

Motor baby likes 4 a.m. refuelings 104

Discovering the realities of the world 106

Columnist turns into crybaby while taking his first vacation . . 108

Search to find God, like circle, is never-ending 110

3-year-old peruses game of politics at Bush rally in Dallas 113

5-year-old adds a little maturity to governor's race 116

Negative campaigners should try to grow up 118

Some art is a laughing matter 121

CHAPTER SEVEN – *Texas Tales* 125

A dream of a lifetime fulfilled 127

Neil's heroic example had power to move a community 130

Cullen Davis smiles for a jury once again 132

Pizza confession: A one-night stand 135

Argyle students learn a lesson from the evangelist 137

Coach Tagg is winner in game of life 140

A life too long to be reduced to a few words 145

Confronting road bullies 147

74-year-old drives herself with precision 150

Common ground links two strangers 152

Bradshaw gets the fur flying at fund-raiser 155

A pilot's wife keeps home fires burning. 157

Dad taught me life's most important lessons 159

This sermon might heal a Watauga congregation 161

Aunt Edith's history as rich as her dessert 163

CHAPTER EIGHT – *Mom*. 167

Thanks, Mom, for your love and nurturing 169

Seeing Mom through her friend's eyes 170

Life: Priceless piece of the big puzzle. 172

Mom called – it was time to say goodbye 174

Trip home puts past in perspective 176

Paying tribute to a mother who encouraged her son 178

CHAPTER NINE – *September 11* 183

Girl offers uplifting message 185

A nightmare envelopes my father's city of dreams 187

Bids fly high for U.S. flag 189

North Richland Hills firefighter grieves alongside brethren. . . . 192

For those forgotten veterans 194

Explaining an empty sky to a little boy 197

CHAPTER TEN – *The Yankee Cowboy*. 201

Lone-Star crusader has lonely battle 203

Rodeo-speak leaves Yankee fit to be tied 205

More than seven wonders for non-Texas visitor 206

Original Lieber-man feeling left out of party 207

Yankee realizes he's become a cowboy. 210

Proud to fall in with this tough crowd. 213

CHAPTER ELEVEN – *Texas Politicians*. 217

Governor's doing all the right things 219

Officials' dinner perk going stale. 221

Hurst officials take freebies at Texas Stadium. 223

Mayor must mend diploma deception. 226

Haltom municipal judge taking ethics to the edge 229

Politician promotes open, responsive government 232

Stereotypes are hard to overcome – just ask the governor. 235

Nothing fond about farewell to Armey 238

CHAPTER TWELVE – *Writer's Life* 241

Tale touches on triumphs, tears in Texas 243

Columnist's death spurs smile, sorrow. 245

A day reserved for honoring columnists 247

Tune in tomorrow and see columnist fall into video stardom . . 249

An apology simply won't be enough for this mistake 251

For shame on the rush to judgment 252

Turtle's tale a crushing, telling tragedy 254

CHAPTER THIRTEEN – *A Magazine Story* 257

Growing up with Poorboy 259

NOTE FROM THE AUTHOR. 281

ABOUT THE AUTHOR. 285

INTRODUCTION

David Leslie Lieber needs no introduction. But he does need some explaining.

By way of explaining, you need to know that the boy was raised and grew up deep in the heart of – New York – Manhattan, to be precise. Go figure.

While still wet behind the ears – I don't know of a Yankee or Yiddish phrase equivalent for it – he left home. He got a degree in American Civilization from the University of Pennsylvania, where he also began his journalism career writing columns for the student newspaper. He interned on *The Atlanta Journal*, was a feature writer for a small paper in Florida and a statehouse reporter for the *Charleston Gazette* in West Virginia. After a 10-year stint as a reporter for *The Philadelphia Inquirer*, he came to the *Fort Worth Star-Telegram* in 1993 as a columnist. Again, go figure. Not born a Texan, he had the good sense to get here as soon as he could.

If Fort Worth proper – and Cowtown, until recently, has never been long on proper – can be identified as Bassville after the famous billionaire Bass family, then Northeast Tarrant County, which Lieber covers, can certainly be called Perotville after mega developer H. Ross Perot Jr., son of the former presidential candidate. Lieber even lives in a master-planned subdivision created by the Perots. Column writing about the Netroplex – a term popularized by Lieber to identify all the towns in Northeast Tarrant County – became his job, his passion, his obligation and duty. On top of that, columnist Lieber fell in love with Texas – I helped the boy all I could – and made his home in the Netroplex and even named his son Austin after – well, you know who. Once again, go figure.

Because David loves the place, maybe decidedly because he does, and is a Real Columnist, he writes about time and place, characters and events, warts and all. That's dangerous, as every journalist worth his/her salt knows; especially dangerous when giants, or those who think they are, walk the earth and find their stomping grounds invaded by someone listening and taking notes. He took them all on, from Big Business and Perot to every peculiarity of each and every one of the towns within his journalistic jurisdiction. About 50 percent of the constituency loves him; the other 50 percent hates him. That is exactly the right balance for a columnist who tells the truth, highlights issues, strips down, layer by layer, the frictions and factions within a community that bring, if not changes, then serious debate about serious issues.

After a time, columnists by the very nature of their work give opinions and make judgments, get reputations for better or worse. Lieber's reputation is sometimes better but often worse. He takes it all in stride, knowing it is a columnist's obligation to stir things up, shock, surprise, startle. David even refers to his paper, and mine, as the Startle-Gram, just as he labels the competing paper The Dallas Morning Snooze.

It was high time – in fact overdue – that David Leslie Lieber gathered together his timely accounts of timeless subjects. The best are in this book. He writes of the personal, of psycho dogs, about his little boy, Austin, his role as stepfather to Jonathan and Desiree, and husband to Karen. He speaks candidly about religious denominations and practitioners, his profession, politics, folklore and folkways, the state's education system or lack of it, of citizens old and young, good and bad, of pride and prejudice, saints and sons-a-bitches, of 9/11 and the acts of courage and citizenship. His alter ego, Yankee Cowboy, makes fun no more of the foibles of the Lone Star State than about his role in them. He is master satirist. Always he tries to understand and make others understand our strengths and weaknesses as Texans, our attempts at being human and inhuman, the best of times, the worst of times for the best and worst of the Lone Star State. Dave Lieber has shown me more about what it means to be a Texan than I ever knew, and, believe me, I ought to know after five generations on this hallowed ground.

That is all the explanation I'm going to give. Go figure – out the rest for yourselves.

Joyce Gibson Roach
Keller, Texas

Chapter One
The Psycho Dog

*"Yesterday I was a dog. Today I'm a dog.
Tomorrow I'll probably still be a dog. Sigh!
There's so little hope for advancement."*

—Snoopy (Charles Schultz)

Dog's not all I need to fill hole in my life

Here in Texas, I've met the woman of my dreams. Unfortunately, she lives with the dog of my nightmares.

Karen, a woman I've known only six months, is calm and self-assured. A godsend. To me, she easily is the First Lady of Watauga. She lives in Watauga, is first in my life and is very much a lady.

Sadie, a Labrador retriever, is her dog. And she easily is the Last Dog of Watauga. She is last in my life and very much an obstacle. The Psycho Dog.

While Karen and her two children appear to love me very much, Psycho Dog hates and fears me.

Sadie the Psycho Dog

The First Lady, who like me is divorced, rescued the Last Dog at age 6 months from an early life of apparent abuse – probably at the hands of some mean male. At age 2, Sadie is still skittish, hyperactive and impossible to deal with. Karen says the Last Dog is a lot like me.

But Sadie and I share the most important thing: We both love Karen with all the force of life. And we both gather strength from her thoughtful ways and tender hugs. If only the dog and I could get along.

The truth is, I didn't like Sadie. So how could she like me?

With Karen's two children, it didn't appear to matter that I have never been a father. We got along well from the start. No, Sadie was the problem. Karen says there's a hole in my life when it comes to animals, and filling that hole will make me whole.

Before our first date, Karen and I talked on the phone for hours. When I finally picked her up for a formal dinner in Grapevine, we felt like we'd known one another forever.

At the dinner, we sat with some top executives of this newspaper. A little nervous (well, a lot), I began the meal by spilling water on my editor. Not to be outdone, Karen dropped a pitcher of cream on the lap of my publisher. Knowing that the embarrassment was now off of me alone and shared by both of us, Karen turned and gave me a high-five. I knew then that it was love.

That's her style. From the start, we shared everything – unless it was something that Karen could do better. Amazed that it took me three hours to mow my lawn, she bet $20 that she could do it in less than an hour. She clocked in at 49 minutes and 32 seconds.

Then one night, when I had a bad cold, Karen gently applied vapor rub to my chest – a daring act in this age of selfishness. In one stroke, she became my Florence Nightingale of Texas. "I don't want you to call me that," she said. "I want to be *Doctor Karen*."

We both feel that the search of a lifetime is over; we've found each other. And her children appear to feel the same.

Jonathan, who is 10, longs for a stable father figure. He hugs me when he sees me, asks about my day and kisses me good night.

Desiree, who is 12, has opened my eyes to her world of hormones and mood swings that I never knew existed. And she has taught me the language of youth – her favorite expressions being, "Oh, I'm sure!" and "You're pathetic." She hugs me when she sees me and kisses me good night.

And what of Sadie? The runt of her litter, the Last Dog is half-sized, but she has big, expressive eyes and a pretty, white coat. Karen wanted me to get along with Sadie. Karen talked to me about compromise, about meeting Sadie halfway. I tried – to no avail.

Dog bones, canned meat and my special hamburgers didn't do the trick. Sadie ate them all – but showed me no gratitude.

When I called Sadie "Psycho Dog" to her face, Karen warned me to be careful: "She understands you." And Karen reminded me that filling the hole in my life would make me whole.

Finally, one day, I decided to see the world through Sadie's eyes: I was a big, smelly brute who invaded her turf and came between her and her mother. A brute who didn't like her.

So that day, I sat down beside Sadie and told her that I was sorry. Sorry for the way some man had apparently treated her. And sorry for how I hadn't shown her the proper understanding.

"I'll try to love you, Sadie," I said. "We're both lucky that Karen found us. I love you. I love you." I said it over and over. Those big expressive eyes looked up at me, and she licked my face.

Since that day, I always tell Sadie when I'm about to go – so as not to startle her. Karen says, "I'm glad you and Sadie have made peace."

But now I see the hole in my life needs more than just a dog to fill it. Karen, there's something magical about you, me, the girl, the boy – and even your doggone little dog.

I love you Karen. I'll always tell you when I'm about to go – so as not to startle you. And I promise to come back.

I'll always come back.

I want to stay forever. I really do.

Karen, will you marry me?

October 2, 1994

Postscript: Karen said yes. The couple married in February 1995.

The new family

Psycho Dog won't take it lying down

Note: Sadie the Psycho Dog resents her nickname. She is bitter about her recent notoriety in the press and, most of all, despises the new man in her life, columnist Dave Lieber.

In her first public appearance Monday, Sadie was guest speaker at the monthly meeting of the Hurst-Euless-Bedford Retired School Employees group. The Labrador retriever, adorned in an orange-and-black Halloween bandana, was warmly greeted by 43 older adults at the Bedford Senior Citizens Center.

As Sadie sat quietly beside the podium, Lieber read aloud her speech, titled: "The Press: Unfair Not Only to Humans."

Sadie experienced firsthand (uh, paw) what can happen when the press decides to turn someone's private life into a public spectacle. Because of Sadie's efforts to block Lieber's engagement to Karen, her owner and mother, Sadie found herself written about and photographed – without her permission.

Here are Sadie's prepared remarks:

*L*adies and gentlemen, thank you for this opportunity to clear the record. Before I discuss my negative feelings toward the news media, I'd like to publicly thank my mommy, Karen, for rescuing me from a trip back to the pound. Were it not for her, I wouldn't be here today.

Yes, the rumors are true. As a puppy, I was badly abused. I can talk about it now: My first six months were a doggie hell. My name was Lucky then, but my life was anything but. My master – I WAS his slave – kept me locked outside on a patio. I was not allowed inside.

Then one day, after Master talked about sending me back to the pound – oh, how I hate that term – Mommy came by with the two children and they saved me. It was a few days before Christmas. I love my mommy.

But the subject of my talk today is "The Press: Unfair Not Only to Humans." I chose this topic because I have seen up close the unchallenged power of the so-called Fourth Estate. I now firmly believe that the press is a negative force in our society – not only for humans, but for the entire animal kingdom.

In my own situation, for example, not once did the *Fort Worth Star-Telegram* attempt to contact me for my side of the story.

Now my privacy is shot. I face a dreadful future as a dog who "belongs" to a columnist. And everyone knows that when a columnist has nothing to say, he writes about his dog. Already, the Brute – that's what I call him – has written two columns about me.

I am thinking lawsuit.

I want to sue the Brute for character defamation. The nickname Sadie the Psycho Dog is a libelous affront to millions of psychologically challenged dogs in our society. How insensitive.

But what do you expect from the Brute? The first time we met, he chased me around the coffee table five times. Five times! Is he crazy? But I was too fast for him.

One morning last week, the Brute took me to his office. It was my first visit to the Bedford newsroom of the *Star-Telegram*, and I wanted to make it a memorable one. So I went to the bathroom on the office carpet. Ha! I showed those reporters. Take a whiff of that! That's what I think of the news media.

You should have seen it: The Brute ran about like a madman try-ing to clean it up. I loved it! And when he called me over to rub my nose in it and shout "Bad girl!" at me, I didn't come. Instead, I trot-ted over to visit my new friends in advertising. Ha!

I watch the Brute like a hawk. Somebody should. I don't trust him for a second. In his stories about me, he related how he romanced my mommy – and how I supposedly came around to like him after he proposed. What bunk. I'll never like him.

Our family was fine without him. Now mommy favors him over me. I don't see why: he's so uncouth.

I am shocked and amazed that what I believe should essentially be a private family matter – the engagement of my mommy – was publicly portrayed in the press like some public relations stunt. It's quite apparent – our privacy notwithstanding – that the Brute will do *anything* for a column.

Sometimes, he even acts like a dog. How pathetic. The other day, the family chased him around the house – the same as he chases me. Wow! I jumped in and bit the Brute's hand, yanked at his shirt and pawed him flat to the ground. It was exhilarating. My tail wagged so hard I nearly broke a window.

In conclusion, I resent how my life has become a public soap opera. Dogs have feelings, too, you know. Thanks for inviting me, woof, woof, and God bless.

At the conclusion of Sadie's remarks, a show of hands determined that the former teachers overwhelmingly supported her sentiments.

Lois Nixon of Bedford affectionately called Sadie "a real character." Ruth Berrier of North Richland Hills said she believed the dog because, "She has an earnest look on her face."

And Lou Dodson of Hurst opined that press treatment of Sadie's predicament reminded her of the circumstances surrounding the O.J. Simpson case.

October 19, 1994

Beloved dog has one lesson left to teach

Sadie, near the end of her life

The dog of your boyhood, Willie Morris wrote in his book *My Dog Skip*, teaches you a great deal about friendship, about love, and death.

Because I didn't get my first dog until I was 37 years old, I never learned those important lessons until very late. Maybe a little too late.

It took me several years before I allowed Sadie, the little runt of a retriever who came in a package deal with my wife and two stepchildren, to teach me those lessons about friendship and love. The lesson about death, I fear, is coming soon.

Sadie, the only dog I ever had, the only dog I ever loved, is dying.

You first met this little pooch when I introduced her in a 1994 column in which I proposed marriage to my future wife, Karen. I introduced her as Sadie the Psycho Dog, the dog of my nightmares who was doing her doggone best to come between me and my intended new family.

While Karen and her two children appeared to love me very much, Psycho Dog hated and feared me. She was 2 years old when I met her, and from the start, she couldn't stand the sight of me.

Until my arrival, she was quite happy with the way things were. There were no men around to torment her. From her point of view, I ruined everything.

Apparently, I reminded Sadie of her initial owner, an Irving man who abused her without mercy before Karen and the kids rescued her. Sadie wanted nothing to do with me, running in circles to avoid me, yapping at my ankles, secreting a strange and horrible odor from her glands that was designed to push me away. All of this behavior worked exceedingly well.

With no prior dog experience, I was as confused and hurt as she was. During the wedding, when the judge looked around and asked if anyone had any objection, I stole a worried glance at Sadie, who fortunately wasn't paying attention.

Yet for all these difficulties, Sadie was a lovely dog, with big expressive eyes that told you everything you needed to know about her mood and opinions. Those eyes looked upon me with scorn and unending annoyance.

As a cure for the situation, Karen had the idea that if Sadie were to spend more time with me, she would grow to like me and vice versa. That began an eight-year relationship between the dog and me that remains as tortured as any Elizabeth Taylor marriage.

I walk and feed her. Give her treats and toys. Take her to the doctor. Keep her company by day, when she lies beneath my desk, and at night, when I drag out her bed and place it beside ours. Yet she is loyal to only one: Sadie lives for Karen's approval and nothing more.

I understand that Sadie is scarred by her early days as an abused puppy. I can see how she resents the way I interrupted her family when I joined the party. And I know that retrievers in general are said to remain loyal to only one.

Yet perhaps because she is the first dog I ever had, I am fascinated by her every move and quirk. I watch her day and night and talk to her constantly, even if she ignores me. I keep hoping that deep down, she understands that despite our rough start, our tortured middle and our apparently difficult ending, she knows that I love her.

But now I worry about her constantly. These worries began a year ago, when I thought her allergy problems were worse than usual. She is almost 10 years old, and it's not uncommon for older dogs in this region to suffer from breathing difficulties in the springtime. I took her to the doctor, who gave her a shot. She appeared to get better.

By Christmas, it became evident that she was getting worse. Her condition had deteriorated to where she sneezed constantly and coughed up blood. But after we visited the doctor again and discussed the possibilities, she suddenly became better. Her recovery began on Christmas morning, so we called it a Christmas miracle.

Now she is suffering again. Her breathing is labored, and there is a growing bump on her nose that doctors say could be a nasal tumor. She is losing weight, too.

This week, we took her to a Southlake animal hospital, where the doctor said there was a nine out of 10 chance that she has cancer.

We are faced with many options, the last of which I cannot bear to write here. Next week, I will take her to a cancer specialist in Dallas.

I no longer call her Psycho Dog, because it is a term of disrespect for a family member whom I have come to admire. Actually, I had given her the formal name of Sadie Denise Lieber after my mother, who died of cancer in 1996. The sad irony is that Mom's canine namesake may leave us in much the same way.

So here I am at 44 years old, and I fear that something is about to occur that usually happens to most people during their childhood years. I am about to lose my first and only dog I ever loved.

Sadie has already taught me about friendship and love. Now there appears to be one sad lesson left for me to learn.

April 5, 2002

Bidding farewell to a 'doggone little dog'

Sadie the Psycho Dog, a retriever who belonged to *Star-Telegram* columnist Dave Lieber and his family, died of cancer this month at the Animal Clinic of Watauga. She was 9.

Sadie was introduced to the public in a 1994 column by Dave called "Dog's not all I need to fill hole in my life."

On the surface, the column was about Dave's troubled relationship with his girlfriend's dog. It began, "Here in Texas, I've met the woman of my dreams. Unfortunately, she lives with the dog of my nightmares."

Detailing Dave's relationship with Karen and her family, the column continued, "While Karen and her two children appear to love me very much, Psycho Dog hates and fears me." The column ended with a surprise marriage proposal to Karen, the children and "your doggone little dog."

The column generated tremendous reader response and earned Dave the top prize the next year in a writing contest sponsored by the National Society of Newspaper Columnists.

After that debut, Dave and Sadie embarked on a string of public appearances. Sadie played the role of America's premier canine press critic, but it was not an act. She really didn't like Dave, whom she called "The Brute."

In their first appearance, before the Hurst-Euless-Bedford Retired School Employees group, Sadie sat nearby as Dave read a speech on the dog's behalf titled, "The Press: Unfair Not Only to Humans."

Sadie recounted the details of her early life. A family in Irving had abused her until Karen and her children rescued her a few days before Christmas 1992 when she was 6 months old. To give her a fresh start, Karen changed the dog's name from Lucky to Sadie.

In that speech, Sadie also told how during her first visit to the *Star-Telegram* with Dave, she went to the bathroom on the newsroom carpet.

"Ha!" the text of her speech stated. "I showed those reporters. Take a whiff of that! That's what I think of the news media."

In an attempt to improve their relationship, Dave and Sadie enrolled in a dog obedience class at North Richland Hills Recreation Center. The course was taught by Ernie Barr, an 82-year-old who took one look at the pair and commented, "We've got a lot of ground to cover."

Months later, Dave and Sadie appeared at Mutt & Strutt '95, an event sponsored by the Humane Society of North Texas. The pair entered a costume contest dressed as bride and groom. Sadie wore a lace wedding veil, and Dave wore a tuxedo.

At that event, Sadie sat next to Island Girl, a well-known German shepherd who had lived on a median near Interstate 30 and Texas 183 in west Fort Worth before she was rescued, becoming – like Sadie – a role model for pet adoptions. As Sadie sniffed Island Girl, Island Girl snapped at Sadie's face. Both dogs barked and glared before Dave moved Sadie to a neutral corner.

Dave and Sadie's next public appearance went much better. On the eve of the 1996 debut of her new Web site, Sadie's Backyard, Sadie appeared before 400 students at Shady Grove Elementary School in Keller to deliver a speech called "What a Dog Can Teach About Reading and Writing."

Sadie's Web site on StarText.net garnered nationwide attention. Hers was one of the nation's first pet Web sites, and she used it to communicate with other animals. The *Star-Telegram* heavily promoted Sadie's Backyard, which caused Dave to grow jealous because his Web site was not nearly as popular.

With her popularity growing, Sadie was the featured attraction at a July 1996 event at the Barnes & Noble bookstore in North Richland Hills. More than 100 people attended the *Star-Telegram* event, which was promoted in newspaper advertisements that announced, "Come Meet Dave and Sadie." More than half of those who attended said they cared only about meeting the dog.

Not long after that, Sadie retreated from the public eye, and her appearances in Dave's column became rare.

Several weeks ago, after Dave wrote a column revealing Sadie's illness, she returned to the keyboard and responded to a flurry of sympathetic e-mails with a message that included the following:

"I don't feel quite comfortable with my illness being paraded in the newspaper. I knew something was up when Dave made me sit with him as he wrote that column. He started crying as he wrote it, but he wouldn't read it to me, which is fine because I usually don't like his stuff anyway."

She continued, "I wasn't pleased. I am a private dog. I retired from public life several years ago to spend more time with my family. But for some reason, Dave insists on trotting me out every so often for a column. He is a desperate man, always looking for something to fill his space in the paper. But I get no residuals, so what good does public exposure do for me?"

At Sadie's passing, Dave was by her side. Afterward, amid the tears, Karen told Dave, "You owe her everything. She put you on the map."

Sadie was buried April 18 at Pine Hill Cemetery in Bowie. That is the day recognized each year by the National Society of Newspaper Columnists as National Columnists Day. Dave was instrumental in helping to create that day in 1995 as a way to call attention to the role of newspaper columnists in society. April 18 is the day that legendary newspaper columnist Ernie Pyle was killed in World War II.

Sadie's survivors include Karen; Dave; their children, Desiree, Jonathan and Austin; two cats, Terry Bradshaw and Anastasia; and grandparents, John and Joan Pasciutti of Keller.

The family asks that in lieu of flowers, donations be sent in Sadie's memory to the Humane Society of North Texas, 1840 E. Lancaster Ave., Fort Worth, TX 76103, so other pets may get adopted and receive a second chance similar to Sadie's.

April 28, 2002

Chapter Two
Karen, My Soul Mate

"Well, if you ever want to motor west;
travel my way, take the highway that's the best.
Get your kicks on Route 66!"

— Songwriter Bobby Short

Matchless act results in perfect match

Patti Smith

*T*he deed performed by Patti Smith is so big, so monumental that *Woman of the Year*, *Woman of the Decade* or even *Woman of the Century* doesn't quite cut it.

So, on a recent night as lightning filled the sky – but there was no rain – Smith was named *Woman of the Millennium*.

An award given every 1,000 years. Lightning strikes. And now the engraved plaque hangs on her wall.

Patti does unending charity work. She delivers meals to senior citizens, serves as secretary of the Keller library board and leads the Greater Keller Women's Club. But her volunteer work had never touched off lightning strikes.

To understand why she won this award, you have to know the story of how Patti Smith came to be crouched behind a parked car early one morning in Watauga, just before sunrise, waiting for a horse.

You have to know why Patti clutched her black riding helmet under her arm and waited, along with a man, who also crouched behind a car, for the horse to arrive from Grapevine.

The man, whom Patti barely knew, kept telling her that the horse was due any moment. So Patti and the man crouched because they didn't want a certain woman, just awakening in a house across the street, to see them. It was part of a grand birthday surprise, and Patti waited because she had a stake in it.

But the horse never showed.

Patti knew the woman inside the house from the Keller women's club. The woman, divorced with two children, had told Patti that she had given up on men. "Just my kids and myself," the woman said. "And a dog and two cats. I don't need a man in my life. I've made it on my own."

But Patti didn't believe her.

If Patti had walked away, if she had listened to her husband, Dave Smith, who had warned her that in this day and age, it wasn't smart to fix up two people you barely knew... then there would be no *Woman of the Millennium.*

But Patti said to the woman, "I know someone who'd be perfect for you." And she said to the man, "I know someone who'd be perfect for you."

At a luncheon, Patti introduced the man to the woman. Then she stepped aside.

Lightning struck – the kind without rain.

And much to Patti's surprise, the woman and the man fell in love with each other.

The man often called Patti to thank her profusely for helping change the course of his life. As a gesture of appreciation, he invited Patti, who owns a quarter horse, to accompany him to the woman's house for that early morning birthday surprise. "Bring your riding helmet," said the man, envisioning birthday rides around the neighborhood.

The woman in the house had confided to the man that she dreamed of owning a horse. And the man, starry-eyed and in love, wanted to make her dream come true – even if only for a rented hour.

So the man booked the horse at a stable in Grapevine. And at the appointed hour, he and Patti crouched behind a car and waited. Patti had a stake in it.

But the horse never showed.

When the man finally gave up and knocked on the woman's door to wish her happy birthday, he told his pitiful story – and Patti's presence in the doorway, smiling sheepishly and clutching her riding helmet, proved the man's far-fetched tale of love to be true.

So on a recent night as lightning filled the sky – but there was no rain – the man and the woman were guests at an evening meeting of the Keller women's club, where they were invited to tell the story of how the club president had taken a risk, and how it had paid off. After their talk, the woman and the man gave Patti an award of gratitude.

Last night, the woman and the man stood by the fireplace in their new Northeast Tarrant County home, and before a small gathering of family members, the two were married. Patti Smith and her husband were the only nonfamily members in attendance.

I guess you could call this my wedding day announcement. By the time you read this, the woman and the man – Karen and me – will be married. But really, this is in gratitude to Patti Smith of Keller for arranging the greatest day of our lives.

She took a chance. Lightning struck. And now the engraved plaque hangs on her wall:

> *Woman of the Millennium*
> *To Patti Smith*
> *Eternal thanks,*
> *Karen and Dave*

February 19, 1995

Get your kicks
on Route 66

Getting our kicks on old Route 66

ALONG HISTORIC ROUTE 66 – "If only your friends at the Greater Keller Women's Club could see you now," I told Karen as she drove our little rental car through the red rocks of New Mexico.

Teasing her, I said in my best women's club voice: "She could have spent an extra afternoon shopping in Santa Fe, but, no-o-o-o, instead he's got her doing a U-turn in a Stuckey's parking lot."

This was our honeymoon, after all. Instead, at my behest, she had just made a U-turn to drive past a sign that warned:

Dead End
3 Miles Ahead

But that U-turn was one of the most tender expressions of love anyone has ever shown me. It proved her willingness to accept the part of me that's determined to go where I'm not supposed to go, and maybe once I get there, see things I'm not supposed to see.

From past experience, this natural curiosity of mine doesn't always jibe with the difficult art of marriage.

For most people, a sign saying, "Dead End, 3 Miles Ahead" is a warning to turn back, not an invitation to some preserved and enchanted place.

So when I asked Karen to make a U-turn onto the little two-lane road that stripped alongside Interstate 40, I wasn't sure she'd say yes.

She did.

The little road seemed nearly forgotten. It was still passable – but it had cracks and overgrown weeds.

Why bother? Especially with the interstate highway right next door.

But the little road was old U.S. 66 . . . Route 66 . . . once the Main Street of America.

Officially, there hasn't been a Route 66 since the last portion was decommissioned 10 years ago in Arizona and replaced by Interstate 40. The signs are gone, and the road maps no longer show a U.S. 66.

Once the main road west, stretching from Chicago to the Santa Monica Pier in California, Route 66 is still alive in souvenirs, books and, mostly, the memories of three generations of Americans.

Too many Dust Bowl refugees in the Depression, military men and women during World War II, and tourists in the 1950s and '60s traveled this treasured roadway to have it vanish. *If you ever want to motor west; travel my way, take the highway that's the best. Get your kicks on Route 66!*

Still, a honeymoon is not the time for misadventure. We did the usual tourist stuff. Visited Pueblo Indian ruins. Ate dinner at the Pink Adobe in Santa Fe. Admired the purple mountains' majesty of the New Mexico mesas. But I'll always remember that sign outside the Stuckey's parking lot:

Dead End

3 Miles Ahead

A warning to some, an invitation to me.

The nearby buildings fronted the old road, not the new interstate highway. *Old Route 66!!*

Two roads diverged in a wood, Robert Frost wrote. *I took the one less traveled by, and that has made all the difference.*

So I asked Karen to make the U-turn, but I wasn't sure she'd say yes. She did.

Before Karen, I knew only women who warned "Turn back" or "Slow down" – even when it wasn't necessary.

No longer.

We drove peacefully down the little road, knowing there was nothing but a memory waiting on the other end. The big rigs and the tourists whizzed by us on the interstate, but we took our sweet time on the road with no signs.

Finally, at the dead end, we stepped out and stood by a mound of dirt.

"Did you get your kicks on Route 66?" Karen asked. And she laughed in a carefree way that I'll always remember.

We took the road less traveled by, and that has made all the difference.

March 5, 1995

Loosening the reins on my wife's dream

Karen Lieber

My wife wants a horse.

"You can't have a horse," I said.

"Why not?"

"Because we live in a subdivision," I said.

"My dream has always been to have a horse," Karen said.

Our youngest, Austin James, a 3-year-old meteor who never flames out, was listening.

"Daddy, I want a horse, too," he said. "Let's get a horse today, OK?"

"Listen," I said to both of them. "A horse costs money. If you and Mommy want a horse, then Austin, you need to get a job."

"Can I get a job today, Daddy?"

"You'll get one when you turn 16 years old."

"Is that tomorrow?"

"No, that's in 13 years. Until then, no horse."

* * *

That was a few months ago. Now I look back on the conversation and realize that I was the dream killer.

If Karen dreams about a horse and she lives in Texas where more than a few people have one, why can't she have a horse?

If Austin James, the only native Texan in the family, wants to own a horse and be true to his heritage, who am I to stop him?

I didn't figure this out on my own. You might say that a higher power nudged me along.

Several weeks ago, doctors were alarmed to learn that Karen's heart beats slowly, sometimes too slowly. When she sleeps, her heart stops for several long seconds.

A nurse who saw Karen's test results telephoned her in a panic. Stop driving, she said. Lie down and rest. Come see the doctor first thing in the morning.

"This is nothing new," Karen told me. "There is nothing wrong with me. This is how my heart beats."

She had a major heart operation when she was 5. It was a success, and Karen is healthy. But she knows that her heart beats slowly. She knows that one day she might need further medical attention.

We met with doctors. She underwent more tests. There were a few anxious nights as we wondered whether she would need a pacemaker.

In the end, the doctors did what Karen hoped they would. They did nothing. They understand that her heart is not like most but that it gets the job done.

During this period, though, something unexpected happened to me. When I saw Karen, worried about her heart because doctors were worried, I saw her in a different way.

She was sitting atop her horse, enjoying the rest of her long life.

*   *   *

Three years ago, Karen said she wanted to move to a house with more land. I said "no." You know, the dream killer.

In recent weeks, I have become a changed man. The dream maker. When I told Karen about my sudden reversal, she asked whether I felt OK.

As I began to see it, if Dell Computer builds its planned service center at Alliance, other computer-related industries will move here, and land values will soar.

I figured how much I would make living in my house for five more years and how much I would make living on a miniature ranch near Haslet or Northlake during the same time.

The difference was impressive enough that I quickly began seeing myself on a horse, too. Her dream was now my dream. I even visited a boot store.

Besides, the other reason has to do with Karen. Life is too short, and I love her.

*   *   *

We looked at a 5-acre lot in a rural subdivision in Northlake. The lot was on a small hill, and we could imagine the wonderful sunsets. That is about the time I visited the boot store.

A week later, we traveled west and found the housing boom in the Haslet area. Large houses with luxury features in a price range that young families can afford. And most lots offer enough land for a horse!

We were riding high – until we checked with our school district and learned the residency rules. Our son Jonathan would have to transfer to another district. That is not a topic for discussion because Jon is committed to his school and, especially, to its baseball team. We respect his desire for stability.

After he graduates, however, we're gone.

*   *   *

Every week, my wife has a new plan to get us closer to the dream.

Two weeks ago, Karen planned to install wood floors to increase the resale value while we waited for Mr. Baseball to finish his high school career.

Then last week, Karen announced her latest plan. We are not going to make major home improvements. Why? Because we are moving, she said, to another part of the school district.

She says we will paint our house, clean the carpets, plant flowers and sell it for a neat profit.

We will then buy another house, allowing Mr. Baseball to maintain his residency. While he hits home runs, we will fix up the new place, and maybe near his graduation day, sell that house for another neat profit.

Then we could move to the country.

And get the horse.

As part of that scenario, last week we selected a favored house plan in a development about a mile away. But of course, that was last week's plan. I do not know what Karen will want to do this week.

Whatever it is, I am ready in my new role as the dream maker.

Life is too short. I love her. And two hearts beat quicker than one.

March 11, 2001

Gala with Bob is a hair-praising experience

Unexpectedly, I went on a date Saturday night with my wife, Karen, and also Bob.

Funny the way this started. One moment, I was tooling down Airport Freeway without a care in the world. A free man on a Saturday afternoon. Then the cellphone rang. Karen was calling from home.

"Honey," she began. "Want to go out on a date tonight?"

"Sure," I said. "Where to?"

"The Heart Gala," she replied.

I gasped. A ticket to the benefit for the American Heart Association, Northeast Tarrant Division, cost $150. It's a great cause but an expensive night.

"Don't worry," Karen said. "Kelley Herring has two extra tickets. Call her and tell her we're going. Then come home and change into your tuxedo because we leave in an hour, OK?"

"But you know I don't like galas," I said.

"Listen," Karen said, "I was a model in the fashion show this morning, and everybody tells me my hair looks great. So we're going out tonight, OK?"

"Uh, OK."

I called Herring, the *Star-Telegram/Northeast* marketing director. When I started to complain, Herring scolded me.

"You need to take her out!" she said. "Besides, her hair looks great!"

Huh?

"You know, her hair," Herring said. "She looks amazing. You do know what I'm talking about, don't you?"

"Uh, sure," I said.

Really, I didn't. I knew that my wife had a haircut earlier in the week by the Queen of Hair, Rebecca Boles at Healing Hands Day Spa in Hurst. It was a lovely haircut.

Also, I knew that Karen was a model that morning in the Greater Keller Women's Club fashion show. Maybe somebody did something to her hair before the show while I stayed at home with the kids.

Looking back now, I say to myself, "Uh, duh."

I forgot the rule whereby a woman does not walk out on a fashion runway unless somebody does something to her hair.

In Karen's case, that somebody was Candace Smith of Terrace Retreat Salon and Day Spa in Colleyville. She introduced Karen to Bob.

"Like my hair, honey?" my wife asked when I arrived home.

Whoa! Her hair was layered and lifted so artfully. My already lovely wife was suddenly Miss Eye Candy.

"What style is that?" I asked.

"It's called the layered bob."

"The what?"

"The layered bob."

So that is how Karen, Bob and I went to the gala.

I'm not a gala guy. I don't dance. I don't bid in live auctions. There is not a lot I can do at these things. But this night at the Renaissance Worthington Hotel in Fort Worth, there was not much pressure.

Karen's real date was Bob.

Moments after we entered, a woman neither of us knew walked up to Karen and said, "My daughter wants your hair."

To me, that sounded like a potential scalping. The two women, understanding the secret code of women, began chatting about Bob. That moment, as I stood looking at my shoes, I realized that Bob was taking over.

Throughout the night, women approached Karen to talk about Bob. When Karen was busy talking to one woman, another walked up to me and said, "I just love her hair."

"You mean Bob?" I said.

Karen and I sat at the *Star-Telegram* table. Herring told Karen how much she liked Bob. Janet Carroll Richardson, the community relations manager, commented about Bob. Then Joy Donovan, who writes the Out & About column about these galas, asked Karen how Bob spells his name.

While I was sitting at the table, watching Bob shine in the candlelight, my initial jealousy about Bob was replaced by an inner peace that I had never felt at a gala, wedding or bar mitzvah. I realized that if Karen wanted to dance, she could dance with Bob. If Karen wanted conversation, she could talk to somebody about Bob. I was there for the ride.

I hope that Bob enjoyed the gala. He didn't eat much and didn't bid on anything.

But aside from Colleyville Mayor Donna Arp and two space creatures hired by party organizers for the "2001: A Heart Odyssey" theme, nobody attracted as much attention as Bob.

I think that Arp liked the hairstyle, too.

In a hall, the mayor, who is running for re-election, looked at my wife and turned to me.

"Karen is far too attractive to be married to you," Arp said.

"I'm going to put that in the paper," I told the mayor, explaining that I was doing a column on Bob.

"That's OK," Arp said. "I'll say it again. Karen is far too attractive to be married to you."

Her opponent, Councilman Mike Taylor, worked another part of the ballroom and was unavailable to comment on Bob.

As we prepared to leave, Karen said, "You wouldn't believe the people who came up to me tonight to talk about my hair. That was great. I got the oomph I needed."

I wanted to thank Bob, but I never got the chance.

The next morning, when Karen woke up, he was gone.

March 20, 2001

Chapter Three
The Teen-agers

*"Insanity is hereditary. You can get it
from your children."*

— Comedian Sam Levinson

Stepdaughter gives daddy a dance lesson

Young Desiree

A little girl has entered my life – only she's not so little. Desiree Lauren is 12 years old, but at 5-foot-9, she's already an inch taller than me. She looks down at me and calls me "Little Man."

This is my future.

In a matter of days, I will marry her mother, but I can't help but feel I am marrying Desiree and her brother, too.

Her 10-year-old brother still looks up to me. He's quite simple, actually, when compared with the giant 12-year-old who calls me "Little Man."

I never had a sister, and I didn't have a girlfriend when I was 12. So I really know nothing about preteen girls. Nothing.

Worse, my future stepdaughter is incredibly like me: We share the same initials, fight over Oreos and don't like to be told what to do. We're both left-handed, and thus a little clumsy. We're both get-in-the-last-word people, so our arguments tend to go on forever.

A female version of me. Scary.

Lately, she keeps telling me that after I marry her mother, she will smooth out my rough edges.

And she's not kidding. She can do it. Here's a recent note she wrote me:

I think you should take Mom's advice about washing your hands after you read your newspapers. Because we don't want to clean the counters every time you read …. If you have any questions, talk to me in private!!! Desiree.

Last weekend, I escorted her to the Daddy-Daughter Valentine Dance at North Richland Hills Recreation Center. Of course, I knew I'd be the only daddy dwarfed by his dance partner.

Desiree looked beautiful in her corsage, baggy green sweater and red kilt skirt. She could be a model or an actress. Last year, she won the local Facefinders National Model Search and went to Palm Springs, Calif., for the national convention. When she met an agent scouting for Cybill Shepherd's new television show, the agent asked, "Would you like to try out for Cybill's daughter?"

"No, I'm not interested in acting," my future stepdaughter said. Later, when she realized what she had done, she cried a lot of tears in that dry desert.

In the hours before the daddy-daughter dance, Desiree and I argued about stupid things. Nothing new for us. But as we left the house, her mother warned her: "Don't call him 'Little Man.' Don't argue. Don't put him down in front of people."

My future.

At the dance, we argued. She wanted to lead. I explained how the man leads.

"Noooooooo!" she shouted. "I can't dance like that!"

All the other couples quietly danced, but our argument continued. (At least she didn't call me "Little Man.")

I wish I could tell you that we bonded over Elvis and the Beatles. But the truth is, she ran into a friend from her old school, and they had a lot of catching up to do. We danced some, but I also sat and talked to her friend's father.

He pointed to the girl Desiree was talking to, his daughter, and said: "She's 12 going on 18 – or at least she thinks and acts like she is. It scares me to death.

"And lately, there's been this 15-year-old creep calling, and I don't know what to do. If you forbid it, they do it anyway. So I don't know what to do."

He looked at me, half-expecting some advice, I think. Because he saw I had a daughter, Desiree, he figured I must know something. I didn't say anything.

That was the first time I had ever talked to another father about our daughters, and I was totally bewildered. I know nothing about preteen girls. Nothing.

When we got home from the dance, she gave her mother a full report: "It was a success," Desiree said, as I listened insecurely from the next room. "No fighting. No crying."

Maybe it doesn't matter that I don't know anything. Maybe things will work themselves out through common sense – hers and mine. All I know is, I love the big little girl in a way I never loved a child before.

And she says she loves her Little Man.

Hey David, I just wanted to tell you that I'm going to miss you tomorrow. I also have a present for you. I got it at the book fair …. Can you take us to school tomorrow? Love, Desiree.

The other night, when she and her brother were docked from watching television, she baked a chocolate cake that tasted so good, the only way to thank her for its arrival on the kitchen counter was to say the words that every child wants to hear: "OK, you can watch TV again."

She looked down at me, smiled and said: "Thank you for letting me watch TV. Thank you for letting me bake a cake. And thank you for letting me be myself!"

Then she pinched my cheeks. The old rule was, nobody looks down at me and pinches my cheeks. But this was Desiree, my new daughter. And I kinda liked it.

Still, I know nothing about preteen girls. Nothing. But Desiree's mother keeps telling me that my fatherly instincts aren't too far off. She says that letting Desiree be herself is the greatest Valentine's Day gift I could give our daughter.

February 12, 1995

Heart of gold turns blue after birthday lapse

Young Jonathan

*I*n the days preceding his 11th birthday, the boy became obsessed with details about the United Parcel Service.

When does the truck come? Can I open the front door for a delivery? Will I have to sign anything?

Several times, the boy's stepfather came down the stairs and saw him sitting midway with his chin in his hands and his elbows on his knees. He was waiting for the UPS truck. Waiting for a birthday gift from his biological father.

The boy is blond-haired and blue-eyed, the perfect young sportsman, with a heart of gold, as good as they come.

He doesn't call his stepfather "Dad," probably because if he did it would acknowledge the loss of his biological father, who lives about 1,500 miles away. The boy has seen him once in two years.

They talk on the telephone sporadically. In one recent conversation, the biological father asked the boy what he wanted for his birthday. The boy told him about a fancy electronic game. The father said he would see what he could do.

Thus began the stakeout of the UPS truck. Every day, the boy waited with his chin in his hands.

On his birthday, the boy complained of a sore throat and a headache. He took the day off from school. This allowed him to maintain a minute-by-minute vigil on the stairway, with close access to the phone.

But the phone didn't ring. And the UPS truck didn't come. There was no card in the mail, either. That night, the boy went to bed without the one thing he wanted most.

The next day, the biological father called with birthday greetings from 1,500 miles away. The boy acted as if nothing were wrong.

The father called again later, but this time, the boy's mother answered.

"Why didn't you call him on his birthday?" she asked quickly.

"I did," he replied. "I called him this morning."

"Since when is his birthday on the 30th?" she asked. "His birthday is the 29th!"

The father had forgotten his son's birthday. When he apologized to the boy, the boy quickly excused him.

"That's OK," the boy kept saying. "That's OK. That's OK. That's OK."

Perhaps the boy wanted it to be OK, because it hurt so much to admit that his father had forgotten something so important.

But certainly, it was not OK.

A father should never forget a child's birthday. The stepfather wishes the father would get more involved in the boy's life. The perfect young sportsman with a heart of gold, this boy is a father's pride.

The stepfather feels quite lucky, actually. And he reinforced that with the boy after his birthday.

"I love you and I'll try to be the best dad that I can be," he said.

The boy put his arm around the man, smiled and called him "my beloved David."

And maybe with time, one day, he'll call me Dad.

September 5, 1995

Greatest gift of all warms a dad's heart

Desiree, in her teens

When I have flashbacks about my daughter's life, they don't begin – like those of most fathers – on the day she was born.

I didn't meet Desiree Lauren Bertschinger until she was 11 years old.

She was nearly formed, with messy closets, strong opinions and high ideals.

So I must skip ahead a few songs on her life's album to her middle school cheerleading days ... singing in the high school choir ... first days of driving ... graduation day from high school.

My flashbacks are snippets of a little girl grown big, a girl who does not hear from her biological father, a man who lost the only important things he ever had – a terrific wife, Karen; a great daughter, Des; and a wonderful son, Jonathan. And he lost them all to me.

After I married Karen, Desiree went through a brief period where she tormented me. Once I asked her why, and she said, "I want to see if you are going to stay."

There's no genetic link between us, but there are similarities. She is left-handed and a little clumsy. Like me. She's also a back-talker. Like me. (Our arguments have no endings.) We both love practical jokes.

People see her with me and do double takes because she is 2 inches taller. I explain that she's my stepdaughter, and they say, "Oh, that makes sense."

Fortunately, Desiree no longer uses her original nickname for me, "Little Man."

Until recently, she called me David. In the past year, however, she began calling me "Daddy." Maybe she's making up for lost time.

Exactly a month ago, on her 18th birthday, my present to her was not something that fits in any box. There was no gift-wrapping or fancy bow. It is not something you usually give to another person.

Our family, including Karen's parents, John and Joan Pasciutti of Keller, gathered in the living room, and I handed Des a brown envelope.

Des cut her finger on the envelope's metal clasp, then accidentally let go of a helium balloon she was holding. A big frown spread across her face.

I remember the frown because of what happened next. Her face changed dramatically as she pulled a document out of the envelope and began reading it. She smiled, turned to me and said, "Thank you!"

Then she began crying. She brought her hand to her mouth, then covered her eyes. Tears toppled onto the document.

Karen hugged her. Austin, her 3-year-old brother, asked, "Why is she crying?"

I put my arm around her and explained, "All you have to do is take this to a notary public and sign it. We mail it back to the lawyer. And then she files it in court and it becomes official."

Des read the document again:

Original Petition for Change of Name of Adult

Petitioner requests the Court to grant a change of Petitioner's name to Desiree Lauren Lieber.

The reason for the requested change is that Petitioner wants the same last name as her mother and stepfather.

A few legal words on two sheets of paper. The start of the second side of songs on her life's album.

"You and I need to get dual bathrobes with our initials mono-grammed on them!" I joked.

See, we both would be DLL.

In the weeks that followed, Des practiced signing her name the way a bride practices before her wedding.

Desiree Lauren Lieber.

Desiree Lauren Lieber.

At the Tarrant County Courthouse on Thursday, my father-in-law and I made a side bet over which woman in the family – Des, Karen or Joan – would cry first at the hearing. Silly me. I let him pick Des.

"All rise, please," the bailiff said.

"Thank you. Be seated," Judge Frank Sullivan said.

The bailiff looked out and called, "The Bertschinger case."

Desiree walked with our family lawyer, Lori A. Spearman of Grapevine, to the judge's bench.

"Are you Desiree Lauren Bertschinger?" Spearman asked her for what would be the last time she could legally say yes.

"Yes."

"Are you 18 years old?"

"Yes."

"Tell me," Spearman said, rolling through the required questions, "have you ever been convicted of a felony?"

At that moment, Desiree burst out crying. The lawyer told me later that she thought that maybe Desiree was hiding a criminal record.

Actually, though, Desiree suddenly realized what was happening.

The judge asked, "Why do you want your name changed?"

Desiree turned, pointed at me in the front row and answered, "Because that's my rightful father."

Thinking about it a few days later, I'm certain that those are the five greatest words anyone has ever said about me.

Desiree was the one who received the new name. But now I see that I am the one who actually received the greater gift.

She gets the name, but I get a daughter.

Desiree Lauren Lieber. Desiree Lauren Lieber. What an honor.

For me. Her rightful father.

September 17, 2000

Boy's baseball quest teaches important lesson

Jon at bat

There comes a moment when a boy becomes a man. Fathers usually do not get to witness such a moment. I was lucky.

I was there at 2:40 p.m. Monday when my son, Jonathan, stepped across the threshold. It wasn't so much what happened at that moment. It was how hard he worked to get there.

You have watched Jonathan grow in this column from a pip-squeak 9-year-old when I first met him and married his mother to a towering 6-foot-4-inch high school sophomore sandwiched between the twin terrors of an older sister and a toddler brother. Poor guy.

He has logged more hours baby-sitting his little brother than any 16-year-old I know. He vacuums once a day, does his laundry and rarely talks back. Nowadays, what more could a father ask?

Outside of family, the only thing he cares about is sports. He knows every player on every team in every major sport. Like ESPN, he is all sports, all the time.

Not surprisingly, Jonathan wants to be a professional baseball player.

He and 20 million others.

The most trying times in our stepfather-stepson relationship have revolved around my trying to show him that if he wanted to make anything of himself, he had to get off the couch, stay away from the television and the video games, and actually live a life dedicated to the pursuit of his dream.

He had to work, study and plan. He had to hustle and be happy doing it. In his case, he had to love the game of baseball more than anything.

Oh, and he had to give up football and basketball.

When I first suggested this a year ago in our household, my wife treated this talk as heresy. As a single mom, Karen had trained Jonathan for football in a manner that would have made Pop Warner proud.

Jonathan played great football, but he didn't love the game. He was the only 11-year-old on his team in the Bronco-league Super Bowl, a game played in mud and rain, who didn't get his white uniform dirty. Jonathan is a finesse player.

Whenever I brought up specializing in one sport, Karen would say, "But my dream has always been to see him play high school football."

I could tell the only reason that he planned to play sophomore football was to please Karen.

But one night, when our family was at a restaurant, everyone went to the powder room except Jonathan and me.

I pulled my chair close so I could look him in the eye.

"I know you are only playing football for Mom," I said.

He didn't answer.

"But you are the athlete. You play the game. Not her. What do you want to do?"

"I want to play baseball," he said.

"Why don't you?"

He answered with a torrent of emotions and fears. He didn't want to disappoint Mom. The football coach would be ticked at him. His friends who played football might not like him anymore.

I told him we could work all that out.

"You think about it for a few days, and if you still want to do it, we'll write a letter to the football coach explaining your decision," I said. "I'll talk to your mother and convince her. But you have to promise to work hard so this proves to be the right decision."

"I will. I promise," he said.

Disappointed, Karen still went to the Friday night football games and watched Fossil Ridge High School make the playoffs for the first time. But Jonathan played no part.

He was working out for baseball. Almost every day for six months, through the football and basketball seasons, he worked with others who share his dream.

At school, he practiced every day during his baseball athletics period.

After school, he stayed to lift weights, bat and throw.

In his bedroom, he lifted more weights and exercised. He took batting lessons, read baseball books and changed his diet to emphasize nutrition.

He worked with a core group of fathers and sons who share this year-round pursuit of the dream: Curtis and Robert Bogan, Ed and David Bloom, Dennis and Mike Bentley and Robert and Daniel Morales. (I appreciate the time and baseball wisdom these folks share with Jonathan.)

Jonathan's work was noticed. Baseball coach Doug Dulany walked up to him in the locker room and shook his hand.

"He told me he was proud of me," Jonathan said. "And since then I've been busting my tail even more."

Karen is coming around. How can she not? We have never seen him so focused and committed.

That's why the first day of baseball tryouts, which began at 2:40 p.m. Monday, was the moment I believe that Jonathan stepped across the threshold of manhood.

"Show us what you've got," Dulany told the 100 boys assembled. "We need a lot of hustle, a lot of shake."

While Jonathan warmed up, as he has for the previous 200 days, Dulany told me that he was impressed with Jonathan's work ethic.

"He works as hard as anyone," the coach said.

As a sophomore, Jonathan might not make the varsity team. But that doesn't matter for now.

What matters is how hard he worked to get there.

When a boy learns that lesson, he becomes a man.

February 4, 2001

Teen-ager hits detour in effort to get license

On Thanksgiving Day, I gave thanks for my family's health, our freedoms and, most important, the fact that my 17-year-old son, because of an ongoing conspiracy in my household, still does not have his driver's license.

Jonathan, the boy who believes he is a man, is 17 years, 2 months and 26 days old. That's an astounding 451 days past his 16th birthday, when, according to Texas law, he was allowed to become a legal driver.

Keeping him away from the car was difficult, but not impossible. We were concerned about his safety and the insurance costs.

Of course, he has complained at least once a day for the past 451 days, but that's why somebody invented the expression "fallen on deaf ears."

I'll tell you: The tactics employed by my wife and I were brilliant.

A few years ago, Texas law was changed so parents could be allowed to teach their children to drive. My wife decided that she would teach Jon rather than send him to the driving school down the street.

Every night, Karen returned home from work, and Jon asked, "Mom, can you take me driving tonight?"

"Not tonight, honey," Karen always replied. "I'm tired."

"You're always tired," he complained.

"One day I won't be," she would say.

This lasted for months. My poor tired wife. Tsk-tsk.

Then she and I would run to the bedroom, close the door and giggle. We talked driving statistics. (Did you know that traffic accidents are the leading cause of death among teen-age drivers?) And when we ran out of stats, we discussed how our annual automobile insurance bill would surpass the gross national product of Sri Lanka.

Of course, the boy grew wise. So Karen altered her story.

"Mom, can you take me driving tonight?"

"Not tonight, honey," she said. "I have to vacuum."

This lasted more months. In the meantime, our house was as clean as a hospital.

Finally, one night, when Karen was not tired and there was not a speck of dust left to vacuum, she took Jon to the parking lot of his high school. For the first time, he sat in the driver's seat.

"First, I want you to check your rearview mirror," Karen said.

"How do I know what I'm looking at?" Jon asked.

I was in the back seat for this historic occasion. Karen looked at me, and I whispered in our secret code: "Karen, you look tired, and the house is dirty. Let's go home, vacuum and go to bed early."

Months went by. Each night, after vacuuming, we retired early to bed.

Finally, one night, Jon angrily exploded: "YOU DON'T WANT ME TO DRIVE!"

So to quiet him, we enrolled him in a driving school. But that didn't really help him. We simply entered Phase 2 of our plan.

Phase 2 involved the unwitting cooperation of the Texas Department of Public Safety, especially those kindly bureaucrats who work at the office near North East Mall in Hurst.

I would drive Jon to the office to apply for his learner's permit, and the woman at the front desk would always check his papers. Always, always, there would be something missing, and he would return home, angry and miserable.

The first time, he didn't have a required form from school.

The second time, he didn't have an original copy of his birth certificate.

The third time, he didn't have his Social Security card.

The fourth time, his school form had expired. (Of course, I waited until it lapsed.)

By that time, the clerks at DPS knew what I expected of them.

On the fifth trip, Jon was rejected because his left shoelace was untied.

The sixth time, they said, "Sorry. We're closed."

Sadly, this month, Jon got his act together. He compiled a checklist before he left for the Department of Public Safety. He carried an unexpired school form, an original copy of his birth certificate and his Social Security card. His shoelaces were tied, and the DPS office was open.

There was one more chance to stop him.

We stood in line. When his number was called, we stepped forward. The clerk checked Jon's papers and glanced at his shoelaces. Everything was OK.

Then she told both of us to raise our right hands.

"Why me?" I asked. "I already have a license."

"Because I need you to swear that you are his parent or legal guardian," she answered. "Do you swear that you are?"

I paused and thought of my wife. I knew what she expected of me, but I could not lie under oath. I admit for a brief moment I thought of saying, "Honestly, lady, I have never seen this kid in my life." But the words came tumbling out of my mouth.

"I do."

Minutes later, Jon passed his driver's test. Now he is the proud owner of a learner's permit – the precursor to a license.

Our conspiracy is almost over. I say "almost" because until Jon gets a job, I keep the keys to his future car hidden under my mattress. He does not read this column, so our secret is safe.

November 23, 2001

Her shiny red convertible is a cut above

The day before my daughter secured her driving learner's permit last week, I promised that a momentous gift would be waiting for her in the garage.

"A shiny new red convertible," I said.

Desiree looked at me, wide-eyed and disbelieving.

"It's a toy car, right?"

"No, honey," I replied. "It's the real thing. This is something you've told me you've wanted for a long time."

She didn't believe me.

This girl knows me.

But I went on with my sales pitch. I told her she deserves this special gift, which she would receive the next day upon obtaining her permit. And deserve it she does.

Last semester in school, Desiree made the honor roll. She pitches in around the house, too. Every day after school, she comes home and vacuums. She also watches her baby brother. She alternates with her other brother to empty the dishwasher. She cleans up after meals. Twice a week, she mows the lawn. The list goes on.

I was driving her to driver's education class when I described her gift.

"I'm getting a good deal for it on a trade-in," I told her. "I shopped around and finally found the perfect model for you.

"First of all, it's cherry red. Heads will turn when you go by.

"And because it's a convertible, the wind will blow through your hair on hot summer days.

"It's brand new, too. Never been driven."

She still didn't believe me.

"It's a child's car or something, right?" she asked.

"No, it's full size," I said. "I saw it on the showroom floor and I knew it was perfect for you. It's got all the bells and whistles.

"It's not like a hot rod where you need special gas. It takes regular unleaded. But this baby has a lot of horsepower. Still, it ought to get great gas mileage.

"It has electronic ignition, so it starts right up. The engine is so quiet you can hear it purr. And it meets all clean-air standards.

"Every part is guaranteed for two years, so all you'll need to do is change the oil and the air filter. I can show you how.

"The tires are radials, with shiny hubcaps.

"It's American-made. None of this import stuff.

"It's got automatic transmission, so you don't have to worry about a stick shift."

She liked that. The idea of driving sounds fun, but a stick shift has always troubled her.

"Did I tell you about the handling?" I asked. "This baby is smooth around the curves. It handles real effortlessly. All the neighbors will look at you with envy.

"There's just one thing."

"Uh-oh, here it comes," she said. "I knew there was a catch."

"It's not a big deal," I said. "But when the time comes, I'd like you to share it with your brothers. It's yours, but you can let them use it, too, OK?"

I could tell she didn't like that idea, but she agreed.

"When do I get it?" she asked.

"Tomorrow, when you come home from school. It will be waiting for you in the garage. I'll tie ribbons around it. I guarantee that you'll love it."

The next day, everything was ready when she came home. Before we left for her driver's education class, I led her to the garage.

Slowly, I opened the door.

And there it was!

Shiny and new. Gleaming red. Bedecked with ribbons. Just as I promised.

Desiree let out a howl of laughter. And mock anger, too.

There was her new Toro walk-behind power lawn mower.

"OH, YOU'RE SO MEAN!!!" she yelled.

Fortunately, she hadn't bothered to tell her friends in school about her "shiny new red convertible." Like I said, she knows me.

But she did say one thing to me afterward that put me on notice.

She wasn't laughing when she said it. In fact, I detected frostiness in her voice when she uttered these words: "I owe you one."

September 10, 1999

Sharp teen drives point home to dad

A lot of readers are still sore about a practical joke I played on my daughter two years ago. That's the one where I promised her a gift when she secured her driving learner's permit.

"A shiny, new red convertible," I told Desiree. "And because it's a convertible, the wind will blow through your hair on hot summer days."

I described how she would find it in the garage, tied up with ribbons. I bragged about its special features – electronic ignition, radial tires and shiny hubcaps and the way it handled sweetly on the turns.

When the moment arrived, we walked into the garage for the unveiling. There it was. Shiny and new. Bedecked with ribbons. Just as I had promised.

Desiree looked at her gift. She screamed, "Oh, you're so mean!"

It was a new Toro walk-behind power lawn mower.

In conversations with appalled readers after this story appeared, I tried to explain that Des appreciated the mower as a gift because she is the family member responsible for mowing each week. It has made her life easier.

Yet readers often ask if she kept her promise of revenge. Her last words to me in the story were uttered in a frosty tone, "I owe you one."

Until now, the answer was no. But if you ever wondered about that moment, well, that moment is here.

*   *   *

First, a little background.

Before I came to Texas, I drove a Honda. But I yearned to move to Texas and start a new life and drive a sport utility vehicle. To me, the two were synonymous. An SUV represented a transformation from my cramped urban world.

To foster my dream, I kept a Matchbox SUV on my desk in Philadelphia and constantly played with the toy. And dreamed.

When I got hired by the *Star-Telegram*, the very first thing I did when I moved here was go out and buy an SUV.

I met the legendary Dallas car dealer Sam Jock, who said to me, "Boy, we're going to get you a horse."

That day in 1993, I drove off tall in the saddle and began my new life. Little man in a big car.

Eight years passed, and I was still driving my SUV. I loved every mile on my big horse. Even when gasoline prices shot to record levels, I didn't care. I was pouring my kids' future college tuition into a gas tank, but I couldn't imagine it any other way.

Desiree, on the other hand, had done very well for herself. For her commute to her day job and her night college classes, she bought herself a little black Honda with tinted windows. Pretty good for an 18-year-old, I thought.

Though I would never drive it – I gave up Hondas, remember? –

I admired the little car. It never broke down. Not once. I knew we couldn't let it leave the family.

Desiree had her own plan. She wanted to sell the Honda and replace it with her dream car, a Beetle.

"What if I can find a Bug and the payments are cheaper?" she asked.

"Cheaper?" She said the magic word.

"Go for it," I shouted.

Well, she did. She found a lime green Beetle, 1 year old, in excellent condition with low mileage and cheaper payments.

She faced one hitch. I told her she had to do all the work: Make the phone calls. Get the car checked out by a garage. Check with the insurance company. Make all the arrangements with my company credit union. Only then, I said, would I do my part: co-sign my name on a loan.

Well, she did. When we drove to pick up the car, I complimented her.

"Oh, I'm very proud of myself," she said. "You tried to talk me out of it, and that's not going to happen. If I'm going to do something, I'm going to do it."

Then she said more magic words: "I have to keep doing things on my own."

Things turned quiet for a moment. Then she said, "Now you, on the other hand, I don't know if you're going to like all this."

"Like what?" I asked.

"Your new car."

Which was how I came to find out that Desiree and her mother had cooked up a plan in which I would begin driving the Honda and my SUV would go to her brother Jonathan when he starts driving in late summer.

"Think about it," Des told me. "With the Honda, you have better gas mileage and a more dependable car. It's going to work out, I guess."

I guess.

My wife backed her up, saying I had no choice. If I drove the SUV, I was a gas guzzling idiot. She's right. And Desiree got the last laugh.

This week, I began driving the little black Honda. I am 9 inches off the road. So low that drive-through window employees look down on me.

The first day, the driver of an SUV in front of me on Colleyville Boulevard didn't see me sitting 9 inches off the ground and ran me off the road.

"How's the car?" Desiree asks with a wide grin.

Every time she sees me get into her old car, she laughs. Little man in a big car. Then she jumps in her cosmic green Beetle and leaves me in the dust.

May 18, 2001

Columnist's stepson is a hit with his dad

Jon, in senior year

One dreary afternoon, my son Jonathan came home from school, stomped up the stairs to my office and stood in the doorway looking at me with fierce eyes.

"Why did you write that about me?" he demanded.

"Write what?"

"That crack in today's column about me not wanting to take showers," he said.

"It was just a joke," I said.

He explained that he had been teased in school and didn't like it. As he turned away, he shouted, "I HATE COLUMNISTS!"

There are three ways for a child to get in the newspaper. Do something really good. Do something really bad. Or have the misfortune of being the child of a columnist.

Since becoming my stepson, Jon has never asked me to write about him, but that hasn't protected him from the invasion of his privacy that has marked the last seven years he has lived with me. He has appeared in enough of these columns to fill a book. His teachers know things about him that they don't know about other students. The same goes for his friends' parents.

Although he has given me permission to write about him in every instance, Jon often complains that all this shared information sometimes freaks him out.

I couldn't help it. He was always good for a cute remark and a great story. My other motivation was that I hoped readers would see part of themselves and their children through the shared experiences I had with Jonathan as he grew from a pipsqueak into a young man who is now, I must say, 8 inches taller than me.

Back in 1994, a week after I proposed to his mother in a column, I wrote, "Last weekend was a big one for Jonathan, too. He scored his first touchdown in a youth league. We have a precious videotape of him explaining how in one weekend, 'I got a touchdown and a father.' "

When Jon was 13, I took him to a Pat Buchanan for President rally. Talk about fun! But, as always, I was in dire need of a column.

Unintentionally, I portrayed him as an opponent of a one-world government, even though he didn't even know what that was. I wrote, "Possibly tired of sitting, Jon stood up and started dancing and cheering as loudly as anyone. He didn't know or care that the roar was against the United Nations. A little too young for this, he just wanted to have some fun."

I didn't score any points with Jon when I visited his school for Texas Parent Involvement Day. All parents were invited, but I was one of about five who actually showed up – and the only one to tell about it in the *Star-Telegram*. I wrote the following about his athletics class:

"What I saw shocked me. I learned what is wrong with our school system. The boys do push-ups WITH THEIR KNEES ON THE GROUND! Push-ups must be done without knees touching. Everyone knows that. How will our children compete in the 21st century?"

After the column appeared, the athletics teacher forced all the boys to do proper push-ups. When the other boys complained, the teacher responded, "You can thank Jonathan's dad for this."

Later, when he came home, that was the first time I heard that phrase, "I hate columnists!"

Because I constantly harp on his lack of homework, administrators at his high school do their best to place him in classes where teachers give lots of it.

"I hate columnists!"

When I wrote about how my wife and I prevented Jon from getting his driver's license for more than a year after his 16th birthday, this drew a strong rebuttal from readers, both for and against the idea of postponing a teen-ager's driving debut. He didn't like that one either.

"I hate columnists!"

The poor kid couldn't even buy me a parents appreciation plaque as part of a telephone marketing scam without me writing about the lecture I gave him about buying things from strangers.

"I hate columnists!"

But then eight days ago, something beautiful and unexpected happened. Jon got his name in the newspaper without me. In small agate print in the sports section, his name was listed as a District 5-5A first-team selection for varsity baseball.

Jon led the Fossil Ridge High School Panthers in batting. He was a clutch performer and showed a dedication to the game and also to the pursuit of his dream that I had never properly depicted in all those other columns.

Yes, Jon was in the newspaper again. But this time, he did it on his own, getting there for all the right reasons. Congratulations, kid. There is no better story to tell.

May 26, 2002

In bottom of 9th, a prayer for victory

Rick Moon

Future New York Yankee?

George Steinbrenner, the boss of the New York Yankees, was sitting in a war room in Tampa, Fla., on Wednesday looking at a big board with the names of 150 amateur baseball players targeted by his scouts in the draft. My son's name was on that board.

Three weeks ago, the Yankees scout for North Texas, Mark Batchko, gave Jonathan a private tryout at Keller High School. Jon jacked three balls out of the park, and Batchko was smiling. All the balls went deep to right field, and the Yankees love left-handed hitters because of that famous short right-field porch in Yankee Stadium.

The scout told Jon, his mother and me that he was impressed. He told us to wait by the phone.

The draft was Tuesday and Wednesday. During the first 20 rounds Tuesday, Jon and I listened on the Internet. Every time the Yankees made a pick, Jon let out a groan that shook the house.

"Don't worry," I said. "They're taking pitchers now." Jon is an out-fielder and a first baseman.

On day two, we set up our monitoring station by the computer again and listened. Team after team. Player after player. Soon, Jon was lying on the couch in my office, his hands covering his face. By the 30th round, he gave up in despair.

"Where are you going?" I asked when he started to leave.

"I'm sick and tired of hearing it," he said.

I stuck with it. Glad I did.

*   *   *

Maybe you remember the story I told two years ago about how I persuaded Jon to drop football and basketball and concentrate on his true love of baseball.

We've had many strains in our father-stepson relationship, but the biggest has been my constant urging that he do what he really wants to do. One night, when our family was at a restaurant and everyone went to the powder room except Jon and me, I pulled my chair close so I could look in his eyes.

"I know you are only playing football for Mom," I said.

He didn't answer.

"But you are the athlete. You play the game. Not her. What do you want to do?"

"I want to play baseball," he said quietly.

"Why don't you?"

He answered with a torrent of fears and emotions. He didn't want to disappoint Mom. The football coach would be mad. His friends who played football might not like him anymore.

I told him we could work all that out.

*   *   *

By the 35th round, Jon was lying on his bed, complaining of a headache.

By the 40th round, he moaned, "I'm not going to be drafted."

"You are!" I said.

Then I did something I have never done in front of him. I knelt down and prayed aloud, asking that my son be able to realize his dream. He watched but said nothing.

During a break after the 45th round, the announcer said the final rounds were reserved for good players that the other teams didn't know about.

"Here you go," I said.

He still didn't believe.

In the 46th round, the San Francisco Giants selected a pitcher.

"The Yankees are next," Jon said quietly.

We heard a voice from the baseball commissioner's office say: "Yankees?"

Then a voice from the Yankees war room in Tampa said the words we will never forget: "Yankees select Bertschinger, Jonathan, left fielder at Fossil Ridge High School in Fort Worth."

What happened next was the greatest feeling of pure joy either of us has ever known. When you give birth to a child, you have months to prepare. When you get married, an engagement period allows time to ponder the significance. But this was something we were never sure would happen. So in one moment, all the joy and delight from years of dreaming were released in one loud, long shout of ecstasy.

I jumped on top of him like he had just won the World Series. He looked at me like I was nuts. He'd never seen me celebrate like that before. He had never seen me react when one of my prayers – and one of his dreams – was answered.

"You did it! You did it!" I kept repeating, as I hugged him with all my might.

We called his mother at work. Karen was thrilled — but not speechless. She still had the wherewithal to make a wisecrack.

"Just because you are a Yankee doesn't mean you can get out of doing your household chores," she warned, half-serious.

Jon plans to attend Navarro Junior College, where he earned a full baseball scholarship. The following year, if all goes right, he will join the Yankees' minor league system.

There are several people Jon says helped him achieve his dream: Curtis Bogan, his former Little League coach who continued to work with him; Eric Persyn, his assistant coach at Fossil Ridge High who never gave up on him; Andy Adams, his hitting instructor; Dave Acton, the manager of the Arlington A's select team that Jon plays for; and the scout, Batchko.

"I see in him what I see in a big leaguer," Batchko told me. "That's a guy with a good work ethic, humility and a knowledge that he's got to work hard to get better. He's got to prove himself every day when he goes out on the field.

"He's young, and he's definitely got a chance to be something some day. That's what I saw."

Here's what I see. A boy who, like most boys, took a long time to get serious about his life. But once he did, he never looked back. Adversity, injuries, naysayers. Nothing could stop him. Hopefully, nothing ever will.

I told Jon that I needed a comment from him for this column.

He said: "I gotta go do a bunch of household chores."

Can you imagine Mickey Mantle saying that?

Jokes aside, I look up to my son in awe.

June 8, 2003

The Blessing is bestowed upon us all

About 25 years ago, a boy moved to a small town in Central Texas. He was a fifth-grader, and he moved to the town because his parents had separated. It was a tough move, for it meant that the boy never saw his father.

The town's children hated the new boy, an outsider. They tried to beat him up three times every day – before school, at lunch and after school. If the boy could run home fast enough, he managed to avoid that third daily beating.

Not surprisingly, the boy found his new school terribly difficult. Formerly a top student, the boy began failing. He became sick with a stomach infection and lost a lot of weight.

Once, a teacher even told the boy, "I don't like you. I wish you weren't in my school. You will drop out one day."

The boy knew that she spoke the truth. There was no evidence to the contrary.

Then a music teacher stepped into the boy's life. With her long hair and embroidered skirts, the teacher was considered a hippie in the small town. She smoked cigarettes and never visited with the other teachers, who disliked her immensely.

The music teacher entered the boy's life by asking him, "Would you like to walk home with me?"

The boy lived nearby, so he and the teacher walked home together. The teacher began helping the boy with his musical scales. As he walked along the street, the boy sang out the notes. *Every good boy does fine.*

When the teacher reached her front door, she asked, "Would you like to walk me home tomorrow?"

For the next three months, in sunshine and rain, cold and heat, the teacher and the boy walked home after school. The teacher talked to the boy about English, history, science, math and spelling.

Sometimes, she hugged the boy. Other times, she told him how smart he was. Once, she told the boy that the teacher who predicted he would drop out of school was a liar.

Every day, the music teacher reminded the boy that he could make something out of his life. Every day, she told the boy everything would be OK.

The boy eventually earned five college degrees and a doctorate in ministry.

The man told his story one night last week to two dozen parents at Colleyville Heritage High School, gathered for the "Parenting Through Turbulent Times" seminar.

Eric Cupp, a professor at Amber University in Dallas, has long, dark hair that flows to his shoulders. Handsome and immaculately dressed, he cut an impressive figure before the parents in Colleyville.

Cupp presented "The Blessing," five steps to help raise and love your child. The Blessing is so simple and obvious, it's a wonder these steps aren't better known.

The first involves *meaningful touch*. A typical father stops hugging his daughter when she is 8 years old, Cupp said.

Second comes *the spoken message*. "You can never tell a child that you love them too many times," he said.

Next is *picturing a specific future*. Tell your child he or she can become a great writer or a great parent or a great anything. "Put a light bulb way out there," he said.

The fourth step is to *honor your child*. "Give them value. Not because of what they do but because of who they are."

Lastly, *show active commitment* in raising your child. At the end of a long day, say, "I'm tired, but I'll do one more thing with you because I love you."

"I know The Blessing works," Cupp told the parents. "I'm standing here because of it. That music teacher instilled self-confidence in me. I like school because of what school does for me. She taught me that."

The parents were gripped by his words, caught in emotions bubbling to the surface as if they had just watched a great film.

Sitting in the room that night, I too felt those powerful emotions. That night, I went home and talked with my children, hugged them, loved them and put that light bulb out there for them. Certainly, though, it must not stop there.

For some reason, The Blessing had been passed to me. Now, the only thing to do is pass it to you.

So simple and obvious, The Blessing made all the difference in the life of the troubled boy in that small town in Central Texas. All these years later, The Blessing still offers a way for parents, teachers or anybody to do the most important thing that we can do: Bring meaning and hope to the lives of the little ones we love and care for most.

It's a blessing all its own.

February 2, 1997

Chapter Four
Texas Edukation

"The greatest service that you can do mankind is to expose hypocrisy, question authority, and blow the whistle."

— Actor Ed Asner

Education system is failing teachers

*T*oday I am calling for a teachers' revolt.

I have come to realize that the biggest dreamers in our society, public school teachers who entered the work force with a noble calling to nurture young minds and prepare them for the world, are no longer allowed to do much of that.

Instead, teachers have become standardized-test preparation specialists, seekers of exemplary ratings and blue ribbons. They are pawns in the political empires that our school districts have become.

This movement for a teachers' revolution has been building in my mind for some time as I watch bright and wonderful teachers slowly being worn down by an educational bureaucracy that sucks the academic life out of them.

I can't appeal to principals and other school administrators because they answer to upper management and if they balk, they lose their jobs.

I can't appeal to superintendents because they breathe a rarified air with annual salaries and benefits that approach $200,000 and a coterie of door holders and sycophants who rarely tell them what they do not want to hear.

I can't appeal to school board members because, more often than not, they do what the superintendent wants them to do.

I can't appeal to the state politicians who appoint the bureaucrats who set educational standards because these politicians are so far removed from education that they wouldn't know a homeroom door if it smacked them in the rear.

I can't appeal to the parents because I believe most modern parents have given up on the idea that tougher schooling makes for smarter children.

For every parent who complains that his or her child does not get enough homework, there are probably five who believe what little homework the child gets is already too much. Besides, they believe that homework interferes with dance recitals, band practices or sports activities.

And I can't appeal to the students because no child I know actually wants to do more schoolwork.

So all that is left are the teachers, and that is probably the best choice of all, because they are the purest and most idealistic of the bunch. Teachers entered a tough profession knowing they wouldn't earn much money or change the world, except maybe one child at a time.

And as conditions deteriorate and government-sponsored test standards rise, they tough it out even though they don't get the resources, time or support from everyone named above to do the job they originally set out to do.

This is a most appropriate week for me to call for a teachers' revolt. As a principal put it so perfectly in a school newsletter, "If it's April, it must be time for TAAS!"

In that particular school, as in most schools, the biggest effort of the year has been to create the perfect testing world for the Texas Assessment of Academic Skills.

In the coming days, TAAS will be given to thousands of greater Northeast Tarrant County students. Preparations have gone beyond reading, writing and arithmetic.

There are snack packets for children that include bottled water, granola bars, yogurt, and orange and apple slices.

Instructions sent to parents include the following nuggets of wisdom:

"Please make sure that your child has a good breakfast the morning of the test."

"Please make sure they have 2 pencils and a highlighter."

"Make sure they dress for success!"

And at the end of the week, this particular school will hold what it calls a TAAS Celebration Dance.

To which I ask: How about a "Reading and Writing Celebration Dance"? How about a "Library Dance" or a "Term Paper Dance" or a "We Read an Entire Book Dance"?

If you are an English teacher and you make your students watch the movie instead of reading the book, I say revolt and open that classic novel to teach the joy of reading.

If you are a teacher and you have not been correcting spelling and grammar in as tough a manner as possible, I say revolt and pull out the red pen.

If you are a teacher who does not assign homework because the students refuse to do it, I say revolt and build a learning fire in your classroom.

If you are a teacher who has ceased calling parents about their child's poor performance because you are tired of hearing the parent ask, "What do you want me to do about it?" – well, I say, tell them what you want them to do about it.

If you are a teacher who gives your students a copy of a test several days ahead of time so they can properly "prepare," I say make tests what they are supposed to be – a challenge to learn the material.

If you are a teacher who allows open-book tests, I say stop because real life is not an open book.

If you are a teacher who has lost sight of your goals and dreams because of external pressures from principals, superintendents, school board members, state bureaucrats, parents and students, I say rise up and lead the revolt in your classroom.

You are our last line of defense against an ignorant world.

Stand up for schooling! If you don't, no one else will. The dance should be about celebrating you, not some test that has nearly ruined everything you wanted to do.

Remember your noble calling. Remember your passion. Remember, please remember, why you originally decided to become a teacher.

April 14, 2002

Teacher Lynn Ryals

Keller first-graders educate teacher for a day

"**N**ervous?"

Lynn Ryals, the teacher with whom I traded jobs, was giving me last-minute instructions. Before I could answer, 22 first-graders at Keller-Harvel Elementary School walked through the door with worried faces.

It was about 8 a.m. The next seven hours passed in a blur. There wasn't a one-minute break to catch my breath. I never worked so hard.

We began with the Pledge of Allegiance, the school song and the attendance check, and then I took a lunch count.

"Who is eating chicken rings?" I asked.

I told the children to answer the questions on the blackboard. At that point, it became clear who was in charge.

"It's a blueboard, not a blackboard," one corrected.

So began a day when these 6-year-olds reminded me over and over whose classroom I was invading. If I dared do something a little differently from the way Mrs. Ryals did her job, I was told in no uncertain terms.

Twenty-two first-graders nitpicked me to death.

Mr. Lieber, Mrs. Ryals always lets us sharpen our pencils first.

Mr. Lieber, Mrs. Ryals takes the lunch count AFTER the morning work.

Mr. Lieber, when is Mrs. Ryals coming back?

One boy, in particular, granted me no leeway. Every little detail that wasn't done EXACTLY as Mrs. Ryals would do it was pointed out. I called him Mr. Protocol. One day, he will make a great diplomat.

Mr. Protocol was especially unnerved when I taught phonics. The lesson was about the "oa" sound in words such as soap, coal and toad.

Mr. Lieber, that's not the way Mrs. Ryals teaches us!

"Well, guess what? I'm not Mrs. Ryals!"

After phonics, it was time for something called Reading Center Rotation. The students divided into three groups.

The first group sat with me at a reading table. We read a book together. Meanwhile, the second group worked on a sheet in which they practiced word contractions. The third group answered questions about a story.

I set a timer for 20 minutes and said, "Go!" When 20 minutes ended, everybody was supposed to switch.

But I had to work with all three groups AT THE SAME TIME!

My reading group was trying to read. Meanwhile, children in the second group were interrupting to ask how to turn "cannot" into "can't." And the third group was shoving papers at me to verify that they had answered story questions correctly.

The only bribery tool I had was a jar of gummy bears candy that Mrs. Ryals left with a sticky note attached telling me that gummy bears go to children who remembered to bring their reading books.

Too complicated. So I gave gummy bears to everyone after they finished reading. Mr. Protocol went berserk!

Mr. Lieber, that's not how Mrs. Ryals hands out the gummy bears.

"True," I replied, "but if you accept this gummy bear that I am holding before you, this means you accept the fact that I am not Mrs. Ryals, and today is different than usual."

Mr. Protocol thought for a long time. He frowned. He thought some more. Then he accepted the gummy bear. However, all that time spent with him created a backlog.

Mr. Lieber, I lost my pencil.

Mr. Lieber, my notebook ran out of paper.

Mr. Lieber, have I been good?

Lunch time. The cafeteria workers were not, I mean, weren't happy to see me. They did not (didn't) like my joke in Sunday's column about their precious chicken rings. They demanded that I try the chicken rings. Fortunately, the quick lunch ended before I could even swallow.

After recess, the children went to music class. For the first time all day, I was surrounded by quiet. Just Red the guinea pig and me. Then I thought I heard him talking.

Mr. Lieber, my food pellets are gone.

Mr. Lieber, my water bottle is empty.

Mr. Lieber, when is Mrs. Ryals coming back?

The children returned. I grabbed a gummy bear for energy, smiled sweetly at Mr. Protocol and helped the children pack for the buses. As a reward for a great day, I gave them each *Star-Telegram* sticky notepads and advised how they could leave notes around the house such as "Great dinner, Mom!" and "Hey, big sister: Clean up your room!"

After I walked the children to the buses, I returned to the classroom where some had left sticky notes on their chairs:

"I love you, Mr. Lieber."

I missed them already. But my body ached and my legs could no longer support me. I grabbed a gummy bear for nourishment.

Time to keep my promise that the children would get their names in the paper – if they behaved. They behaved, so here goes:

Caleb "Mr. Protocol" Christensen, Blaine Briddell, Cassie

Chamblee, Kacie Coker, Molly Covington, Rachel Dahl, Elizabeth Doughty, Katie Gaby, Kristen Keithan, Paige Lawrence, M'Kaly Lewis, Erin Lowry, Cameron Marshall, Lauren Null, Luis Perez, Maddison Riggie, Kirina Rojas, Brittany Salvesen, Phillip Seward, Katrina Williamson, Michael Zaring and Jillian Zozaya.

Yes, these children are terrific, but four days later, I'm still exhausted.

One final thought: Texas teachers' pay ranks in the bottom one-third among the 50 states. That's a Lone Star disgrace. Texas lawmakers had better correct that.

Or they won't get their gummy bears.

March 5, 1999

Zero tolerance means educators cannot practice what they preach

I keep waiting for Rod Serling to pop out in the story of L.D. Bell High School student Taylor Hess and tell us it is another episode from his old television show, *The Twilight Zone*. Hess was expelled from school because his grandmother's bread knife was found in his pickup parked on school property.

"Respectfully submitted for your perusal," Serling would say. "This is Taylor Hess, age 16, an honors student who has never spent a single moment in school detention. Yet on this day, he is in alternative school because of a good deed gone awry, a good Samaritan type of act in which he was merely trying to help his elderly, stroke-ridden grandmother and clean out his family's garage.

"The problem here," Serling would continue, "is that both young Mr. Hess and you will reach a point where it might be difficult to decide which is reality and which is nightmare, a problem uncommon but rather peculiar to the Twilight Zone."

Perhaps we ought to begin with Hess' actual words, as told to school officials in a statement he wrote on Feb. 26:

"In February of 2001, my grandmother suffered a stroke. My family decided to move her into an assisted-living complex near our home so we could be closer to her. Her new apartment was much smaller than her original house, so many of her possessions were kept in our family's garage.

"On Sunday, Feb. 24, 2002, my father and I were cleaning out our garage and we decided to donate some of my grandmother's old possessions to Goodwill.

"Towards the later part of the evening, my father and I loaded up the bed of my 1993 Ford truck with boxes of items. Among these items was a box of kitchen items that included my grandmother's old cutting knives.

"At approximately 7 p.m., my father and I unloaded these items at the Goodwill institution in Hurst. One of the knives had fallen out of the box either during the drive there or as we handled the box to unload. It was dark and therefore I did not know the knife was lying in the bed of my truck."

The next day, a school security guard found the 10-inch knife, notified Hurst police and reported the incident to school administrators. Under the Hurst-Euless-Bedford school district's zero-tolerance policy, any student found to be in possession of such a knife, no matter the circumstances, is to be expelled from school. This is what happened to our student lost in the Twilight Zone.

"What they're trying to do is incomprehensible," Robert Hess, Taylor's father, told me. "I just can't believe it. Zero tolerance doesn't mean zero brains. You have to use your judgment."

Jim Short, L.D. Bell principal, said at Taylor's disciplinary hearing that he had no choice. "There isn't a good feeling in my body about this," he said.

At the hearing, Short explained that school officials like the blanket rule of zero tolerance.

"School safety does have to come first," Short said at the hearing. "We all agree on that. It makes it important for us to not be able to sort out the average [student] from the stellar. I can look myself in the mirror and know that I treated the students as equally as I possibly could.

"And so in that regard, I'm kind of grateful that I don't have to ... you know ... special circumstances are really hard to sort out because people are not always truthful to you. And so in some ways, truthfully, sometimes zero tolerance makes you feel like you lose some of the judgment. It's a love-hate thing, I guess."

This is so sad, what our public education system has been reduced to, as administrators and teachers try to cope with the very real threat of student violence.

We have taken away from them the very concepts that we try to teach our children. We have removed their ability to use their own good judgment, their reasoning powers and their ability to make decisions on a case-by-case basis.

If justice is not examined on a case-by-case basis, then it is not true justice.

In two other cases of student misbehavior studied recently in this column, there was at least some evidence of possible wrongdoing.

In the case of the seven Richland High School baseball players who placed feces on dollar bills and left them outside a store, there was videotaped evidence, and police citations were issued for disorderly conduct. In the case of a Fossil Ridge High School baseball player, police arrested him on suspicion of assault after a 16-year-old girl went to a hospital for treatment of her injuries. The baseball player has denied that he was involved.

But in this case, there is nobody saying that Hess brought the knife to school as a weapon. There is nobody saying that he knew the knife was lying in plain view, not hidden, in the bed of his pickup. And most importantly, Hurst police have declined to pursue charges.

School security officers ought to be commended for finding the knife. The administration has done well by investigating the matter fully and not ignoring this. But enough is enough. Taylor Hess has an appeal hearing scheduled for Thursday. This has already gone too far.

I keep waiting for Rod Serling to pop out and end this *Twilight Zone* episode with a closing statement similar to one he delivered on a show 40 years ago.

"There are many bromides applicable here – too much of a good thing, tiger by the tail, as you sow so shall ye reap," he said. "The point is that too often man becomes clever instead of becoming wise. He becomes inventive but not thoughtful. And sometimes, as in this case, he can create himself right out of existence. Today's tale of oddness and obsolescence from the Twilight Zone."

March 19, 2002

Postscript: At his appeal hearing, the charges against Taylor Hess were reduced by the district. In addition, the school board voted unanimously to revise the district expulsion policy, giving administrators more flexibility in levying punishment.

Educators should serve as examples to students

The Ponder schoolboy's essay that landed him in a juvenile detention facility was troubling. But his spelling was atrocious, too.

His essay included three misspellings: aircondtionar, acessdently and steeling.

I was more surprised, however, when I saw the written statement released by Ponder Superintendent Byron Welch.

"The school in turn is reviewing the matter and planning a hearing with the Beaman's to provide Chris with a chance to state his side of the matter," the release states.

The boy's name is Beamon, not Beaman. And there should be no apostrophe because the name, as used, is not possessive.

"Ponder High School is a recognized campus that has a history of outstanding academic success by it's students," the release also states.

Attention superintendent: Go back and study the proper use of apostrophes.

If school administrators do not bother to proofread, why should we expect any better from their students?

Last week, at Dove Elementary School in the Grapevine-Colleyville school district, an administrator sent home a one-page flier to parents that begins, "Dear Students and Parent."

Is every Dove Elementary student living in a single-parent household?

The letter continues, "If you are a volunteer at Dove, please turn it the number of hours you have volunteered."

A teacher at Dove Elementary sent home a letter last week informing parents about a class project to create a newspaper. "You are a newspaper columnist," the letter begins.

Should I be worried about future competition? Not necessarily.

"As you research your topic, answer the following questions," the letter states. One question: "What are the three important fact about this event?"

The granddaddy of mistake-riddled school papers is the team handbook given to high school football players and their parents in the Keller school district.

The booklet was written by district Athletic Director Dennis Parker. He told me he wrote it 18 years ago and that he has distributed it to thousands of students in every school district where he has worked, including these last two years as the Keller district's athletic director.

Before I pass on Parker's extraordinary reaction to my questions about the poor grammar in his booklet, let me share some examples:

- "Each player receive a diploma and an education."
- "Once learned how to play correctly; there is nothing more fun."
- "The individual who motivates his Teammates to do better, is always enthusiastic and ready,, will make a greater contribution that on who does not possess this quality."
- "Know in your mind if we are close going into the 4th quarter, the advantage is our."
- "Your teammates needs you when he has made a mistake."

Parker's booklet ends with these words: "Hold coaches accountable for everything in his handbook."

So I did.

When I visited Parker last week and asked about these mistakes, he acknowledged that the booklet has never been proofread.

Then he made a statement that I will quote in full:

"I apologize for the grammatical errors. They are my fault. I take responsibility. And as a matter of fact, we'll start proofreading it right now.

"We shouldn't have grammatical errors in anything. It's embarrassing.

"If we want excellence out of the kids, we've got to be willing to give it ourselves."

Bravo, coach.

The values espoused in the handbook are good and honest. But the reader, whether player or parent, cannot get past the mistakes to follow the meaning.

Errors such as these are not limited to the three North Texas school districts cited above. Each column I write is edited by at least three editors, but much to my embarrassment, mistakes I make still get published from time to time.

Sadly, I believe the errors by adult educators shamefully reflect the overall declining standards in schools today. They are one more reason why educational expectations for students have fallen.

As Parker said so eloquently, if we want excellence out of the kids, we've got to be willing to give it ourselves.

November 14, 1999

High schools are failing a key test

*F*or years now, I have harped in this space that many of our children are unprepared for college-level work after they graduate from public high schools. My theory was based on observations in my own household.

If teachers don't assign books to read and papers to research and write, the students will not know how to do either.

Imagine my delight last year when my son's 11th-grade English teacher informed me at meet-the-teacher night that Jonathan would be studying classic works of American fiction such as *The Scarlet Letter* and *The Great Gatsby*. Finally.

But my delight turned to disgust. In Jon's class, each student was assigned one chapter of *The Scarlet Letter* to read. That student then delivered an oral report in class on the chapter. When all the oral reports were delivered in numerical order, the students had "read" the book.

When it came time to study *The Great Gatsby* – in my opinion, the greatest novel ever written – the book was never opened. The students simply watched the movie.

My daughter graduated in the top quarter of the Class of 2000 with a 90 grade-point average. But open-book tests, literary-movie watching and the lack of homework assignments caught up with her when she took the state test that determined her fitness for college. Desiree, along with many of her classmates, failed the Texas Academic Skills Program test, also known as the TASP.

The TASP is required for all high school graduates who fail to make the minimum scores on the SAT, the ACT or the Texas Assessment of Academic Skills and who wish to attend Texas public institutions of higher learning, including junior colleges, four-year colleges and technical schools.

Desiree had to take a year of remedial classes in English and math at Tarrant County College before she finally passed all sections of the TASP and could take courses for college credit. Unfortunately, she had loads of company.

Star-Telegram reporter Paula Caballero's analysis of TASP scores from the Class of 2000 for area school districts ("Students' college readiness is lagging," Dec. 22, 2002) sent a chill up my spine. For the first time, data became available that revealed the dirty little secret of Texas high schools.

Many, if not most, of the students who earn a high school diploma will probably not be eligible to take college-credit courses. In the six districts that make up greater Northeast Tarrant County, nearly 1,600 members of the Class of 2000 took the TASP. More than half failed at least one portion.

In the Keller school district, 72 percent of Desiree's classmates failed at least one portion.

In the vaunted Carroll school district, 58 percent failed at least one portion.

In the Birdville school district, the rate was 83 percent.

In the Grapevine-Colleyville and Hurst-Euless-Bedford school districts, 68 percent failed one or more parts.

In the Northwest school district, 69 percent failed.

Imagine the shock when your high school graduate enrolls in college, takes the test and finds out that he or she must relearn what was supposed to have been learned in high school.

Larry Darlage, president of Tarrant County College Northeast Campus, told me, "It can be somewhat depressing when you think of students who enroll in college and they have to kind of back up and pick up math class or reading or writing so they can function in the college environment."

Darlage estimates that of the 10,000 students enrolled at the Northeast Campus, 3,333 are in remedial classes. A two-year associate's degree program can easily stretch into four years.

As taxpayers, we are paying double for these students' high school educations. Statewide, there are 40,000 high school graduates in remedial classes at an annual cost of $92 million.

Please don't tell me that this is the parents' responsibility. The schools have our children for seven hours a day, 35 hours a week, 140 hours a month. We pay school taxes, and the districts use that money to hire trained personnel who are supposed to know how to educate our children.

Yes, this is a statewide problem. But in greater Northeast Tarrant County, we have been brainwashed into believing that our schools are so much better.

Now the dirty little secret is out. All those awards and banners and honors earned by our schools apparently did not take college preparedness into account. How else can you explain why Northwest High School was named a National Blue Ribbon campus last year and why the Northwest school board was honored as one of five Honor Boards by the Texas Association of School Administrators? Yet, almost seven of 10 Northwest students who took the TASP two years ago couldn't pass all three parts.

Is it the responsibility of a school district to help its students pass the TAAS – soon to be the TAKS – and push them out the door with a diploma? No, the responsibility is to prepare them for the next level. This is why I have been complaining so loudly that school board members who act as cheerleaders and don't hold administrators, principals and teachers accountable are guilty of a tremendous disservice to the youth they profess to serve.

As educators Allan E. Parker Jr. and Stephen Ratliff wrote in a study of the TASP crisis, "Districts are supposed to ensure that high school students with diplomas are prepared for college and life. Otherwise a high school diploma has little credibility.... It is time that the citizens of Texas demand greater accountability from their local school districts."

The two educators suggested that if school districts pass students with B or above averages and if those students need remediation, the districts should pay for the remedial courses. "Truth in grading," the educators called it. The current proposed solutions don't go that far. The more rigorous Texas Assessment of Knowledge and Skills is supposed to help. So, too, are new rules in which parents must sign waivers if they want their children to take only the minimum required courses to graduate.

In the Keller district, officials are beefing up Advanced Placement programs, urging more students to enroll in those classes earlier and studying successful AP programs statewide.

What we really need to do, however, is end the charade that our area schools are wonderful, fantastic, exemplary. Let's quit the self-promotion and public-relations puffery, acknowledge the long road ahead and talk more about where we need to improve. It may not be pretty, but pretty doesn't pass the test.

When you have such high failure rates for the TASP, the dirty little secret is that in the area of college preparedness, our well-regarded schools are – dare I say it? – mediocre and low-performing.

January 19, 2003

Tough love will be needed to fix our public schools

*T*oday I share my solutions for improving the Texas public school system. The following ideas, some major, some minor, would require a new way of thinking by the Texas Legislature, school boards, superintendents, principals, teachers, students and parents.

I call it the "tough-love approach to education."

The first several years in transition would be extremely difficult, but in the end, the education system would be tougher, stronger and more rewarding for everyone.

1. Put the tough-love approach back into teaching. Homework for everybody. Books to read. Term papers to research and write. If you fail, you repeat the class. If you fail enough classes, you repeat the grade. Count on increased failures in the first five years of this system, until students and parents get the tough-love message.

2. Deal with the increased dropout rate. Everyone says the above would cause more students to drop out. Maybe so, but you create a system in which you nurture those on the edge and help them do what needs to be done. You restore the value of a high school diploma so that earning one really means something.

3. When parents complain, tell them about tough love. Stop thinking of students and parents as customers. The public school system is a monopoly and, as harsh as that sounds, that comes with some advantages. When the inevitable complaints from parents come rolling in – too much homework, my kid's grade is too low, how dare you fail him? – don't give in. Drop the after-school activities if they get in the way of schoolwork. Under tough love, school is the focus of a young person's life.

4. Stop making decisions based on parent surveys. Sorry, but what do parents know about education? We went to school once, too, but does that make us experts? Do parents ask school districts how to run their households?

5. Hire community advocates to handle the inevitable flood of complaints. Despite my tough talk on parental complaints, there still would be many, if not more, under this new system. These independent advocates assigned to handle complaints would not depend on the approval of the school superintendent to keep their jobs. They would field complaints, investigate independently and make recommendations to the school board. This independence would bring fairness into the system. Right now, complaints are often whitewashed to protect those in power.

6. Stop hiring career superintendents who bounce from district to district. It's time to convince leaders in the corporate world that they must do turns as school superintendents as a form of public service. They would bring their knowledge of accounting, efficiency and motivational techniques into what are essentially multimillion-dollar corporations. Let the deputy and associate superintendents run the education side while this new breed of superintendents rotates in, then back to the business world.

7. Eliminate at-large school board seats. Each elected trustee would represent a distinct section of the district, instead of serving at-large. That means voters would know who is responsible for their area.

8. Make attendance at meet-the-teacher nights mandatory for parents. Hold these nights two or three times each semester, including once on a Saturday. Send strong reminder notes to parents who miss the first one. Parents need to understand what is expected of their children each semester.

9. End block scheduling. It's a failure. Class periods of 90 minutes are too long. It's a joke to have three long classes each semester, not including electives or sports. Students need to take science, math and English year-round, not just one semester each year in these longer classes, where teachers sometimes use up the time by letting their students do homework or play games.

10. Eliminate team practices during school hours. My son's varsity baseball team is currently practicing every school day between 1:30 and 2:30 p.m., which means he loses five hours of educational instruction a week. Practices should be after school.

11. Require districts to hire outside auditors to conduct curriculum audits every five years. These audits study how a curriculum meshes with local and state goals. Many districts do not want to do them because they fear upheaval and negative publicity. Make them mandatory.

12. Show all school board meetings on television. The technology is there. Let's use it. If you, as a trustee, want to rubber-stamp the superintendent's decisions, let everyone with a television see that you have no backbone.

13. Use e-mail to improve communication. Part of registration requirements should be the submission of parents' business and home e-mail addresses so school authorities, especially teachers and principals, can keep in constant contact with parents in an inexpensive way.

14. Don't even think of lowering passing levels on state tests. Watch how Texas superintendents shout in the coming months that the new Texas Assessment of Knowledge and Skills requirements are too tough. Hey, tough love, remember?

15. Restore the concept of requiring junior and senior term papers to graduate. Make them at least 15 pages in length, and allow students to rewrite after the initial grading for a higher grade. If you can't read books, go to the library, do research and place original ideas on paper, then you can't graduate. Thinking is part of scholarship.

16. Remove the television from classrooms. At first, it was a wonderful idea to use videos in school, but too many teachers rely on them as a crutch. Keep television rooms where students can go to watch special videos, but keeping a television in each room makes it too easy.

17. Create a required reading list for all Texas high school graduates. Let educators select the list, but no child should be allowed to graduate without reading at least one book by Ernest Hemingway, F. Scott Fitzgerald and Robert Frost. That's just for starters.

18. Roll back top staff salaries and increase teachers' pay. No way that superintendents' salaries and perks should be approaching $200,000, with deputy superintendents making $100,000. Bring a sense of civic obligation to the job: those who lead do so for public service, not money. When they are done, they can go into the private sector and make real money. Reward teachers as a way of attracting the best into the field. They are the front-line soldiers.

19. Beef up community service requirements for students. Follow Birdville High School's lead and reward students who engage in a significant amount of community service with varsity letter jackets for volunteering.

20. Finally, eliminate the "excuse" mentality that exists in public education today. Everybody has an excuse about why things don't work. Parents blame teachers. Teachers blame parents and administrators. Administrators blame state requirements. Create a can-do spirit. Think positive, and you'll act positively.

In the end, the kids won't have a problem with the above. Children can rise up and achieve if they know what is expected of them. It's the adults I'm worried about.

February 2, 2003

Chapter Five

Intolerance, Texas Style

"Who loves his region more — he who fights those things in it which are ugly and wrong and unjust or he who says, 'Let us dwell on our lovely sunsets and our beautiful fields and not advertise our faults?' "

— The great Southern editor
Ralph McGill of *The Atlanta Constitution*

For neighbors, hateful act has opposite effect

So, punk, you come into my Park Glen neighborhood and break into a neighbor's house and cover the walls with your filth by penning swastikas and misspelled slogans about blacks dying and going home, even though they already are home.

You deface the carpets, rip the linoleum, hammer holes into kitchen cabinets, tear up pillows and break glass frames that show Martin Luther King Jr. and a baby on whom you have so thoughtfully drawn a Hitler-like mustache.

The moment I hear, I dash over and knock on the Davises' front door and offer to help paint over your stupidity. Daniel and Rolanda Davis invite me in, and somebody asks, "Who's got paint trays?" So I rush out and get paint trays and tarpaulins, and I'm running across the store parking lot in a fury because I am on a mission to repair, repaint and rebuild everything you did so your act becomes as meaningless and wasted as possible.

I return to the house and meet the neighbors from across the street, Marnie and Chris Pettit and David Polzin, and Brad Brittain, associate pastor of nearby Alliance United Methodist Church, and together we start painting over your evil and making each other laugh and bonding with neighbors I never knew in seven years of living in the neighborhood.

It dawns on me halfway through the afternoon, when the white paint is dripping down my arm and the paint fumes are starting to get to me and the sound of laughter in the house is so loud that the TV reporters downstairs are asking us to be quiet because it doesn't jibe with the solemn nature of the story they are trying to report, that what you have accomplished is exactly what you did not want to do.

I'm not talking about how you have proven yourself to be the dumbest of the dumb. I'm talking about how you unintentionally introduced us to this wonderful family who moved into our neighborhood a year ago and whom we never had the privilege of meeting.

We live in a world where people such as Daniel and Rolanda are the kind of people who are not only raising their two children, ages

8 and 14. They are so kind and so giving that they also are foster parents who share their love and hugs with children abandoned by others.

Truly amazing people.

We now know that Daniel, a mechanic for American Airlines, was a little startled several years ago when Rolanda broached the subject of opening up their home to foster children.

We know that when the first of many foster children entered their house – a 5-year-old girl named Mira, who felt scared and unloved – the Davis family scooped her up and changed her life forever. Mira learned to love and to hug and to kiss. When she eventually left for adoption and a permanent home, she was a happy girl.

"It just tugged at my heart," Daniel recalled.

He was so moved that he and his family could make a difference in the life of someone else that, from then on, he was hooked on helping the unwanted children of others. Such unselfish people in a selfish world.

Punk, last week when you broke into their house and tromped from room to room, spilling red nail polish so it looked like blood and stabbing pillows with the fury of a madman, you invaded the fragile world of three foster children who need no more trauma in their young lives – a week-old baby, a month-old premature baby and an 18-month-old about to move to another home and start all over again with a new mommy and daddy.

Were it not for Daniel and Rolanda, where would these little ones be?

So I'm standing in Daniel and Rolanda's bedroom, and I'm painting over your swastikas, retracing your madness again and again until the hate doesn't show on the walls anymore.

Daniel walks by, sees the freshly painted walls and whispers, "All right. Excellent."

Marnie the schoolteacher and Chris the auditor are downstairs shielding the Davises from reporters like professional public relations people. Brad the associate pastor is upstairs telling me about how he wants to strangle you, punk, but he has learned such a valuable lesson that it has tempered his anger.

"I don't see a lot of hate in them," he says of Daniel and Rolanda. "I'm impressed with how they have handled this."

Punk, you failed in the biggest way.

Thank you for inadvertently introducing us to these beautiful people. What a privilege and an honor to meet them. I pray that your bigotry and hate do not drive them away. We cannot afford to lose such extraordinary neighbors.

September 10, 2000

Maybe by waving hello, we can tell past goodbye

You can see the men in trucks each evening as you drive home from work. At a red light, your car pulls up beside their pickup. Several men sit in the front of the truck. More sit in the rear, facing backward. They wear baseball caps, and sweat stains their clothes after a full day in the sun.

Just yards away, they do not look at you. You do not look at them.

Possibly some of them are undocumented workers from Mexico and other Latin American countries. Their numbers in Fort Worth-Dallas are at an all-time high.

When was the last time you talked to them or waved hello?

"I know there are people who don't like these folks," Southlake home builder Kosse Maykus says. "But these workers are human beings. They're good people. They have good families. They're trying to do good."

Maykus, former president of the Southlake Chamber of Commerce, is a third-generation Czech-American whose grandfather Frank Majkusova immigrated to the United States in 1918 to work as a sharecropper. For this reason, Maykus says he is especially sensitive to the plight of newcomers.

Some among the new generation of foreign workers probably work for Maykus and other home builders. Builders such as Maykus say they always ask to see these workers' papers. The federal government has made Maykus and his colleagues de facto enforcers of tepid government policies.

"I don't like it at all," he says. "I don't believe in a police state."

Maykus makes it a point to say hello when he sees these men in stores and on jobs. He knows they are here for the same reasons his grandfather came to America. He knows that, illegal or not, they represent the last great wave of immigration of this century.

The lack of personal attention we give these individuals in our daily lives – our ambivalence and hesitation to take notice – mirrors the attitude of our government and its policies toward immigration for most of the past 100 years.

The stories in today's *Star-Telegram* about a sophisticated system of recruiters who supply workers for jobs amid today's labor shortage show that, if anything, very little has changed since the days of Ellis Island. If illegal workers are forbidden, but this underground system enables them to find work so easily, then government policies restricting undocumented workers are hardly worth the paper they are written on.

Too often, our economy has used cheap labor – first slavery then child labor. When both were outlawed, we turned to undocumented workers. In this, are we so different from a Third World nation?

Whether it be meatpacking or garment industry jobs in the early part of the century, or home building and landscaping in the later part, what has changed?

Tomas, a 33-year-old construction worker from Mexico, lives in the Metroplex after working at a turkey processing plant in North Carolina.

"I worked where it was hot – where the turkeys were killed and cleaned," he says. "It was very hard. I bled from my nose because it was so hot…. There were many [workers] who lasted two days or just hours."

A century ago, Upton Sinclair wrote in his classic novel *The Jungle*, "It was a sweltering day in July, and the place ran with steaming hot blood – one waded with it on the floor. The stench was almost overpowering, but to Jurgis it was nothing. His whole soul was dancing with joy – he was at work at last! He was at work and earning money."

In 1908, three years after the book was published, a New York congressman declared that the United States had always required the immigrant in order to amass wealth and probably always would.

During World War II, the *Saturday Evening Post* declared, "We cannot expand industrially without a continually expanding supply of labor."

Today's wave of Hispanic workers to North Texas jobs is the latest step in longtime Mexican immigration patterns that began when Mexicans crossed the Rio Grande for farming, mining and construction jobs.

After that, the railroads "lent" surplus Mexican workers to American farmers and introduced the use of Mexican labor for agricultural work throughout the heartland.

Mexican workers came to the United States during World War I to help in the factories while U.S. troops fought in Europe. In the 1920s, Mexicans migrated to northern manufacturing plants and built cars, forged steel and packed meat.

During the Depression, many were sent back to Mexico. Often, Mexicans were favored by U.S. management to break labor strikes.

A second wave of Mexican immigrants came to the United States from 1942 to 1964. A third wave began after that and continues today.

It was always the same. Mexicans responded quickly to news that jobs were available, sometimes at pay rates up to 10 times what they could earn at home. If they were exploited by employers who took a cut of their earnings to justify "the risk," or by landlords who allowed squalid conditions at their quarters, who among us cared enough to protest?

"Weak, often half-hearted attempts at immigration enforcement have not been able to deflect the powerful market incentives: cheap labor as seen by U.S. employers and high wages as seen by Mexican workers," historian Walter Fogel wrote in 1980. "These parties have managed to get together, with or without imprimatur of legality."

We have such mixed feelings about this. So in the face of our ambivalence, we do nothing.

When we pull up beside that pickup at the end of the day, and we neither wave nor nod hello, it's a fitting nongesture of vacillation. If we say nothing, if we do nothing, it is because this is what we have always done.

June 27, 1999

Bible Belt can sometimes feel too tight for comfort

Leslie had lived in Texas all of a month when the kindhearted married couple down the street invited him to a get-acquainted dinner.

He had no family, no friends in Texas, so he welcomed the opportunity to begin his life anew. His dinner host was an airline pilot, a former military man who had lived with his wife in various places around the world before settling in Texas. Their beautifully decorated home reflected a worldliness that impressed Leslie.

"We are glad you could come," the wife began as she passed a plate to Leslie. "We want to welcome you to Texas."

"Thank you," Leslie said, grateful for the hospitality.

"But there's something important we want to talk to you about," she said.

"What's that?" Leslie asked.

"Well," she said, "you seem like such a nice young man, and it's a shame ... why, it's a shame that you are ..."

She fumbled for words.

"Go on," Leslie said.

"Well, it's a shame that you are going to hell!"

"What?" Leslie asked, thinking he had misheard.

"You are Jewish, right?" she asked.

"Yes," Leslie replied.

"Well, until you accept Jesus Christ as your lord and savior, you cannot go to heaven, so even though you seem like a perfectly decent and respectable young man, you will end up in hell for all eternity. And that seems like a terrible waste."

Leslie almost choked on his dinner.

Welcome to Texas, guy.

In the years since, Leslie has come to understand the meaning of the expression that Texas is the buckle of the Bible Belt. Perhaps, he often tells himself, that belt is strapped too tight.

Leslie talks to himself about such matters. He rarely shares his feelings about religion with others.

Indeed, one of his favorite Bible passages is Matthew 6:1, which states, "Be careful not to make a show of your religion before men;

if you do, no reward awaits you in your Father's house in heaven."

To Leslie, at least, many in Texas appear to make a show of their religion.

Leslie often attends government and civic meetings, and at almost every school board or city council meeting, someone will lead an opening prayer that states, "In Jesus' name we pray."

Those five words hurt Leslie more than any Christian could understand. Those five words stab at Leslie's heart. They are the majority's way of denying the minority a place at the public meeting.

He knows that the speakers mean no harm. As consolation, he keeps telling himself, They don't realize what they are doing. They don't even know.

He feels alone. Alone with his God in a place where the belt is too tight.

He felt alone that night at Richland High School when the father of a student who had killed himself in a school bathroom stood before hundreds of parents at a community meeting and said that what is wrong with society is the lack of religion in public schools.

Hundreds of parents responded with a standing ovation. Even the Birdville school district superintendent stood and applauded.

Leslie sat in the back. He did not stand or clap. He knew that to these well-meaning people, adding prayer to the schools means adding Christianity.

As the ovation went on, it appeared to Leslie that many of the people who stood and applauded looked around to see who was not joining them. Leslie could feel their disapproving eyes upon him.

He felt the same way a few months ago when results were announced for the Texas Republican primary's nonbinding resolution about student-led prayer at public school sporting events.

Because Leslie knew that those prayers would be "in Jesus' name," he had voted no.

Nearly a million Texas Republican primary voters cast ballots in favor of the measure, while only 63,901 voted against it.

In the same vein, Leslie skipped the baccalaureate service for his daughter's high school graduation last month because it was at a Baptist church, and he knew that those five words would be said and, again, he would feel alone.

He believes that prayer is for church and for home – or for any other place, as long as it is handled in a private manner. He respects the religious beliefs of others and, as a guest, frequently attends services for other religious denominations. His wife, whom he met after moving to Texas, is a member of a Southlake church, and he sometimes visits there, too.

Last week, when the U.S. Supreme Court ruled against student-initiated prayers at public school athletic events, Leslie felt a little less alone. The court majority decreed in a Texas case that such prayers improperly amount to a government endorsement of religion rather than free speech.

Leslie listened to the outcry against the ruling and reminded himself that the high court did not take away anybody's right to pray.

Where does it say that prayer must be uttered through a public address system for God to hear? Why not pray as described in Matthew 6:6?

"When you pray, go into a room by yourself, shut the door, and pray to your Father who is there in the secret place; and your Father who sees what is secret will reward you."

I know that the loneliness felt by Leslie, a minority in a place where the buckle is tight, is exactly as described above.

You see, this is my story.

Leslie is my middle name.

I am Leslie.

June 25, 2000

Colleyville family reaches out to family hurt by bigot

Dear XYZ family,

I'm not using your name because I know you wouldn't want me to. But let me state how angry I am about what happened to you 15 days ago in Colleyville. All the people I talked to about this feel terrible, so I'm writing on behalf of them, too.

You were about to get a big piece of the American dream – building your dream home – and then the biggest idiot in town ruined it for you. But really, this human trash shouldn't be allowed to get away with what he did. Besides, the sincere reaction from others shows what kind of town Colleyville really is.

Your family consists of you, the husband, an American-born doctor of Indian descent, and your wife, who is a doctor, too. You planned to buy a half-acre lot in Montclair Parc and build a beautiful million-dollar home.

On July 27, you took your relatives there to show them the exclusive gated community, the wonderful French-style homes, the terrific diversity of the neighborhood, which includes Asian-Americans, African-Americans, Jews and families of Middle Eastern descent.

A white man, who was estimated to be 50 to 55 years old and was wearing a baseball cap and sunglasses, rode a bicycle toward you. Believing he was coming to welcome you to the neighborhood, you stuck out your hand and waited for his welcome. He never gave it, and what he said next shook your world – and ours.

He said, "Your kind is not welcome in the neighborhood. Your kind has attacked Americans and killed Americans. You have to get out of here now! And I'm going to make sure that the neighborhood association's architectural board does not approve your house plans. And even if they do, I will make sure that your house will never be built."

You replied, "I'm sorry, but there is a misunderstanding. We are Americans of Indian descent. I was born and raised in Southern California."

The man countered, "We don't care what you are. We don't want your kind in the neighborhood."

Understandably, you were frightened. You ordered your family into the car and drove off. You pulled out of the real estate deal, and the $10,000 you spent on architectural fees went to waste. You swore you would never return to Montclair Parc.

The viciousness and ignorance of this one-man unwelcoming committee are despicable. But please, let's focus on what happened next. The bigot has not been publicly identified, but Colleyville's response is what really matters.

The lot owners, Dr. Y. Anthony Nakamura and his wife, Tammy, wrote a letter to each of the 68 property owners in Montclair Parc. It stated, "We are angry! We are very unhappy that our property will not be sold at this time. However, it is more disturbing to think that there is someone who lives in this neighborhood with such a small and dangerous mind."

Dr. Nakamura told me, "I want him ostracized like he's trying to ostracize these other people. That was the purpose of the letter."

Tammy Nakamura told me, "I want him exposed for the type of person he is. You don't run around and say these sorts of things to people and get away with it."

Kim Gill, president of the Montclair Parc Homeowners Association, mailed the Nakamuras' letter to all property owners and added a cover sheet of his own. It stated, "It is with heavy hearts that we share this letter from the Nakamuras. This terrible incident is disgusting and reflects poorly on all who live in this neighborhood. As a board, we are hopeful that each and every neighbor will be as disgusted as we were after hearing this story and will join us in trying to help identify the person who did this."

The condemnations do not stop there.

Colleyville Mayor Donna Arp told me, "It's a personal assault on every human being, whether they live in Colleyville or anywhere else. I think that every person is damaged when this kind of thing happens. There's never a place for it. It's embarrassing for Colleyville. I feel so badly for this family, and I'm afraid they have the wrong impression of our city."

Because you haven't filed a police report, Colleyville Police Chief John Young said his department could not act. Even with a complaint, the police might not be able to do anything because it does not appear that a specific threat of violence was uttered, Young said.

The chief told me, "Personally, there are a lot of things I find very offensive, but I can't do anything because there's no criminal violation. When people get to that point, they have lost what our community and our nation is all about. It's about diversity and about freedom. But unfortunately, some people are pretty closed-minded about that."

It's hard for a white person such as me to understand why your family won't fight this. Dr. Nakamura, who grew up in Japan, explained: "They were very frightened. They felt threatened for their lives, and they backed out of the deal. The husband said that if anything ever were to happen to any member of his family, knowing that this guy was around in the neighborhood, he would never forgive himself."

Kal Malik, a Dallas lawyer who was born in what is now Pakistan when it was still part of India under British rule, told me that Americans whose ancestors hail from the Indian subcontinent feel especially vulnerable.

"We have many Americans who come from that region who are very loyal and patriotic," he said. "And for a society to take the view that anybody from that part of the world ought to be looked at with suspicion is unfair and against the American ideals. My concern is that this will go unpunished and that people don't have as harsh a view of that bigotry as they did before Sept. 11."

To the XYZ family, I pray that you reconsider. Perhaps you can tell from the widespread condemnation by others that Colleyville really is the city for you. Please understand that one idiot is one idiot. Nothing more.

August 11, 2002

Chapter Six

Austin James Lieber, Native Texan

"I feel good, Daddy. I feel like a chicken."

— Austin James Lieber, before he
announced he was running for
governor of Texas

Fatherhood suddenly has new meaning

My darling *little Beaver Cleaver Lieber,*

I haven't told the world about you until now because your pending arrival is just starting to sink in. Your existence hit me full force last week when your mother and I visited the obstetrician's office. We looked at a sonogram screen showing an image of you inside of her. My goodness, you look about the size of my finger.

"That's the fetus," the doctor said. "See the little flicker?"

I saw your little heart thumping away. I saw your little head and arms, your emerging eye sockets and tiny nose. Kid, you are the most incredible thing I have ever seen.

Since we don't have a name for you, I'm going with the working title of Beaver Cleaver Lieber after one of my favorite television characters. Beaver's father, Ward, always took a genuine interest in his son's activities and escapades. And that's the way I view fatherhood, too.

Last week, in your honor, I placed an old photograph of Ward and little Beaver on our fireplace mantle. In the photograph, Ward looks sternly at Beaver because, inevitably, the Beav has stumbled into trouble again.

Little one, I was always hesitant to have a child of my own because of my late mother's great prophesy. As a child, whenever I misbehaved, my mother warned, "God is going to punish you when you have children."

Now I have two stepchildren, and they are so wonderful and even-tempered that, obviously, they do not share my genetic material.

But you, little Beav, you have the power to make my mother's words come true. So this is my first official request as your daddy. *Please be calm.* My mother didn't have to be right about everything.

Your half sister, Desiree, and half brother, Jonathan, eagerly await your arrival next spring. But we won't ever use that "half" word again, because there will be nothing halfway about their love for you.

Your sister is a 14-year-old high school freshman. She's very tall and wants to be a model. Further proof that she does not carry my genetic material.

Your brother is a 12-year-old Little League all-star. He definitely expects you to pitch by the 1998 season.

Both are trying to come up with your name: Jonathan likes Scooter; Desiree favors Alessandra.

"It can't be a run-of-the-mill name," your mother says.

Until we decide, I'll call you Beav.

Speaking of your mother, you're quite lucky to have her. Karen is a nurturing and kind-hearted woman. But you know that, don't you?

Your grandparents – Karen's parents – can't wait to meet you. And your other grandfather – my father – cried when he first heard about you, probably because I told him on my late mother's birthday.

Finally, in our household, there is Dr. Nero, the elderly black cat with an honorary degree in philosophy, and Sadie the Psycho Dog, whose story is too complicated for now. They will love you and care for you, too.

Nobody, though, awaits you more than me. Desiree and Jonathan are the wonders of my life, but I can't take credit for their success. Since I only married into the family 20 months ago, I missed their important early years.

What kind of father will I be from scratch?

I can't wait to see your first breath, your first steps, your first day at school. Can't wait to push your little bicycle with the training wheels. Can't wait for the day when the wheels come off, and I let you go.

I want to get us, I mean you, an old-fashioned red wagon and pull you around the neighborhood. Since you will be the first native Texan in our family, we can go in search of the Alamo.

Little Beav, there's so much more to say. Just know that I cannot wait to meet you, hug you, kiss you. Welcome to our family.

October 6, 1996

Little Lieber proud to be born a Texan
By Austin James Lieber, 2 days old

Howdy, everybody.

I'm Austin James Lieber, one of Northeast Tarrant County's newest residents. Yes, I'm finally here. At last, we get to meet.

On Friday, I gave Mommy the greatest gift I could. I arrived on her 41st birthday. The clock read 1:02 p.m.

"Welcome to the world, kid!" Daddy said.

My journey out here hurt. It was real scary. But I was getting too crowded inside. Native Texan that I am, I wanted more real estate.

Slowly at first, Mommy pushed and squeezed me toward my new life. I was quite unsure what awaited me. But I was eager to meet my new family and new friends.

Mommy asked me to work with her, so I tried my best.

"You're a good boy," she kept saying during our shared four-hour struggle. "A very good boy."

Once I heard her scream, "Ooooh!!! I hate the pain. I know he does, too. Come on, Austin! Hurry up! Come out!"

So I did. Already, I'm starting to forget the pain.

Hello, world. I'm happy to be here.

I weigh 7 pounds 2 ounces and am 19 inches long. I have blue eyes and dark curly hair. I have Daddy's grin, but not necessarily his personality, because I hardly ever complain.

It's wonderful to match my family's voices with their faces.

Moments after I arrived, my deliveryman, Dr. Robert Hardie, placed me on Mommy's tummy. I lay staring at her and smiling. She is prettier than I ever dreamed.

My big sister is really cool. Desiree held me tight, and I held her back. My big brother was so happy to see me that he cried. At first, I thought he wanted milk, but Daddy explained that Jonathan cries for joy at momentous occasions.

Daddy, Jonathan and I have already formed a secret boys club called the Lieber-teers. Daddy is president. Jonathan is vice president, and I'm secretary-treasurer. What's a secretary-treasurer?

Daddy read somewhere that babies are most aware of their surroundings during their first two hours of life. So he crammed my brain full of necessary information.

He told me where I live and about my name. Austin is the capital of Texas, he said, and I'm the first native Texan in the family. He told me to be proud.

Daddy also sat with me in a rocking chair and read aloud the Ten Commandments. He said I needed a proper start in life.

But when he read the one about honoring thy mother and father, I looked up and wanted to say, "Duh, Dad."

"Wonderful introduction to the world," said my nurse, Eulee Phillips of Bedford. Yeah, maybe so, but I had to admit that I have a higher priority.

I turned to Mommy and cried out, "Got milk?"

I have a silver rattle that makes a funny noise. It's the same rattle Daddy played with almost 40 years ago. I'm surprised it still works.

But life is about more than playing. There's work to do. Daddy made me write this column for you.

"What should I write about?" I asked.

"Write about your life and times," he suggested.

"What life and times?" I asked. "I'm only a day old. I haven't done anything yet."

That doesn't stop other newspaper columnists, he said.

Well, there's something I can say that Daddy never can.

I'm a native Texan.

I understand what that means. It's an honor. And I promise to do my very best to make y'all proud.

Oh, one more thing.

Got milk?

May 4, 1997

Motor baby likes 4 a.m. refuelings

*T*he other night, I stood 20 feet from the pit crews at Texas Motor Speedway watching the professionals change tires and refuel race cars in seconds.

It was the first night racing event at Texas Motor Speedway, but for me it was a *déjà vu* experience.

Every night, I handle racing pit stops with my month-old Motor Baby.

When his tires squeal, I pull Motor Baby off his sleep track and refuel him with bottled milk. Sometimes I also must change his rear spoilers as quickly as possible, so I can push him back on the track for the rest of the race.

During tomorrow night's major Indy race at Texas Motor Speedway, it will take a six-member pit crew to change a car's tires and refuel. The other night, for example, I watched top pole qualifier Tony Stewart's team do a pit stop in an amazing 12.9 seconds.

I could probably do it in that time, too, if I had a half-dozen helpmates. But all I have is Karen, my wife and team manager, who whispers my orders when she says simply, "Your turn."

So I roll out of my garage bay, warm the refueling bottle and place a cloth over Motor Baby's hood. I open a valve cap and start refueling.

I have learned that using warm fuel is crucial to ensuring the best chance for a proper re-start. Within seconds, Motor Baby's camshaft begins making sweet sucking sounds.

During this portion of the pit stop, my chief focus is to keep air out of his engine. But sometimes during these nighttime stops, I feel little emissions coming from Motor Baby's rear exhaust, which means that I must add precious seconds by changing his rear spoilers, too.

My equipment is nearby – cleaning cloths, a fresh rear spoiler and, of course, the handy used-emissions drum container. Technical innovations on racing equipment help to save valuable time – especially Velcro fasteners.

When I'm done with the changing, I dash back to the pit with Motor Baby to continue refueling. One eye is on the clock (it's usually 4 a.m.) and the other is on Motor Baby, as I gently tell him that soon it will be time to get back out on the track for more nighttime racing.

A tricky part comes near the end when I have to hold Motor Baby with his headlights facing skyward and gently push out air blockages from his engine. It's the part of a pit stop where I'm weakest, often costing me cherished seconds.

But the toughest part comes at the end of the pit stop, when I gently push Motor Baby back on the track. It's usually well after 4 a.m., and I have to do the re-start smoothly enough so that Motor Baby doesn't even realize he's going to race again.

"Go! Go! Go!" I whisper, as I tuck his racing cloths into position. I rock Motor Baby to give him a good push start and, after a moment of anxiety, I tiptoe from the track.

The other night at Texas Motor Speedway, I searched for pointers from the pit crew pros. I watched their muscles tense. Observed their fierce yet calculated movements. And witnessed the anxious looks on their faces.

How do I look during the throes of my competition? Well, I don't perform in front of thousands. The only post-pit review comes after I slide back into the garage bay and whisper results to the team manager:

"Twenty-two minutes," I report to Karen. "But no burp."

"Hmmmm," she replies.

I don't know if her reply is good or bad. Usually, I ponder it for a moment, then return to my own race toward dawn.

Sometimes, though, I learn quickly when my performance isn't up to top standards: Motor Baby's headlights turn back on and his tires start squealing again.

No surprise, really. I'm a rookie in this racing league.

Like a professional pit man who drops a tire, I have messed up. Usually, this means I have to get up and do it all over again.

Yes, nighttime racing is the most difficult sport I have ever played.

June 6, 1997

Little Austin

Discovering the realities of the world

By Austin James Lieber, 15 months old

I've had some trauma in my little life. First, I lost someone who meant a lot to me. I never lost somebody I loved before. Shari Lewis, the puppet woman, died this month.

There's a hole in my life every day when her television show no longer comes on. I often wonder, does this mean that Lamb Chop died, too?

Second, do you remember how Daddy watched me in the day-time while Mommy went off to her office job?

That has ended, too.

For weeks, Mommy kept telling Daddy, "Austin is too big for you now, and he needs to go to Miss Debbie's Home Day Care every day. It's time for a new arrangement."

Daddy kept pretending that he didn't hear her. Me, too.

He liked taking me places. I liked going with him. But I'm almost 16 months old. I realize now that I am born to run.

The last important function Daddy and I attended was the grand opening of the Colleyville Area Chamber of Commerce building.

It was a hot day, and I was teething. I'll admit that I wasn't wearing my best chamber of commerce smile. Not until I found the cookie plate at the reception.

After that, I heard Daddy ask Miss Debbie how much it would cost for me to stay with her full time. I love Miss Debbie. She lives a few blocks from us, and I've been visiting her several hours a week for more than a year. But I wasn't ready for any new arrangement.

Neither was Daddy.

The first Monday that he dropped me off, I cried real tears. I'm a little kid. I'm supposed to cry. But what's Daddy's excuse?

I later heard him tell a friend on the telephone that he felt like he got punched in the gut. He said he hadn't felt so lonely since he was 9 and a member of the "Homesick Club" during his first summer at sleep-away camp.

The first week of the new arrangement, Daddy kept picking me up several hours early. He took me out for ice cream or for a stroll at the mall.

Finally, I looked up and asked, "Ima jaba do braba?" – which means, "Get a grip, old man! How do you expect me to adjust if you can't?"

Mommy is another story. Every morning around the time Barney comes on television, she goes to work. She doesn't come home for a long, long time. It seems like forever.

My feelings are hurt. When she smiles at me, I turn my head away. I'm hoping that if I keep this up, she might not leave when Barney comes on.

It's working. I heard Mommy tell Daddy, "In 20 years, he'll be telling the psychiatrist that his problem is his mother went to work."

Actually, Miss Debbie runs a fun place. I don't cry anymore when Mommy or Daddy drop me off in the morning. Well, maybe a little – but not real tears.

I play with my new friends: Abby, Shelby, Stephanie and the ones Daddy calls "the two little presidents" – Carter and Kennedy.

Miss Debbie has been doing this for 13 years, and she's fantastic. Even when she gets mad at me.

A week ago, I hit one of my friends – accidentally, you know – and I had my first timeout. Miss Debbie took me aside and repeated softly: "Austin, we don't hit our friends. We have to be nice to our friends. And we don't hit."

I knew that.

The older kids tell me the score. Our dads and moms work to get money to buy toys for us. No work means no toys. That's why I have to put in my time at Miss Debbie's.

After only a few weeks with her, I can say, "A, B, C" and "1, 2, 3."

Yes, I miss my old life with Daddy, and, no, I don't like making Mommy feel guilty.

But we all need to get on with our lives. I am discovering that there's a whole new world beyond my playpen.

August 23, 1998

Columnist turns into crybaby while taking his first vacation
By Austin James Lieber, 2 years old

*F*or weeks, my family prepped me for my first vacation.

"Austin, you are going to Kentucky," Daddy said. "You are going with me and the rest of the family to the annual columnists convention. You, as America's youngest newspaper columnist, are up for an award. I nominated your three best humor columns from last year. Please prepare your acceptance speech, just in case."

"OK, Daddy," I said.

"Austin, you are going to stay with us in a hotel," Mommy said. "You must be a good boy. You must mind Mommy. You must sleep through the night in the little room with Mommy, Daddy, Sissy and Bubba-Man."

"OK, Mommy," I said.

I didn't know what I was agreeing to. Kentucky? Convention? Hotel room? Acceptance speech? What were they talking about? I'm 2 years old.

But when my sister told me about the airplane, now that was something that excited me!

"Austin, you are going to fly in your first airplane," Sissy said. "You must wear your seat belt. You must not cry. You must be a good boy."

"OK, Sissy."

I love airplanes. I look for them in the sky. When I see one, I shout, "Pair-plane!"

Everyone says this is cute.

For a week, I shouted to anyone who would listen, "Pair-plane to Tucky! Pair-plane to Tucky!" What I meant was, "I am taking an airplane to Kentucky on my first family vacation." But as a writer, I have been trained to use the fewest words possible.

On the pair-plane to Tucky, yes, I became the child from heck. It was a fitting way to start what Daddy now calls the vacation from heck.

It's a one-hour, 40-minute ride to Louisville, Ky. I cried the entire way.

"That's it!" Mommy shouted. "Tomorrow, we're driving back to Texas in a rental car."

I quieted down because the trillion-mile drive from Tucky to Texas with an angry Mommy did not sound fun.

Don't let me forget to mention that I finally fell asleep as the pair-plane landed.

When we arrived at the Tucky hotel, there was no crib in my room. Daddy had a fight with the hotel manager. Seven hours later, a crib was brought up. Of course, I had no use for it.

"Mommy, I sleep in bed with you. Mommy, I sleep in bed with you." Guess where I slept?

The air conditioner did not work. The toilet was clogged and Daddy foolishly forgot to pack a plunger. The food was terrible. The hotel elevators took forever.

This is what y'all mean by vacation?

Every night at 3 a.m., I woke up in a crying fit that lasted an hour.

"Home, Mommy!" I screamed.

"Vacation from heck," Mommy and Daddy kept saying.

They left me in the room with my brother, Bubba-Man, who watched sports day and night on television.

Daddy went to seminars. Mommy and Sissy went shopping.

I love horses, but they went to Churchill Downs without me.

I love baseball, but they went to the Louisville Slugger bat museum without me.

I love boats, but they rode the *Spirit of Jefferson* sternwheeler on the Ohio River without me.

I paid them back with those 3 a.m. wake-up calls.

When the time came to fly the pair-plane back to Texas, everyone made me promise to behave.

"I promise," I said.

On the pair-plane, I cried and cried.

A flight attendant whispered to Daddy, "Trust me, I know what I'm doing."

Then she said, "Little boy, you better be good or I will take you away!" She scared me.

Now every time I see a pair-plane, I shout "Pair-plane!" And then fearfully add, "Lady come get me?"

By the way, I didn't win the award, but I had a speech prepared: "I would like to thank the editors of the *Star-Telegram* for putting their faith in a 2-year-old."

Apparently, the contest judge did not think my columns were funny.

At this point, nobody else in my family thinks I'm very funny either.

June 25, 1999

Search to find God,
like circle, is never-ending

One recent summer afternoon, when the Texas sun burned hot enough to touch my soul, I took Austin, my 2-year-old son, on an adventure to find God.

I had read in my wife's church newsletter about a recently completed labyrinth built by parishioners at St. Anne's Episcopal Church in Lake Worth.

A photograph in the periodical showed parishioners walking contemplatively on the labyrinth's circular paths toward the center. The journey represents a pilgrimage to Jerusalem.

I told my little boy that we were going to play a game where we would walk in circles.

"Why?" he asked, as he always does.

I answered, "Because we're going to find God."

"OK," he said.

We had never talked about God. I mean, the boy is 2 years old. But is a child ever too young to understand?

We drove on Northwest Loop 820 and exited at Azle Avenue. I had never been to St. Anne's, but the labyrinth wasn't hard to find. The series of circles was painted on asphalt in the rear parking lot.

"Let's play the circle game," I told Austin.

And so we began to walk.

Sometimes I followed him on the paths, and sometimes Austin, wearing his Winnie the Pooh baseball cap to shield the sun, followed me.

Sometimes I walked alone, while he stopped to pick up rocks or play with the church kitty who had come out to walk with us.

After a bit, he asked, "Daddy, where's God?"

I pointed to the sky and replied, "God is everywhere, Austin."

He looked up and then back at me. He didn't appear satisfied with the answer. We continued our walk.

A man with bright eyes and a salt-and-pepper beard emerged from the church. He introduced himself as the Rev. William S. Winston and welcomed us to the labyrinth.

He told us that when we get thirsty, we should come inside for a glass of water.

Austin and I continued on our journey.

"Going to find God?" Austin asked again. "Where's God?"

"God is everywhere," I repeated.

"That's the circle?" he asked.

"Yes."

"Daddy, I thirsty."

Holding his Pooh hat, he began walking toward the church's front door. The kitty followed, as did I.

"Going to find God," he said again, but this time it wasn't a question.

Inside, Winston ushered us in and asked Austin, "Would you like cold water?"

"Uh-huh."

The priest left to fetch drinks.

Austin looked at me and said, "God get the water."

When Winston returned with water, Austin took a drink, promptly spilling some on a couch. The priest smiled and said, "That's why we have the utilitarian stuff in here. The French provincial is in the other room."

I asked how the labyrinth came to be.

He explained that church members learned of other churches with similar meditation paths. The best known, he said, is at Chartres Cathedral in France. It measures 42 feet across, the same size as the one in his church parking lot.

Members plotted out the lines and then painted them in time for a dedication blessing on July 4.

"Where did the kitty go?" Austin asked.

"Would you like to play with the kitty?" Winston asked.

"Uh-huh."

Winston brought the kitty in from the hallway and handed Austin a table tennis ball.

"Throw it," Winston said.

Austin threw the ball, and the kitty chased it.

Winston told me that the concept of a labyrinth dates many centuries.

"Most people come early in the morning when it's coolest," he said. "It's a walking meditation. It's simply another tool for listening to God. Around here, most people's ideas of praying to God is talking to God and making requests or demands, rather than listening. And this is just a tool to listen."

Austin was getting impatient. Winston walked to a shelf and pulled down a rice-paper ball, given to him by St. Anne's sister church in Japan. The priest deflated the ball by squeezing. Then he blew it up again.

"See?" he asked Austin. "Nifty, huh?"

"Uh-huh."

Austin wanted the ball, of course, but the priest said he couldn't have it because the ball was a gift to the church. He walked back to his shelf and pulled down a small paper crane, also given by the sister church. He handed the origami artwork to my boy.

"One of their legends," Winston said, "is that if you make a thousand cranes, your wish will come true."

We thanked the priest and said our goodbyes. He invited us to come again.

Traveling home in the car, Austin kept repeating, "Daddy, I go circles! I go circles! We go circles at home?"

"Yeah," I answered as I drove. "You can look for God any time, anywhere."

"My bird, Daddy," he said. "Please give me my bird."

I handed him the paper bird, and thought about the legend of the thousand cranes and the wish that can come true.

My wish is that Austin will never cease the adventure that he has now begun. I pray that my little boy will never stop his search to find God.

August 29, 1999

3-year-old peruses game of politics at Bush rally in Dallas
By Austin James Lieber, 3 years old

I want to tell you the story of how I came face to face with Gov. George W. Bush last week in Dallas.

This story begins a few days before, when Daddy and I watched the Democratic convention together on television.

"That's Joe Lieberman!" Daddy said.

My last name is Lieber, so I was confused.

"Is he my grandpa?" I asked Daddy.

"No," Daddy said.

"Who is he?" I asked.

Little Austin

"He's running for vice president of the United States."

"Is he my friend?" I asked.

"That's for you to decide," Daddy said.

He told me how people run for president and vice president, and then we decide whether we want to vote for them. I'm 3 years old, so, of course, I got a little bored.

"Daddy, can you switch the television to sports?"

Daddy laughed and said that's what most people want to do when they see people making speeches. But he said he wanted me to understand the way the game works.

OK, I like games.

A few days later, he woke up early and said, "We're going to Dallas today."

"To see the Mavericks?" I asked.

"No," he said. "I want you to see George W. Bush. He's the governor of Texas, and he's running for president."

"Is he my friend?" I asked.

"That's for you to decide," he said.

In the car, Daddy explained that we were going to a rally where many people would sit and listen to other people talk. He told me to behave.

"Are there sports there?"

"It's in a basketball gym, but there's no sports today," he said.

"Where are the players?" I asked.

"Not there," he said.

When we arrived at Moody Coliseum in Dallas, I saw many people waiting to get in. There was a band playing.

"I'm so excited," I said. "This is like a parade!"

Across the street, I saw people holding signs.

"See those protesters there?" Daddy asked. "They don't like George W. Bush."

"They think he's mean?" I asked.

"Yes."

"Is he mean, Daddy?"

"No, Austin. He's a compassionate conservative."

"What?"

Daddy started to explain, but then a nice lady handed me an American flag.

We found seats in the gym.

That man from television, Walker the Texas Ranger, was talking.

"So let's make George W. Bush the next president of the United States," he said.

"Daddy, where are the basketball players?"

"Sh!"

"Daddy, I'm hungry."

"Quiet, please."

People from something called a Congress were talking. One after another. I didn't know them. I didn't like listening to them.

"Daddy, where's George W. Bush?"

"He's coming."

"Daddy, let's go home."

"Soon."

"No, not soon. Now!"

Daddy ignored me.

The people in the gym started screaming: "Bush! Bush! Bush!"

"That's him!" Daddy said.

I saw George W. Bush on the stage far away. He looked little.

"Daddy, what's he saying?"

"He said he wants to help sick people," Daddy said.

"Oh."

"Now he's saying he wants to help old people."

"Oh."

"Now he says he wants to help kids in school."

"Oh."

I tried to listen, but I wondered where the basketball players were. Then something really great happened. George W. Bush stopped talking and a cannon shot lots of paper stars in the air. Daddy called it confetti. I loved that!

Finally, we left the gym. It was hot, and we walked many blocks to our car.

At North Central Expressway and Mockingbird Lane, I saw lots of policemen.

Daddy said, "Something big is about to happen."

"What Daddy?"

There were no cars on the street. Then policemen on motorcycles rode by. I heard sirens. Then a long line of black cars passed by slowly.

In one car, I saw a man in the back seat. His window was open, and the man was very close to me – just a few feet away.

I looked at the man. The man looked at me.

I knew him. It was George W. Bush!

I was holding my flag. He waved at me and smiled.

I waved back.

Then he was gone.

"Daddy, why did George W. Bush wave at me?"

"He wants to be your friend."

"Is he my friend?"

"Austin, that's for you and everybody else to decide."

OK, now I see how this game is played.

August 25, 2000

5-year-old adds a little maturity to governor's race

I was watching television. A Rick Perry commercial came on. An announcer said Tony Sanchez laundered money through his bank. A Tony Sanchez commercial came next. An announcer said Rick Perry pocketed $1 million from the insurance industry. Enough already.

His campaign poster

Austin, my 5-year-old son, was standing next to me. He said, "I feel good, Daddy. I feel like a chicken."

This statement made more sense than anything the two candidates for Texas governor have said in their ugly and stupid campaigns. My little boy did not care what I thought of his remark. He was just telling me his true feeling at that moment. I know you will agree with me when I suggest we need more of that in politics.

Then it came to me. The best idea I have had in years. Perry and Sanchez are conducting their campaigns like little children. As long as I have a little child myself, I figured, why not run him for governor? Compared with those two, he is equally qualified.

Austin is a Texan, born and bred. Like Perry, he has very good hair. Like Sanchez, he has a substantial sum of money in his personal bank account. Unlike the other two, if my boy feels like a chicken, he will tell you so.

I have a great photograph of Austin in front of the Alamo. He is smiling and wearing a Texas-flag shirt. I called up a friend and asked him to make buttons with that image and the words, "Austin J. Lieber for Governor." That was done, and already, the hard work of our campaign is over.

Today I am here to announce that my son, Austin J. Lieber, is the third candidate for governor. This is a proud moment. I will be his campaign manager, his spokesman and his issues director. My official title is Assistant to the Chicken.

The best part of this campaign is that the candidate does not care about any of this. I have told him what I plan to do with his name and image, but he only nods and returns to the Cartoon Network. I believe he likes the Cartoon Network because political commercials do not appear on that channel.

I am selling the buttons for $5 each. The money goes to Summer Santa, Northeast Tarrant County's largest children's charity, which I co-founded. I have sold several dozen to members of two groups, the Greater Southlake Women's Society and the Women's Division of the Grapevine Chamber of Commerce. From these early sales, I can see that my son is a big hit with an important part of the electorate – women with a sense of humor, known to pollsters by the acronym WASH.

Before I explain how you can order an Austin-for-governor button, I should share his position on the issues. But let me make one quick promise. We will never place a single hateful commercial on television. As shown by what has appeared on television for months, it is a childish way to conduct a campaign. And while Sanchez may draw from his own bank account, we do not want to touch Austin's bank account.

OK, you need to know that Austin is pro-education. Last week in kindergarten, he learned how to read the following words: bat, can, sad and fan. On Friday in school, he tried to read his first book. From what I can tell, this would place him in a tie with Perry when it comes to the candidates' literacy.

As for fiscal matters, Austin is cost-conscious. Whenever he wants a new toy, he asks how much it costs and then asks, "Is that expensive?" If all our politicians did that, we would have fewer problems.

Austin will never say a negative word about his opponents. But if he slips and calls either of them his favorite derogatory name – "poo-poo head" – I promise he will take a bath and go to bed early.

Taking a bath is part of our campaign strategy. Our motto is, "Vote for Austin. He's clean. He takes a bath every night."

Now if the other poo-poo heads, I mean candidates, declare that they are clean because they also take baths every night, they would be lying. Their campaign commercials are so dirty, they need at least two baths a night to wipe off the mud.

Good people of Texas, please follow the lead of that important group of voters, WASH, and consider supporting my candidate. If you would like to join the Austin team and buy your campaign button, send a check for $5, payable to Summer Santa (a tax-deductible contribution that will send needy area children to summer camp) to: Dave Lieber, Assistant to the Chicken, *Star-Telegram*, P.O. Box 915007, Fort Worth, TX 76115. I promise that within a week of receiving your check, I will mail you an Austin-at-the-Alamo button.

Maybe with a little boy running against them, Perry and Sanchez will finally grow up.

September 29, 2002

Negative campaigners should try to grow up

Note: The following is a draft of gubernatorial candidate Austin J. Lieber's concession speech, which he is scheduled to deliver tonight after the polls close. These remarks were written by his father, columnist Dave Lieber, who served as his campaign manager.

Victorious in defeat

My fellow Texans, I stand before you tonight to concede the governor's race to (fill in winner's name). I will not be speaking long because, as you know, I am only 5 years old and it is past my bedtime. But I congratulate the winner and wish him the best, because his success will be my success. Anything he can do to help Texas prosper will ultimately help this young Texan prosper, too.

When my daddy and I first discussed entering this race as a write-in candidate seven weeks ago, we knew I wouldn't win. A little boy running for governor of Texas? It was a thought I could not understand. But the point, as my daddy explained, was to add maturity to a race in which two adults were behaving like children.

He told me we would act proudly and positively, and try not to say a bad word about anyone else. Because of this, he said, our campaign would be different and people would notice. He said he hoped that the voters would respond, and to our surprise, many of you did. As the sale of my $5 buttons for charity continued to grow closer to the $1,000 mark, the meaning of my campaign grew clearer.

The Austin J. Lieber campaign represents the beginning of a movement that I hope will not end tonight. Negative campaigning must end. As my daddy explains, for that to happen, it will be up to people like you and me. We cannot count on the politicians who engage in these horrible and childish games of bad-mouthing their opponents to suddenly grow up and do the right thing. This change must be forced on them like the vegetables that are forced upon me at dinnertime.

I would like to thank the hundreds of supporters in greater Northeast Tarrant County who purchased my buttons in these past weeks to help make this statement. And I would like to thank the several dozen voters who wrote my name on their ballots as a symbol of our protest. I know you were not actually voting for me, but for the idea that a state as great as ours deserves leadership that doesn't believe that winning at any cost – no matter how ugly and wrong – is the right way to win.

I'm not perfect. I get my share – no, more than my share – of timeouts at school and at home. But in my short life I have never tried to jump ahead of others by accusing them of crimes that they did not commit or by spending money to buy something that was not my right to buy.

As I mentioned, our campaign has raised almost $1,000 for the Summer Santa charity to send area children in need to summer camp. That sum represents four or five children who will attend camp in 2003 who otherwise would not go. I thank my supporters for this wonderful display of generosity.

But now we must look ahead. As one of my supporters, J.K. of North Richland Hills, wrote to me, "My question remains, Why aren't we as Texans collectively furious about this campaign? I am insulted that both candidates think we are foolish enough to vote for governor based on these commercials. I am proud to declare myself a 'Chickenhead.' "

J.K. was referring to my opening statement in which I said, "I feel good, Daddy. I feel like a chicken." As you may remember, my father used that statement to show my innocence and honesty as a young candidate. It touched many of you and made you laugh. We hope it made you think, too.

Now I call on my fellow Chickenheads to rise up and make clear to the adults running these horrible campaigns that we will no longer stand for their petty games.

Saying bad things about others means that others will believe that you, too, are behaving badly. That is what my parents try to teach me. And although I admit I have trouble learning this lesson, I know that it is an important one. To be good, you must never lie. You must never hurt others to benefit yourself.

I would like to thank my daddy for writing this speech for me. Even though I don't understand most of it, I know that what we are trying to do is right for Texas. Just as adults can act like children, sometimes children can act like adults. I hope I have done so here.

Fellow Chickenheads, thank you for sharing this great honor with me. We must do what we can to make sure that young Texans like me grow up to become strong Texans, happy Texans, and most important, honest and proud Texans.

Please don't let the dream die. God bless you, and God bless Texas. Good night.

November 5, 2002

Some art
is a laughing matter

Austin and Dakota at museum

Despite what some area politicians may tell you, I'm no idiot. I have an Ivy League education, which in Texas I understand is not as prestigious as going to Texas A&M. But I mention it because I know a little something about painting, music, sculpture, theater and other fine arts.

As part of my classical education, I spent a lot of time in modern-art museums gazing at gobs of paint splattered on canvases. Even with my fancy-pants education, I still look at these artworks and mutter, "I could do that. Why is that there?"

If Michelangelo could spend four hours lying on his back atop a scaffold to paint the ceiling of the Sistine Chapel in Rome, nobody has to explain to me why that is an artwork of believable beauty. But if Jackson Pollock had a spat with his lover and was in such a bad mood that he poured paint all over the canvas, I will look at the product and think, "Boy, he sure fooled some rich person into paying too much for that."

When the Modern Art Museum of Fort Worth reopened last month, I was very proud that the city I call home has one more fabulous place that I can use to prove to my relatives elsewhere that we do not live in Yahooville. But I also knew that the slogan for the museum should be "I could do that. Why is that there?"

One area art critic put me in my place when he wrote: "About modern art, people sometimes say: 'I could have done that.' But they didn't do it, didn't even think of it. Modern art is all about seeing new things and seeing old things in new ways. The Modern Art Museum of Fort Worth is a marvelous new place to do both."

Recently, I brought two of my favorite people to see the new museum building – my 5-year-old son, Austin, and his longtime friend, 7-year-old Dakota Wing of Keller. I have tried to instill in Austin a sense of art beyond crayons. He owns an artist's kit to match my own. In recent weeks, we have visited the Kimbell Art Museum and the Amon Carter Museum, where we bring out our sketch kits and try to copy a piece of art we both like.

Dakota, on the other hand, is not much of a museum visitor. He is more of a little cowboy who knows his way around a rodeo. But like any good cowboy, he is always game for new adventures.

On this trip, we first admired the new building, which is quite terrific. The boys really liked the rock pond outside the big glass windows. Cowboy Dakota remarked, "They should put some trout in there."

But as we journeyed throughout the museum, I noticed that the boys were confused.

"Did he paint it?" Austin asked in front of one painting. "It looks like he just threw paint on there."

In front of a sculpture, Austin noted, "That's just a piece of a car!"

"Look how easy that is," Dakota said in front of another painting that looked as if the artist had started to paint but never got around to finishing. Most of the canvas was blank.

"I want to draw that ... and that ... and that," Austin said, pointing at many different pieces.

Dakota, for whom we had brought an extra sketch set, was excited, too. He said: "I want to draw as many things as I can!"

We started in front of the first painting you see near the entrance, Robert Motherwell's *Stephen's Iron Cross*. I'll describe it by calling it a giant Rorschach test where you see large black shapes but you're not sure what they are.

As the boys sat on the floor drawing, a woman in gray woolen pants and a sweater walked up behind them and in a rather loud voice told her male companion: "We had the restoration person give us a lecture, and there's a controversy over whether you restore it or you let the paint have a life of its own. By the way, it's a ballerina."

In museum like this, I like listening to the art snobs more than looking at the art. First, how can she be so certain that these black blobs were a ballerina? Besides, why would a painting of a ballerina be called *Iron Cross*? Second, I believe she was just showing off for her friend. She got to go on a special tour. Wow. She also knew about all the arguments relating to the way the paint had dried. Wow again.

Soon the boys and I moved on to the other painting they wanted to draw – Ellsworth Kelly's *Curved Red on Blue*. The boys wanted to draw it because it looks like a question mark – except, as Dakota pointed out, "The painter forgot the dot."

As the boys sat on a bench and began to draw, I walked over to the wall plaque and read the following: "Although the form initially appears as a question mark without its dot, it is difficult to identify the exact source of the curve. Kelly has acknowledged *Curved Red on Blue* as a seminal work that opened up a career-long investigation of the curve and its graphic possibilities."

Just then, Gray Woolen Pants walked by again and stood behind the boys.

"Look at this and focus," she lectured her companion. "Now move your head very slowly. Do you see the figure transpose? Your brain tells you it moved. Look at it really hard."

I felt like shouting, "Lady, it's just a half-finished question mark! You could go to any pool hall in Texas, drink a couple of beers and do the same thing with a big neon beer sign!"

But I just kept quiet and watched the boys draw. They were having fun. I hope they learned an important lesson about art. Art is often beautiful. But it can also be funny. Perhaps the funniest part is the people who stand around and act so serious about such silly things.

January 7, 2000

Chapter Seven
Texas Tales

"[Jimmy] Breslin made a revolutionary discovery. He made the discovery that it was feasible for a columnist to actually leave the building, go outside and do reporting on his own, genuine legwork. Breslin would go up to the city editor and ask what stories and assignments were coming up, choose one, go out, leave the building, cover the story as a reporter and write about it in his column."

— Tom Wolfe in his anthology
The New Journalism

A dream of a lifetime fulfilled

Note: The following is based on a front-page story that appeared in the February 27, 1997 issue of the Fort Worth Star-Telegram.

*T*he greatest day I spent in a classroom came long after my schooling ended, when I was 39 years old, in an old elementary school in Richland Hills. Theresa Neil, a fifth-grade teacher, was dying of cancer and she had a final wish that wasn't going to come true.

She wanted to meet Emmitt Smith, the Dallas Cowboys' star running back. But so did everyone else. A few of her friends contacted the Cowboys on her behalf but nothing ever happened.

In the mid-1990s, Theresa Neil was well known, too, although not as well known as Smith. Thousands of *Fort Worth Star-Telegram* readers knew about Mrs. Neil because reporter Carlos Illescas and photographer Helen Jau had spent days and nights with her, documenting Mrs. Neil's final months. When their beautifully written and photographed series appeared in the newspaper, readers were enamored by Mrs. Neil's courage and her insistence that she remain on the job. In doing so, she would teach her students and the rest of us wonderful life lessons. Yet although an inspiration to thousands, Mrs. Neil's checklist of to-do's before death remained incomplete:

Teach son Ryan long division. *Check.*

Help daughter Sarah learn how to read. *Check.*

Instruct daughter Candice how to drive a car. *Check.*

Take guitar lessons. *Check.*

Meet Emmitt Smith. Uh, no check.

In early 1997 I learned about this situation from Sue Thompson, a food preparer in the school cafeteria. I called Cowboys public relations director Rich Dalrymple and told him about Mrs. Neil. I sent Rich the *Star-Telegram* series. After reading it, Rich promised to talk to Smith.

Smith read the series and quickly agreed to make a surprise visit to Mrs. Neil's class after working out at the Cowboys' headquarters at Valley Ranch. That winter day, on Feb. 26, 1997, when Smith arrived, we shook hands and I thanked him for coming. Then we walked through the school to Mrs. Neil's class.

As he waited in the corridor, I knocked on her door and went in. In front of the children, I asked Mrs. Neil about her checklist. We ran through it and she kept saying, "Check." Then I mentioned Emmitt Smith and her face dropped.

"But wait!" I said. I opened the door, and there stood Emmitt Smith beaming in the doorway.

Theresa Neil and Emmitt Smith

"How's everybody doing?" he asked nonchalantly.

But no one could hear him. Mrs. Neil's screams of surprise rang throughout the school: "I'm going to have a heart attack!!" she exclaimed. "Oh, my God!"

Smith stood shyly, watching the uproar. Children leapt from their chairs. Some cried with their teacher, and others gawked at the smiling football star.

"My dream!" Mrs. Neil exclaimed. "How did this come about?"

When she found out, she hugged Thompson and me. Then Smith asked if he could speak to the class. What he said next was probably the greatest speech I ever heard.

"I wish I could come here under better circumstances," he began. He gets many requests to visit sick children, but he had never received one on behalf of a dying adult.

"I admire you a great deal because you have a lot of courage," he told Mrs. Neil. "And you kids, look at her, because she's a strong woman. It takes a strong person to understand the situation she's going through.

"To come to school on a day-to-day basis and make sure you guys are learning – and coming in here with a smile on her face – must be very tough.

"Playing football is very easy compared to what she's going through. Doing what I do is very easy compared with what she's going through. I don't know that I would have the courage to do what she's doing right now. So I admire her greatly. That right there is what really got me here."

Mrs. Neil stood across the room with tears in her eyes. Her students hung on Smith's every word.

He acknowledged that he was caught up in the feelings of the moment. Smith pulled off his ball cap and showed everyone that he was sweating, partly from his own emotions. Comparing himself to Mrs. Neil, he joked, "My hair is short, too." Mrs. Neil, who lost her hair from chemotherapy treatments, led the laughter.

"I want you guys to look at her and take something from her," Smith said. "Because she's going to leave a lot with you. Your memories of this teacher and this day are going to stay with you for a long time.

"No matter how old you get, you're going to look back and remember this day. And this day is a very special day. Not only for her, but for you guys. And for me.

"This is the first time for me. I've dealt with kids dying, and I've had some to pass on. And when that happens, it touches me.... When they passed on, a part of me went with them. I felt the grief as well."

Every eye watched Smith, as he continued.

"Obstacles are going to fall in your way," he said. "In the class-room, math is going to get hard. English is going to get hard. But to have the mental and inner strength to keep pressing on – regardless of what your back is up against – is really going to get you through. Sometimes pick yourself out of the first person and start thinking of other people aside from yourself.

"Thank you for inviting me out. It's a day that's going to stay with me for the rest of my life. God bless you," Smith said as he looked up at Mrs. Neil the way she often looked up to him.

Then the teacher asked, "Are we blessed or what?" As the children murmured agreement, she said, "No matter what's given to you in life, you take it and say, 'What can I do with this now? How can I make a difference in my life?'"

"I have one last request," Smith interrupted. "I want to take a pic-ture with the whole group." He wanted the photograph, he told them, for the wall of his home.

The teacher and the football player sat close with their arms around each other. The children gathered in closer. Emmitt Smith was right. It was a special day whose memory would last forever.

Neil's heroic example had power to move a community

"I'm a nobody," the woman said at the front door of the church.

She had traveled from Fort Worth to attend yesterday's memorial service for Theresa Neil, the Glenview Elementary School teacher whose death from cancer evoked great emotions from many in the community.

By sharing her story with others during the past year, Mrs. Neil's reach extended beyond Richland Hills, where she taught, and beyond Watauga, where she lived. Proof of this came from Sharon Finn, the shy woman who walked up to the church and described herself as a nobody.

Finn was not a friend, a relative, neighbor or acquaintance of Theresa Neil. Finn had never met her, but she felt compelled to go to First United Methodist Church of Hurst. It was the first funeral she had attended for someone she did not know.

"This lady is a star to me," she said. "This lady is my idol.

"Her story broke my heart. I was diagnosed with breast cancer a year after she was. She has three kids. I have three kids. She's my hero.

"When she definitely found out she was going to die, everything she did until the end was not for herself. It was for others."

The woman walked through the front door of the church and signed the guest book. She took a program from an usher and sat in the back row. She sighed softly.

"I just had to be a part of this," she whispered.

There was so much about Mrs. Neil that this fan didn't know. She had never heard Mrs. Neil talk or laugh or cry.

She didn't know how Mrs. Neil had met Caryn Yoast, presiding minister at yesterday's service, at a Glenview Elementary School parent-teacher conference. She didn't know how Mrs. Neil and Yoast had spent that first evening several years ago talking not about Yoast's daughter, who was in Mrs. Neil's class, but about God.

Finn didn't know how Mrs. Neil had planned the funeral for months, even joking with the funeral director about climbing into the coffin before she died to see how it felt.

The service began, and Finn clutched a tissue to wipe her eyes. With the other mourners, Finn sang hymns selected by Mrs. Neil. She bowed her head in prayers chosen by Mrs. Neil.

During the service, Finn spoke only once, after Neil's former principal, Juan Mechaca, said that Mrs. Neil "made an indelible mark on every person she met." He called her "Queen Theresa," causing the mourners to laugh.

Finn whispered, "How 'bout Mother Theresa?"

It seemed a little farfetched to compare Mrs. Neil to the saintly nun from India who helps the sick and the dying. But in her own way, Mrs. Neil had helped many others, some of them sick and dying. And some of these people were like Finn, people whom Mrs. Neil had never met.

"We live in communities," Yoast said in a short talk about Mrs. Neil. "We are responsible for one another. We are not strangers."

During Mrs. Neil's final months, the minister said, "I could see through her the goodness of God and the goodness of living with God."

Perhaps a little like Mother Teresa.

There was another hymn and a closing prayer, and the service ended. It was short and to the point, like a Theresa Neil lesson in school.

From her seat in the back row, Sharon Finn, the self-proclaimed nobody, watched patiently as everyone in the rows ahead stood to exit.

First the undertakers pushed the gray coffin carrying her hero past her. Then Mrs. Neil's family – her husband and three children and the rest of Mrs. Neil's extended family – walked past Finn, followed by Mrs. Neil's many, many friends.

Finn was one of the last to leave the church. Outside, she said she didn't like funerals.

"I don't like to deal with death. But I'm getting old. I'm 51 now.

"I had to come. I don't know why. I don't know."

In her own way, Finn stood for a community graced by this dynamic teacher.

We live in communities, the Rev. Yoast said. We are responsible for one another. We are not strangers.

Sharon Finn was the best proof of this.

She was the nobody who is all of us.

August 6, 1997

Cullen Davis smiles
for a jury once again

*T*he judge called a recess, and the jury members stood to exit the courtroom. Cullen Davis stood from his seat on the witness stand and turned to face the jury. He looked each juror in the eye and half-smiled as they walked past.

It was a chilling sight. Cullen Davis was a witness in a jury trial in Tarrant County last week involving an ex-wife – not Priscilla, his second wife who died last year, but Sandra, his nearly forgotten first wife.

There he was, trying to make friends with a jury again. Cullen Davis of Colleyville is very good with juries. He got one jury in the 1970s to believe that he didn't have anything to do with the slaying of 12-year-old Andrea Wilborn.

A mysterious man in black killed the girl, Priscilla's daughter, in August 1976 in Cullen Davis' secluded hilltop mansion off South Hulen Street in Fort Worth overlooking the Colonial Country Club. Another man was killed and two other people were wounded in the same midnight shooting. Three witnesses testified that Cullen Davis was the shooter, something he has always denied.

The best of his four criminal trial juries was the 1977 jury in the murder trial, which was moved to Amarillo after a change of venue. After his acquittal on a capital murder charge, he threw a victory party and invited the jurors.

At a second Fort Worth trial on a solicitation of murder charge, he was acquitted again. Those jurors later invited him to their reunion party.

This new jury is being asked to determine whether Cullen Davis should pay his first wife $492,000 in alimony. Davis acknowledges the debt but says Sandra Davis has to wait until his older brother, Kenneth Davis, gets his debts repaid first.

During the recess, Cullen Davis walked over to where I was sitting, in the second row of a courtroom that was almost empty.

"Must be a slow news day," he said.

"Can't miss Cullen Davis in a courtroom," I explained. "Can we talk?"

"Yeah, I guess," he said. "About my love life?"

"No, I know you're still in love with Karen, right?"

"Right," he said. Karen is his third wife, whom he married in 1979.

We made arrangements to meet after court adjourned for the day. Cullen Davis walked back to the witness stand. He stood for a moment looking at a framed poster on a courtroom wall. The poster contains drawings of Fort Worth icons – cattle, cowboys, the Tarrant County Courthouse and the Will Rogers Coliseum.

You could put his photograph on that poster, too, showing Cullen Davis on a witness stand, angry with an ex-wife. Although the chamber of commerce can't use it, this image is as much a part of Fort Worth history as the daily cattle drive.

The jury returned, and Cullen Davis stood and faced it again, half-smiling.

Cullen Davis testified about his 1987 bankruptcy in which he listed $865 million in debts, including his alimony.

Sandra Davis sat quietly nearby. She appears the opposite of Priscilla Davis, who was notorious for her flamboyance and brazenness. Sandra, who was married to Cullen Davis from 1962 to 1968, appears shy and reserved. She was tastefully dressed in a brown jacket and a long, dark skirt. She wore little makeup and minimal jewelry.

Her lawyers say Cullen and Kenneth Davis concocted a scheme to deprive her of the money. Both men deny such a plan. The trial is expected to continue this week.

Sandra Davis never attracted much attention. Cullen's second and third wives overshadowed her.

But 25 years ago, a former investigator named Jerry Hittson told authorities that Cullen Davis wanted him to kill Sandra, the mother of his two sons, because she was demanding a large divorce settlement. The alleged plot was never carried out, and authorities never took action.

Cullen Davis and I met outside the courtroom. We walked to a parking garage, where he opened the trunk of his cream-colored Cadillac and pulled out a brochure touting his latest product.

After his oil business went bust, he sold hand cream that protected the skin from maladies including fire ant bites, dirt and illnesses, he said. Last year, the company went out of business.

Cullen Davis started selling something new in November – medical discounts. He excitedly showed me the brochure.

"This product is available to everybody," he said. "No rejections. No deductibles. It's for the uninsured, the underinsured, the overinsured. You can be on your deathbed and get it."

Somehow, you think, Cullen Davis should be the last person to use that line in his sales pitch. He continued, "It's a fantastic product because it's going to be the answer to America's health-care crisis. It's going to make insurance irrelevant."

He invited me to his regular Saturday morning meetings in the family room of his Colleyville home, where he recruits customers and salespeople. Karen Davis does the computer work for his new business, he said.

"The money is out-of-sight," he said. "This is a moneymaking deal. This is the best I've ever seen in my life."

"Are you a pretty good salesman?" I asked, already knowing the answer.

He replied, "I can get an appointment with probably anybody without telling them what I'm coming over for."

He smiled again, that same smile he gave the jurors throughout the day. I asked him why he always smiled at the jurors.

"Because I haven't done anything wrong," he said.

"One last question," I said. What did he think of *Star-Telegram* reporter Mike Cochran's report last year about how a chief investigator for the Tarrant County district attorney's office had allegedly spied for Cullen Davis' defense team at his Amarillo capital murder trial? Clearing his conscience, Karen Davis' father, Ray Hudson, told Cochran that he had arranged payments totaling $25,000 for daily information about the prosecution's plans.

The retired investigator, Morris Howeth, vigorously denied the allegation, but several defense lawyers told Cochran that they knew of a secret prosecution source code-named Eyes.

"What about that?" I asked Cullen Davis.

"It happened," he replied. "My attitude is, it's just one of those things that happened. Here I was charged with stuff I didn't do, and I'm going to get help from anybody who will give it. Wouldn't you?"

Cullen Davis looked at me and half-smiled again.

June 16, 2002

Pizza confession:
A one-night stand

Competing pizza men: Tony and Chris

"Where ya been?" Tony the pizza man asked.

I didn't want to hurt Tony, but I had to tell him. Your relationship with your pizza man is based on honesty, even when the truth hurts.

My priorities in life are simple. After God and family, I cherish my pizza parlor. I value a good pizza man the way I value a good woman. In return for her love and his pizza, you must be loyal.

Pizza adultery is a serious offense. I state this now because I have a confession to make.

I grew up in pizza parlors ordering by the slice. When I moved to Texas nine years ago, I tried to order by the slice and found that it could not be done. In these parts, back in 1993, you ordered a whole pie or you hit the door.

My first pizza loyalty went to a joint on Harwood Road. The owner served by the slice, and for many months that became my home away from home. But it was too far from my real home.

Then I found a closer pizza joint on Davis Boulevard and stuck with those guys for a long time.

I like my pizza New York-style. So when a New York-style pizza place opened on Denton Highway, I became a regular. But eventually that place closed.

When I heard about Tony's Pizza & Pasta in the Albertsons shopping center on Rufe Snow Drive and Mid-Cities Boulevard in Watauga, I moved my action there because Tony's offers the best area pizza I have tasted.

Quickly, I became friends with the owners, two brothers named Tony and Fredi Barducci. Their pizza is spectacular, but these guys are also the real thing. They moved from Italy to Brooklyn, N.Y., where they learned their trade before coming to Texas.

After Sept. 11, I went to Tony's to watch the terrible news on his television. Tony wore his New York firefighters' cap and, as former

New Yorkers, we shared our emotions.

Sometimes on a Saturday night, I bring my wife to Tony's. I carry a bottle of wine and a romantic candle. We grab a quiet table in the corner. Tony brings out a corkscrew. The food is served. And all is right with the world. My wife and my pizza man – in that order.

I thought I had my priorities together. But then a few weeks ago, my world turned upside down. I attended a Southlake Chamber of Commerce luncheon and met a loud-talking guy named Mitch Rosenberg from Brooklyn. When I asked him what he did for a living, he said he owned a pizza parlor on Southlake Boulevard.

"For how long?" I asked.

"Three days," he replied.

He invited me to visit, promising me the best pizza in Texas. His place, Angelo & Vito's, is in the Kroger shopping center next to Anne Wayne Salon Spa.

One bite of that first slice, and I knew Tony was in trouble. The pizza is great, as good as or better than Tony's. But the comedy at Angelo & Vito's is unsurpassable.

Unlike Tony and Fredi, Mitch and his partner, Chris, are not the real thing. They purport to be Angelo and Vito, but Mitch is a suburbanite from McKinney, and Chris is his next-door neighbor who grew up in Oklahoma City. Still, when you go there for a slice, you hear a comedy routine that could only happen in Southlake.

Mitch tells stories about how the Southlake teen-agers who work for him, the sons and daughters of wealthy residents, have a tough time adapting to the working world. It's a sitcom called Angelo and Vito Meet the Southlake Dragons.

"I got a dishwasher whose daddy is the former owner of a big communications company," Mitch was telling me the other day. "He's a good kid, but how do you not notice that the sink is flooding while you're cleaning the dishes? Well, he doesn't notice. I walk back there and the water is 2 inches deep on the floor.

"A couple of weeks before, I had to teach him how to use a mop. He was just pushing things from side to side.

"Then there's the daughter of a very powerful businessman. We asked her to do dishes but she refused because there was a good possibility that it would ruin her nails.

"They're nice kids, and we enjoy their company. But they are driving $40,000 cars, better cars than Chris and I drive."

I asked him, "Why do these kids work here for $6.25 an hour?"

He answered, "We'd love to know that ourselves."

Then as I ate a slice, Mitch asked, "Have you been to Tony's lately?"

Suddenly, I lost my appetite.

"Don't worry," Mitch said. "Tony's is like your first wife, and we are your new trophy pizza."

The next day, I went to Tony's and Tony asked, "Where ya been?"

I brought my son along and we ordered a large pie. In front of the brothers, we ate the whole thing. I call it guilt pizza.

Finally, I worked up the courage to tell Tony and Fredi about my new love. They took the story about my pizza infidelities fairly well.

Tony said he forgave me. "Ain't nothing like your first love," he said. "You'll always remember your first pizza."

Fredi said, "Not every pizza is the same. You love different pizzas for different reasons. Remember, I'm here seven days a week. I'll always be here for you."

I am a pizza snake. When I am in Watauga, I visit Tony and Fredi and put on my best face. When I am in Southlake, I visit Angelo and Vito. In both places, I pour on that red pepper and my heart burns in more ways than one.

March 17, 2002

Argyle students learn a lesson from the evangelist

*I*n a previous column, I told you about a prayer breakfast I attended led by Argyle-based television evangelist Mike Murdock. Murdock is raising $625,000 for his move from Argyle to Denton.

During the breakfast, he talked about his new friend, the king of Togo, a nation in Africa. He described his strong friendship with the king.

This month, Murdock brought the man he calls king to meet 80 geography students at Argyle High School.

But before I share the story, you need to know one important fact: Togo doesn't have a king.

Togo is a republic with a president and a prime minister. But no king.

Somehow, Murdock left out that little detail when he asked the Argyle Police Department for protection for his visiting friend.

Murdock didn't mention that when he contacted Argyle High School to arrange the visit.

And Murdock left it out when he introduced Foli-Bebe A. Ayi, dressed in a flowing purple gown, to students as the king of Togo.

This latest Murdock tale began Jan. 31 when Murdock's assistant called Argyle Police Chief Tom Tackett to ask for a security detail of two off-duty officers, whose $25-an-hour services would be paid for by Murdock.

The next day, Murdock's assistant dropped off information about the king at the police station. The packet included a letter on Murdock's letterhead.

"Gentlemen," the letter stated, "enclosed is the information regarding your special guest. His Majesty King Ayi, of Togo, West Africa. Please note all pages including procedures and expected protocol for your convenience."

The letter was signed, "Dr. Mike Murdock."

Let's share some of the rules of protocol in the letter, written on stationery from the Royal Ayi Foundation:

"Forms of address: 'Your majesty' or 'King Ayi.'

"Forms of introduction: His Majesty King Ayi.

"When King Ayi enters or exits a room, everyone (who is able) should stand up, and sit down only after he does, or gives a signal to do so.

"Bowing is traditional and appropriate before the king.

"Hand-shaking is acceptable, but for security reasons should be done after the king extends his hand first."

There were "little warning flags," the police chief said. "I guess I didn't pay any attention to them."

The warnings included the fact that the king lives in Falls Church, Va., and his biography states that he is the first African king enthroned in the United States of America.

The other warning, I would think, is that he is a friend of Murdock's.

The king spoke to the students Feb. 2.

Principal Tom Woody said it was an informative session. His majesty wore a flowing gown. He talked about Africa and answered questions.

Afterward, the police chief and the two officers accompanied the king back to Murdock's Argyle office. The king thanked the officers for being there.

"He wanted to know if we wanted to communicate with the Togo Police Department," Tackett said. "I gave him one of my police patches. So I got scammed as well."

A few days later, a newspaper reporter called Tackett and asked him if he knew that Togo doesn't have a king.

I don't blame the police chief for not knowing. Argyle is a long way from Togo.

Murdock didn't respond to a request for an interview.

The Argyle principal said that the students, at first, were impressed by their royal visitor.

"Since then, when they found out he wasn't a real king, they weren't quite as impressed," Woody said.

"The information about Africa was good, but they are aware that he was saying he was the king, but he wasn't."

The police chief has received lots of ribbing from his officers. They walk by Tackett chanting, "Toga! Toga!" from the movie *Animal House*.

I called the Royal Ayi Foundation in Virginia and learned the story behind the story.

The man who accompanied Murdock to the school is a ceremonial king who traces his lineage to a tribal ruling family that ruled a segment of Togo before it became a country.

"We always try to be very clear, but it doesn't always come across," foundation director Rockley Miller told me. "It's a nuance that unfortunately gets lost in the shuffle. We try to correct people, but we are ultimately responsible for what people say."

Murdock referred to his friend as the king, not the "symbolic" king as the Royal Ayi Foundation Web site describes him.

Murdock and the symbolic king met at a conference for Third World leaders last year in the Bahamas, Miller said. Murdock is a mentor to Ayi.

"They're very close," Miller said. "They've spent time together, visited each other, become very good friends very quickly."

If Murdock believers want to come to Argyle to meet Murdock and invest in his vision, giving him thousands of dollars and whatnot, that's their right.

But when you present somebody or something so patently misleadingly to innocent students at an area high school, you cross the line.

Mike Murdock, may God help you.

February 15, 2000

Coach Tagg with Paula and Jerod

Coach Tagg is winner in game of life

Note: The following is based on two columns that appeared in 2001 and 2002.

The first time I saw Coach Tagg Sawyer, in late spring of 2001, I was a little startled by my initial impression. He dressed and acted as if he were preparing to manage a major-league baseball team.

A plumber by trade, he arrived wearing a muscleman T-shirt, Champion-brand athletic shorts and a crisp, blue Kansas City Royals hat.

As he walked toward the little 3- and 4-year-old players on his Royals T-ball team in the YMCA league in Fort Worth, this first impression was shaken the moment his eyes met those of the team's only little girl. Sitting on the ground, she looked up with Shirley Temple eyes and happily announced, "I found a ladybug!"

"Really?" Coach Tagg asked, as he melted into the grass beside her, looked at the ladybug and gave her a warm hug. Then he told her it was time to bat.

What transpired afterward at that first practice could possibly be described as the single most chaotic hour in the history of organized baseball.

The introduction of this puzzling and difficult game to 3- and 4-year-olds is no small undertaking. Thus, it came as no surprise amid the ensuing bedlam that one of the Royals players accidentally swung the bat into the waiting eyebrow of another player, my son, Austin James.

I swooped Austin into my arms, and within moments had found an ice pack, which I gently began applying to his wound.

Coach Tagg chased after us.

"Are you all right, bud?" he asked. (Bud turned out to be his name for everyone.)

I showed him the ice pack and the little knot starting to form.

Then Coach Tagg held out his arms and politely asked me, "Do you mind?"

It took a moment to register that this unknown man was asking me to hand him my 4-year-old in his time of need. But that's what Coach Tagg wanted, and after another moment's hesitation, I realized I had no reason to stand in the way of this developing coach-player relationship.

As I slipped Austin into his waiting arms, I heard Coach Tagg say, "Thanks, bud."

*   *   *

During the following weeks, I watched Coach Tagg establish similar close bonds with each of the 14 players on his team. He told me that his motivation for this assignment came after watching his son, Jerod, 4, play on his first soccer team for a coach he called "more derogatory than complimentary."

Tagg as soccer coach

"It's their time to play and learn," Coach Tagg said.

He had another motivation, too. Years ago, he made a promise to his father, Thomas Sawyer, before he died on Father's Day in 1996.

"I've never grown up with a father," Coach Tagg explained to me. "My parents were divorced when I was young, and my father picked me up on weekends.

"He bought me my first glove and took me to Kansas City Athletics games. He also coached my first baseball team."

Decades later, when he thanked his father for sharing these things with him, his father's reply startled him.

His father said, "The only way you can thank me is be a better father to your children than I was to you."

The son promised to do so, and a year after Thomas Sawyer died, Paula Sawyer gave birth to Tagg and Paula's first son, Jerod.

Four years later, the time came for Jerod to play on his first baseball team, and Tagg decided to coach.

* * *

That chaotic first practice, however, caused Tagg to question his decision.

"I don't know if I can do this," he told Paula.

But he showed up the next time, and so did his ragtag band of players, and little by little, this team of ultimate rookies started to gel.

Tagg, center, as baseball coach

He taught his players the fundamentals of the game, but more important, he praised them for everything they did and instilled in them their first sense of sportsmanship and fair play.

For his final team talk of the season, the coach gathered his players around him and said it had been "a privilege and an honor" to be their coach.

Privilege and honor are not part of a 4-year-old's vocabulary, but his players could tell by his soft tone of voice that he was pleased.

Then he asked his players to thank "your mommies and daddies for making it possible for you to play."

It was an unusual request, but it made sense for Coach Tagg. By working so diligently with all these little children on his team, he was thanking his own father. He was trying to keep his promise and be the very best father he could be.

* * *

During the winter basketball season, Coach Tagg told me his throat bothered him. Weeks later, after he shifted the 5-year-old boys on his team to the next YMCA league sport – soccer – he complained that the pain was worse. He said he was going to a doctor. By the time spring baseball season arrived, we knew it was cancer.

While he taught 5-year-olds, including my son Austin, how to play baseball, the coach of the YMCA Royals contended with a life of simultaneous chemotherapy and radiation treatments. He sometimes wore a chemotherapy pack under his coach's jersey.

Still, he attended nearly every practice and game that season. He coached each player with his trademark positive words, and as his treatments continued, he said that he felt weaker – he lost 22 pounds in the first three weeks – and that he might spend a game in the dugout.

But he never did. He was always out there. With the kids.

"He tells me he has no time to be weak," says Joe Mead, program director at the local YMCA. "He's got kids looking up to him, and he has to be strong. He always told me not to worry – that he would follow through on his responsibilities and the kids would help him get through it."

*   *   *

Coach Tagg's athletic organization has become a major force in my neighborhood. If your child is lucky enough to get on a Coach Tagg team, you become a member of a mini-sports empire that strives to get the little things right.

There are pre-season meetings and post-season parties. Parents go out to eat together after practices and games. When the season ends, each player gets a yearbook with his photograph on the cover. But the real jewel is the care that the 45-year-old plumber gives to each player, including his 5-year-old son, Jerod.

Even as his throat grew sorer, the radiation shook him and the chemo sometimes knocked him flat, he would stand out there shouting to 5-year-olds for an hour or more:

"Good swing, Bradley."

"Good job, Edward."

"Sebastian, be ready."

"Royals, I'm very proud of you."

Coach Tagg has something kind to say to everybody, including the parents and even the umpires and referees. During baseball season, so many signed up for his team that the YMCA split the players into two teams. Tagg recruited a neighbor to coach the second team.

"If I could duplicate him and have everybody coach like him, I'd be in heaven," Mead told me. "He demonstrates all the core values – caring, honesty, respect and responsibility – and he follows them through to the T. He's the epitome of that as far as a volunteer."

Weeks before he was diagnosed with cancer, the Nowlin YMCA decided to present Coach Tagg with its Volunteer of the Year Award. By the time of the awards ceremony, doctors knew his ailment was serious. After Coach Tagg received the award, Mead recalled watching Tagg's wife, Paula, become teary-eyed.

"He came back and told her, 'This is what it's all about,' " Mead said.

*   *   *

With the help of assistant coaches Cary Walker and Brian Crawford, and Paula and her organizational skills, the Royals, even with a weakened coach, still functioned on all cylinders.

Recently, Coach Tagg rented the Dr Pepper Youth Ballpark beside The Ballpark in Arlington, where the Texas Rangers play, so both teams in his athletic organization could play against each other for fun. It was a perfect Sunday morning for everyone in the prettiest little ballpark ever built. The game was a delight and afterward, the team presented Coach Tagg with a trophy named after his favorite Kansas City Royals player: the George Brett Iron Man Award. Tagg was touched. Then the players and parents attended the Rangers-Royals game at The Ballpark. Of course, the George Brett Iron Man had arranged the details.

The little players on his team know their coach is sick. He told them one day at practice and showed them a chemotherapy pack under his shirt. He said, "This is serious. Please do not get too close to this."

He explained that the liquid inside was supposed to make him better. Then he asked for questions:

"Will you be OK?"

"How does it work?"

"Does it make you feel better?"

After the season's last game, parents pulled July Fourth poppers, supplied by Paula, above the delighted players. Then Coach Tagg gathered everyone and announced: "We won! Don't let anyone tell you different."

Forget the score. The truth is the Royals and their coach really did win, just by being there.

After that, Coach Tagg swore he was going to take some time off. But not much. He faced weeks of radiation and two more weeks of

Tagg, right, as basketball coach

chemotherapy. "I plan to be back for basketball season," he said.

* * *

Throughout the fall and early winter Coach Tagg battled cancer with arduous chemotherapy and radiation treatments. He lost 77 pounds, but he worked hard to beat the illness. He vowed to return to coaching in just a few more weeks.

Forget the pain of the cancer treatments, he said. "Not coaching has been the hardest thing."

A few days before Christmas 2002, he got the good news. For now, he has beat the cancer! How did he celebrate? He signed up to coach in the 5- and 6-year-olds basketball league.

Postscript: In February 2003, Coach Tagg was honored by the Fort Worth Star-Telegram *when he was named the recipient of the Community Spirit Award as the individual who best embodied the spirit of the community.*

A life too long to be reduced to a few words

The obituary was 77 words long. A lifetime in four paragraphs, without a photo.

Doris Jean Johnson of Southlake, a homemaker, died Sunday from cancer. She was 59.

But an obituary does not do a life justice. It just gives the barest of details.

Doris Jean was a Fort Worth native. Survived by her husband, a daughter, a mother and a stepfather, and two grandchildren. Graveside services were Monday at Mount Olivet Cemetery.

Details, but never answers to the meaningful questions.

Was Doris Jean Johnson happy? Did she find fulfillment in her 59 years on this earth? And what did her life mean?

At the service, a green canvas shielded 80 mourners from the open grave. The minister read from the Bible and asked everyone to pray for the family.

The Johnson family is one of Southlake's oldest. A century ago, Jim "Pap" Johnson bought what his descendants now call "the acreage." He also lent his name to well-traveled Johnson Road, which brushes past the acreage as it leads into Keller.

Pap, who came from Kentucky, knew every inch of the acreage, now numbering nine. To pay for the Johnson homestead, Pap and a brother cleared oak trees off the land and turned the wood into charcoal. They hauled the charcoal to Fort Worth on a wagon.

Pap's son, and then his son's son, followed him on the land. One night at a Waxahachie wrestling match in the early 1950s, the grand-son, Jack Johnson, then in his late 20s, met a Fort Worth high school girl, 10 years his junior. "A little-bitty woman," Jack called Doris Jean, "with blond hair like the tail of a palomino pony." They dated, and the night before her 18th birthday, Doris Jean announced, "We're going to get married in the morning." And they did.

In 41 years together, Jack and Doris Jean Johnson had a daughter, Dianne. She married Craig Barrett; they had two children, the fifth-generation family members on the acreage.

When the graveside service ended Monday, three generations of family walked slowly from the site. And Craig told how Doris Jean, like Pap who cleared it, knew every inch of the acreage. She loved to mow it – nearly every day. In 22 years, she wore out three tractors.

Up at 4 a.m. for household chores, Doris Jean usually hopped aboard her green, 18-horsepower mower by 8 a.m. to begin that day's patch. "She'd go to town," Craig recalled. "Other women shop for jewelry," Dianne said. "She shopped for lawn mowers."

When lung cancer was diagnosed nearly four years ago, Doris

Jean, a smoker, watched helplessly as the disease spread to her brain. In 1991, doctors gave her six weeks to live.

"I'm not sick," she told everyone. If she said she wasn't sick, then she wasn't. Doris Jean endured chemotherapy, radiation treatments, pills – all the while insisting upon her good health. Her family went along lovingly.

Doris Jean died at home Sunday morning. "She just took a breath and died," said Dianne, alone with her mother when it happened.

As the family left the grave site Monday, four cemetery workers in white hard hats lifted the casket and carried it behind the protective canvas. The Johnson family, telling stories about how Doris Jean liked to mow and how she had defied her doctors' predictions, didn't take notice.

The grandchildren – Chad, 13, and his sister, Ambrely, 11 – stood quietly among them. Chad often rode with his grandmother on the green tractor. The family said Chad will now tend the Johnson land. But Chad is no Doris Jean. To the boy, life atop the green tractor is a never-ending chore.

"He has to be reminded," his father said.

A 77-word obituary. Four paragraphs and no photo. Details without answers. It doesn't do a life justice.

Doris Jean Johnson lived her life well – so well, in fact, that she squeezed out some extra years. She never gave up.

Now her green tractor is parked on the acreage. And the grass is too tall.

Someone must remind Chad to tend the Johnson land. But the strength of four generations on the land is guiding him. Knowing every inch of the acreage is what the Johnsons of Johnson Road do.

Pap Johnson did it a century ago. Doris Jean Johnson did it the past 20 years. Now it is the boy's turn.

July 13, 1994

Confronting road bullies

I drove to a house six blocks from mine and knocked on the front door. A man opened the door, peered out and asked, "Yes?"

"Hey, remember me?" I said.

"No, I don't," he answered.

"Well," I said, "you ran me off the highway yesterday at milepost 289 on Interstate 20 going west."

"I ran you off the highway yesterday?" he repeated.

"Yes," I said.

"Were you the guy that was in the pickup truck?" he asked.

"No," I replied. "That was obviously somebody else you ran off the road. I was in a compact car. You could have killed me. Now here I am. It took me all of 20 seconds to find you. Why did you do it?"

I guess he was surprised to see me. I would have been shocked if someone with whom I was involved in an anonymous driving encounter some 150 miles from home knocked on my door the next day.

We were on our way to Odessa to watch a high school football game. I was driving in a car with my wife and our 4-year-old son. Our two teen-agers were in a car behind us. We were just outside Abilene.

I had moved into the left lane to pass a slow-moving truck. From nowhere, a man driving a van came up from behind. He was probably traveling 100 mph. I saw him in the rearview mirror and prepared to pull to the right lane to let him pass. Before I could, he jumped ahead in the right lane, then cut back over in front of me. But there wasn't enough distance between his van and the truck, so I braked hard and drove off the road onto the left shoulder.

I was ticked. I sped up and wrote down his license plate number. He saw me and looked back with a wide smirk, as if to say, "What are you going to do about it?"

As he drove off, I fantasized about finding him and asking, "Why?"

Imagine my surprise the next day when I looked up his license plate on the Internet and learned that he lived only six blocks from my house!

I thought about this neighbor last week while on vacation in Disney World. All around me were hundreds, no thousands of people whom I would never see again. Most of the mini-encounters I had with these folks were polite. But every so often I encountered an extremely rude person or two waiting in line or walking on a street who acted as if they could do what they wanted because nobody would ever know who they were.

You know, that used to be true. But with the Internet, it's a lot harder to hide, especially if you are a driver. A few years ago, if you wanted to trace a license plate, you needed a friend who worked for a police department. Now, you can do it yourself with Web sites that offer listings of public records.

The first time I tried this was two years ago. A teen-ager was driving south on Denton Highway around 11 p.m., playing cat-and-mouse with other cars and passing in the middle turn lane.

Ten minutes later, I sat at my home computer and traced the license plate to a Roanoke woman. I found her name in the telephone directory and called. I introduced myself and told her what her son was doing.

"Thank you so much!" she replied excitedly. "There is no way I could know what he does when he's driving my car. I'm going to call him on his cellphone right now!" I always wondered how that conversation went.

By no means am I saying that I am a perfect driver. Once in my early 20s, I accidentally drove a woman off the road and continued on to a restaurant. When I came out an hour later, there was a note on my windshield that said something like, "You stupid driver! You drove me off the road. You better learn how to drive before you get yourself and somebody else killed!"

Last year, I was driving west one night on Southlake Boulevard when a teen-ager was wildly driving a pickup with three teens riding in back.

I caught up with him at the next light, rolled down my window and said, "I'm going to call your mama!"

He smiled and told me to stick a body part in a place where it couldn't go.

A half-hour later, I kept my promise.

After I described her son's antics to the Southlake mother, she told me, "Thank you for calling. He's not allowed to carry passengers in the bed of his truck. And he's certainly not supposed to drive like that!"

"If it were my kid, I'd want to know," I said.

"I appreciate your calling," she said.

My neighbor six blocks away was not so appreciative. "Why?" I asked him. "Why did you do it?"

He replied, "I was rolling down the highway doing a decent speed. You pulled over in front of me. That's all fine. You passed the other car. You were doing 70 and then you decided to play games."

"Play games?" I said in disbelief. "I had no time to play games. You were going too fast. All you had to do was fall in behind and I would have moved over."

He wasn't interested. "Anyway, I'm watching football," he said. "So goodbye."

I didn't move.

"Goodbye! Goodbye!" he shouted. "You so tough! Get out of my yard."

As I walked away, I said, "It's been a pleasure."

And it really was. Maybe next time, he will think twice about these so-called anonymous encounters. Maybe next time, somebody won't get killed because he will drive more safely. This is the part about the loss of privacy that I do not mind.

March 31, 2002

74-year-old drives herself with precision

Miss Audrey drives to church. Miss Audrey drives to the beauty shop. Miss Audrey drives to the doctor.

And wherever she goes, Miss Audrey Jacobs, a 74-year-old Watauga widow, drives her old, yellow Cadillac with the utmost respect for Texas motor vehicle laws. In a driving life that began at age 7, Miss Audrey has a clean record to prove it. No tickets. No chargeable accidents. No imperfections.

This summer, the Texas Highway Patrol (which confirms her record to 1942), Watauga city officials and her auto insurance company presented Miss Audrey with certificates of appreciation. What's her secret?

Let's go driving with Miss Audrey.

It is midafternoon, and Miss Audrey gingerly backs her 1979 car out of the garage. The odometer reads 206,000 miles. She turns the yellow Caddy south on Denton Highway.

Notice her use of the turn signal. "I live by them," she explains.

Observe her concentration. "I watch everybody else driving," she says.

Scrutinize the way she obeys the speed limit. She travels 34 mph in a 45-mph zone.

"I baby this thing," she says of her yellow Caddy, "but when I get on the freeway, I shower down on it." *Shower down?* "I zip it up to the speed limit."

Miss Audrey didn't always drive at a snail's pace. Before 1963, she said, she regularly pushed the pedal to 75 mph – then the legal limit. "Obeying the law is the easiest thing I do," she says. "If it says '30,' it means '30' – so just drive it!"

On Denton Highway, she cruises slowly down the middle of three southbound lanes. Cars whiz by on both sides.

"They're just going to have to sit up there and wait for the red light," she says.

She crosses over Loop 820, remaining on Denton Highway, where three lanes shrink to two. Miss Audrey hugs the left lane. A van whizzes by on the right.

She likes the inside lane, likes it so much that she's in no hurry to leave. A police officer once told her that the inside lane was the safest way to stay out of ditches.

Her father taught her how to drive at age 7 so she could ferry her grandmother to the grocery store every week. Until 1941 – when Texas enacted a strict driver's license law – children drove cars out of necessity. "Nobody thought much about it," she says.

Since then, Miss Audrey has seen a few collisions of her own – she has been rear-ended, front-ended and sideswiped – but it has always been the other driver's fault, she says. She got one ticket, but it didn't stick.

"I was driving the yellow Cadillac, and here comes a cop," she remembers. "He said, 'You didn't stop.' I said, 'I *am* stopped.' Well, he gave me a ticket."

She protested in court. The traffic ticket said Miss Audrey drove a yellow Skylark and made a left turn where there's no left turn – just a drainage ditch. Case dismissed.

Miss Audrey turns north on Rufe Snow Drive, a nightmare of congestion. "Rufe Snow is no problem for me," she says. "Sure, there's heavy traffic and red lights, but just go on."

She continues under the speed limit, and cars continue passing on the right. Sometimes other drivers toot their horns, she says. "I don't pay it no mind. Oh, it's probably somebody I know. I just ignore it and go right on down the road."

But Rufe Snow Drive gets to even the patient Miss Audrey. She tries to avoid the crowded intersection of Rufe Snow and Industrial Park Boulevard. The driver with the perfect record cuts through a Kentucky Fried Chicken parking lot, then exits the wrong way out of the restaurant's drive-through entrance.

Miss Audrey, isn't that illegal?

"Naw," she says, "they don't enforce it."

But isn't it illegal to cut through a commercial parking lot?

"It's illegal – only if you get caught," she says with a laugh.

So the driver with the perfect record isn't completely perfect?

"Nobody is," she says. "There wasn't but one perfect one, and he didn't drive a car."

She zips her yellow Cadillac home at 28 mph, loving that inside lane. Cars pass on the right, and somebody toots. Probably somebody she knows, but she pays it no mind.

Driving with Miss Audrey. A driver for 67 years. Never a ticket or an accident that was her fault. So what if a 15-minute trip takes 25 minutes? So what if she hugs the inside lane at a snail's pace?

For Audrey Jacobs, that's the price of … well, near perfection.

July 27, 1994

Common ground links two strangers

The old-timers were accounted for, but there was a new face, a mystery man, who looked out of place among the regulars.

Everybody was introduced to the new man, Mark Tucker, but nobody said why he had come. What had brought him to the annual meeting of the Lonesome Dove Cemetery Association? Why would the Watauga man, so young at 39, care about the hallowed burial ground beside historic Lonesome Dove Baptist Church in Southlake?

Inside the church hall, the young man quietly ate his dinner with the other members, a dozen people, most in their 70s and 80s. After dinner, the cemetery meeting began.

As always, Jack Cook ran things. Every year, Jack, now 78, makes jokes about how he will die one day, but until then he has every intention of handling the cemetery chores. The cemetery is 2 acres, but Jack likes to mow and weed whack by himself.

At last week's meeting, though, Jack made a historic concession when he acknowledged for the first time, "I wouldn't mind anybody who wanted to help."

As if on cue, Mark Tucker spoke his first words to the group. In a quivering voice, he said: "I'll do anything that you need me to do, sir. Any time you need me to do it."

"We'd appreciate it," Jack replied.

"I'd be honored," the new man said.

The new man's unexplained devotion – and Jack's rare acceptance – only deepened the mystery.

Jack shows the same devotion, and that should have been a clue. The longtime association president has kin buried throughout the pioneer cemetery: his great-great-grandmother; his first wife; his son, Tommy, who died in a fire at age 2.

Jack doesn't like to talk about Tommy's death in 1950. So he mows and weed whacks and does whatever else needs to be done. Jack believes that actions speak louder than words.

After an hour of cemetery business, Jack adjourned the meeting. The other members went home, but the new man said he wanted to go outside in the dark and see the cemetery.

"I buried my daughter two months ago," he said in a quivering voice. "And I asked Mr. Cook if there's anything I could do to help. He gave me the date and time for this meeting."

Emily Ann Tucker died in an auto accident July 5. She was 4 years old.

"She died on a Friday, and I was out here Sunday, and Mr. Cook was picking out a spot," the new man said as he rose from his chair. "By the time he found out it was for my daughter, we both had tears in our eyes."

Lonesome Dove is probably the oldest pioneer cemetery in Tarrant County. For 149 years, the bereaved have buried their loved ones and felt these same emotions.

"I stepped out of the truck, and I knew this was the cemetery I wanted," he said. "This was the first and last I visited."

Since that first visit, he said, "Mr. Cook and I have talked a lot about it. But when it's your daughter… " His voice trailed off and he shook his head side to side.

"All I can do is help here," he said after a moment. "And that's what I want to do."

Jack understood. "It's been 40 or 50 years," he said. "But the hurt is still there."

"I think of you every day," the new man said. "I seriously do. Because you told me you learn to block it. And if you have a job, you put off thinking about it. That's how I learned to cope."

The new man walked outside to the cemetery. It was dark, and he held a flashlight.

"That's Emily," he said glumly as he walked toward a large mound of dirt. A small doll and a long stick had been placed carefully atop the mound.

"She was a Barbie fan, and that's her fishing pole," the father said, pointing at the stick. "Every stick she ever found was her fishing pole."

He remembered her burial: "They said the Lord's Prayer, and a breeze came through, and the birds started singing again. From then on, I saw the birds, the squirrels, everything. It's just something I thought about."

He pointed to four Texas-shaped stone markers in the ground. They are his stakes for future graves.

"That's mine," Mark Tucker said. "This is my wife's, and this is my son's and his future wife's." His son is 9 months old.

The new man said his company had recently offered him a transfer to another state.

"I'm not going," he said. "I'm staying right here." He pointed down at the stone stakes.

"Bye, honey girl," he said as he turned to leave.

For the new man, it was the end of his first cemetery association meeting, held the first Tuesday of every September.

"As long as you need me, Mr. Cook, I'll be here," he told Jack again in the parking lot.

Jack Cook had found his replacement, but not the way he had wanted. The new man, like the old man, had come to this hallowed ground for the very same reasons, knowing actions always speak louder than words.

September 8, 1996

Bradshaw gets the fur flying at fund-raiser

I never saw someone work as hard for an elementary school as Terry Bradshaw did Saturday night.

He was the auctioneer for the PTA fund-raiser for Florence Elementary School in Southlake, which his two daughters, Rachel and Erin, attend. His goal: to beat last year's total of $8,000.

Bradshaw, a Hall of Fame quarterback and Fox television football host, was the star of the evening. Not that the Westlake resident needed any help, but I was Bradshaw's assistant. Or more accurately, his straight man.

I guess I got his dander up when I introduced him as the man who has it all except for one thing: a head of thick, curly hair like mine. Then I pulled out a bald-man wig and wore it the rest of the night.

"Nobody that ugly can be married," he shouted at me, to the delight of everyone. "Tell me you're not married. You haven't fathered any children."

He pointed at my two older children, who attended Florence Elementary years before I met them and married their mother.

"No way those are your kids!" he said.

Bradshaw launched into the auction with a style that was aggressive, seductive, funny, cajoling and pleading – it was a wild act, which fit the Out of Africa theme for the event at Trophy Club Country Club, which was decorated with animal art painted by parent Mike Torrez.

Waving his arms and jumping about like the quarterback he was, he shouted at parents, "GIVE ME A THOUSAND DOLLARS!"

And most of the time, they did.

For two hours, Bradshaw frenetically worked the crowd. His shirt dripped with sweat, and he started losing his voice.

He rolled through auctions of orthodontist visits and barbecue dinners. A helicopter ride, a photography session and restaurant meals. There was even a football for which he promised to get autographs of every Dallas Cowboy and Pittsburgh Steeler in the Hall of Fame.

"It will take some time to get done, and it will be done," he said. "It will be delivered to you, and it will be authentic. I promise you that. Nobody will have this."

As the bidding for the ball climbed to more than $1,000, he became more hypnotist than auctioneer.

"Look at me," he said to one bidder in his softest voice, "Franco Harris. Roger Staubach. I need $1,500."

He worked the crowd more until he finally shouted, "TWO THOUSAND DOLLARS! SOLD!"

He smiled at the powers of his persuasion.

From my point of view, the Bradshaw hypnosis techniques worked a little to well.

For one auction item, Bradshaw held up a kitten that was smaller than his hand. The kitty had a white body with light brown shading and a striped tail that looked like it belonged on a raccoon.

Bradshaw didn't look comfortable holding the kitty, and the kitty wasn't too happy either. So I grabbed the 6-week-old cat and carried him around the room to show bidders.

"Who's got $2?" Bradshaw asked.

Someone shouted, "TWO HUNDRED DOLLARS!"

Bradshaw was startled. Two hundred dollars for an alley cat? "Sold," he said quickly.

Over in the corner, my family cheered. They were the buyers.

Bradshaw said, "Lieber, you got a bad deal."

By night's end, Bradshaw had sweated his way to an amazing total of $19,000. When informed that he had more than doubled last year's amount, he erupted with such glee that you would have thought he had won another Super Bowl.

"UNBELIEVABLE!" he shouted.

Yes, it *was* unbelievable: $200 for a kitty?

"Honey, he's precious," my wife said.

"Who?" I asked.

"Terry," she replied.

"Terry Bradshaw?" I asked.

"No, Terry Bradshaw Lieber."

And so we have a new cat in our household. And that is his name. All for a good cause, I'm sure. But let me tell you: The kitty's namesake is one dangerous man.

April 21, 1998

A pilot's wife keeps home fires burning

*T*he pilot's wife sits by the telephone and waits for word of when the pilot will return from his latest trip.

Their long-distance phone conversations don't always go well.

"I wish you were here," he says. "It's not the same without you. I went out to eat in a beautiful restaurant. Now I'm at the villa."

"When can I expect you home?" she asks.

"I don't know for sure."

They first met in the 1960s. He was a military pilot. She was looking for a dream man. The soul mate of her life. He had charisma. A pilot is exciting. A different breed.

His first love, of course, was flying. She knew that when she married him.

This story is based on Dave's in-laws, Joan and John Pasciutti

But as the couple reach the autumn years of their lives, the pilot said, "I now realize that you come first. You're the wind beneath my wings."

Still, he's out flying.

And a lonely heart waits for him.

Today, they live in Northeast Tarrant County. There are hundreds of couples like them. Pilots who fly for big airlines, corporations or other flying entities. Spouses who, while waiting, carve out lives of their own through work, friends and community volunteer activities.

Together, they worked to reach the goal of their dream house. There's a backyard pool. A luxury car in the garage. A closet filled with designer clothes. Wonderful jewelry, too.

In the early days, when the children were small, they shared a cottage on the military base. It was too small, and the first time they stepped inside, it was all beige walls and brown linoleum floors. It needed a special touch. It needed the touch of the pilot's wife.

The pilot went off on training exercises. He could be gone for days, weeks or even months. Meanwhile, the pilot's wife set the wine bottle with dried flowers on the wooden box in the living room. She painted. She decorated. She redesigned the military quarters to make it look like a mansion for him to come home to. And she waited with love in her heart.

The pilot returned. The pilot's wife, who had served as mother *and* father, watched as the husband adjusted. The children adjusted. The wife tried to adjust.

Just when the adjustment of homecoming began to feel comfortable, he was assigned somewhere else. Another base. Another military cottage. Start all over again. Off into the wild blue yonder.

The 1960s became the 1970s. Little changed in the 1980s. The 1990s arrived, but still, the pilot flew in his own aerial rat race.

By then, the military life had ended in retirement, and a corporate relocation for a second career determined that their home would be in a small town somewhere between Fort Worth and Dallas.

When the couple arrived, they saw that this new place carried the potential of heaven on Earth.

The military cottage had blossomed into practically a mansion. The new stone house contained more bedrooms than children, who were grown and lived elsewhere.

The pilot still has his schedule to keep and the pilot's wife, the wind beneath his wings, is not always included. She has ceased to be only the pilot's wife and has become her own person with her own life. But the pilot's frequent absences are still jarring.

"When can I expect you home?"

"Maybe next week," the pilot replies. "I don't know for sure."

The house may be bigger, but the problems are the same.

Plumbing goes wrong. Lawns need care. Air conditioners fail. But the woman of the house is the only one around to handle these breakdowns.

Then the pilot comes home, smiles and says, "Everything looks terrific. What a good job you've done. It's great to be home."

She looks at him with love in her eyes but dread in her heart, and asks, "When is your next trip?"

July 19, 1998

Dad taught me life's most important lessons

John Pasciutti in his Air Force flying days.

One day, nine years ago, I cleared my throat, straightened my hair and knocked on the big wooden door of the stone house in Keller.

I had been dating Karen Pasciutti for two weeks. I had met her two children. I had met – with regrets – her Psycho Dog. I had even met Karen's mother, Joan. I had met everyone except the man of this house, Karen's father. But it was Karen's birthday, and her parents had invited me to the family celebration.

There was a lot of pressure. Karen had told her parents that after only two weeks of dating me she knew this was the real deal.

So I knocked on the door and held my breath.

And this fellow opened the door.

He welcomed me inside his home.

He looked me dead in the eye and said something I'll never forget. He knew I was Jewish, and he said, "Listen, I hope you don't mind, but we eat pork here."

I said, "I don't mind."

He said, "Good, because we're having ribs tonight, and they say I make the best ribs."

"No," I said. "That's fine. I'll eat your ribs."

But he wasn't done.

"Listen, there's something else," he said. "I know you're from New York, and I'm from New York, too. But that was a long time ago. And I want you to know that we're Republicans in this household."

You could tell he couldn't wait to tell me that.

"OK," I said.

"Good," he said. "Now that you understand. We eat pork, and we're Republicans. So if you have a problem with that, just get over it!"

And then he laughed that big John Pasciutti laugh that you could hear all the way down the street.

And you know, I did get over it.

I got over it because I didn't want to miss the fun.

And I got over it because I soon learned that I had just been granted the privilege of a lifetime – an opportunity to get to know and to love retired Air Force Maj. John L. Pasciutti, who would become one of the most important influences of my life.

I have changed so much in these past years, and probably the biggest reason is that I fell under the influence of this charismatic, principled, idealistic and wonderful man. My father-in-law taught me about American ideals and notions that previously were only book concepts. Dad was a career fighter pilot who had quit college to join Air Force cadet school. In hours of discussions and also in a life that he lived by example, he taught me the meaning of duty, honor and country.

I now regret that I never told Dad of the influence he had on me. But it's too late. He died 10 days ago at age 65.

On Monday, after I delivered the eulogy at his funeral, after the bagpiper played *Amazing Grace*, after Dad's flag-draped casket was carried out to a waiting hearse, we traveled to Dallas-Fort Worth National Cemetery. There, Dad's body joined the waves of military gravesites marked by unending rows of tombstones dotting the hillsides.

We witnessed the missing-man formation, the military flyover in which one jet trails off from the others. We watched the somber folding of the flag. And we sobbed softly during the presentation of the flag to Joan Pasciutti, my mother-in-law. She accepted this final gift from her husband with a look of resignation that showed she always knew this dark moment was coming.

All those years during which Dad flew the skies and demonstrated his love of duty, honor and country made this moment a part of our family's inevitable destiny.

During the more than 20 years Dad and Mom served in the Air Force together, Mom always watched the chaplain's van slowly cruising up and down her neighborhood streets. She prayed that it would never stop at their house.

Monday afternoon, after the gun salute, that flag finally came her way. An Air Force officer, clutching the flag near his heart, slowly marched toward her. He gently knelt at her feet, looked into her eyes and whispered the following:

"On behalf of the president of the United States, the Department of the Air Force and a grateful nation, it is a privilege and my honor to offer this flag for the faithful and dedicated service of your loved one. The personal sacrifices that he made and his contributions to the armed forces in times of peace and war helped to ensure freedom for America and for the world."

Someone had tucked three bullet casings from the gun salute inside a fold of the flag. Those three casings represent duty, honor and country.

Until the day when I first knocked on the big door of that Keller home, those were concepts that I valued but never truly understood. In the years since, retired Air Force Maj. John L. Pasciutti – Dad – brought them to life for me. And in doing so, he changed me. He helped me become a better man, a better father, a better writer and a better American.

As Gen. Douglas MacArthur said in his legendary 1962 retirement speech at West Point:

Duty, honor, country. Those three hallowed words reverently dictate what you ought to be, what you can be, what you will be. They are your rallying points: to build courage when courage seems to fail; to regain faith when there seems to be little cause for faith; to create hope when hope becomes forlorn. ... I bid you farewell.

April 11, 2003

This sermon might heal a Watauga congregation

Note: Former pastor Ollin E. Collins of Harvest Baptist Church in Watauga now acknowledges in court documents that he "engaged in an adulterous relationship" with three women who filed lawsuits against him and the church. After his admission in the documents, lawsuits against Collins were dropped. However, Collins, who was paid an annual church salary of $146,092, according to a document he completed, declines to publicly accept responsibility or apologize.

Here is the sermon that columnist Dave Lieber wishes the ousted pastor would deliver. Lieber wrote these remarks:

Dear friends, thank you for coming today.

As you know, I have spoken from the pulpit thousands of times in my two decades as pastor. But the remarks I have planned for today come from the very depths of my heart and soul.

By my actions, I have hurt so many people. I have hurt everyone here today, and many who are not. I have hurt my wife, Tommie, and my children. I have let down the Southwestern Baptist Theological Seminary, which honored me with the chairmanship of its prestigious board.

But mostly Lord, I have let you down, and the only way to handle this matter is to make a full confession and to throw myself upon your everlasting mercy.

I will begin by apologizing, stepping down from this pulpit, and continuing these remarks from the floor of this sanctuary. I no longer deserve to stand in this or any other pulpit. (Collin steps down and stands before the front pew.)

As Matthew 18:4 says, "Let a man humble himself till he is like a child, and he will be the greatest in the kingdom of heaven."

Dear friends, I publicly admit to the allegations of adultery against me because my failure to do so would only compound my egregious sins.

I shall not deny that I broke two of the Ten Commandments:

"Thou shall not commit adultery."

And "Thou shalt not covet thy neighbor's wife."

I shall not deny that I did harm not only to these members of my former congregation, but also to these women who are the wives of friends of mine who worked and socialized with me.

Dear friends, I lost sight of my mission, which was to do God's work. With your help, we built a $7 million auditorium last year that I insisted must be one of the largest in Tarrant County.

I placed too much pressure on all of you to finance my overblown dreams and now have left you with a huge building debt as my parting legacy.

I became infatuated with personal glory, and forgot that ours was, first and foremost, a house of worship.

I put my face on billboards with the promise that our church was a place, as the signs said, "Where broken lives are mended."

Unfortunately, my actions broke more lives than they mended.

I became enamored of my television ministry and loved the public attention. I forgot that it's not the medium, but the message that counts in the eyes of the Lord.

I degraded the Lord's house by putting a tanning booth in the church to attract new members and then placing a large sign on an exterior wall of the sanctuary that announced, "Tanning." And I foolishly installed a hot tub in the church, which I now realize sent the wrong message.

Fortunately, ours is the God of second chances. Now I will spend the rest of my days on this Earth working for that second chance. I am reminded of the parable in Luke:

Two men go to a temple to pray. One says, "I thank thee, O God, that I am not like the rest of men – greedy, dishonest and adulterous." The other says, "O God, have mercy on me, sinner that I am."

And the Bible says, "It was this second man and not the first who went home acquitted of his sins. For everyone who exalts himself will be humbled; and whoever humbles himself will be exalted."

Dear friends, I will forever work to restore myself in your eyes because we all know that people are far less forgiving than God.

And I am here to promise to all of you that this is the very last time that I will ever address a congregation from the front of a church. I will never preach again as a minister of God. I choose to give up my right to do so because of my sinful ways.

I now seek other ways to serve.

Thank you for coming today to hear my final sermon.

May the healing begin.

April 23, 1999

Aunt Edith's history as rich as her dessert

During lunch at Roanoke Senior Center last week, a woman asked, "Does anybody know anything about Medlin Days?"

"I do," I replied. "I'm going to be a judge in the pie contest."

"Well, I'd like to go," she said.

"What's your name?" I asked.

"Edith Medlin."

"Edith Medlin?"

"Yes," she said.

I had heard about Edith Medlin. She's the last surviving person named Medlin in Northeast Tarrant County, which once boasted of 100 Medlins, descendants of the founding family. Or, as she puts it, "I am the only one that wears the Medlin name left in this vicinity."

Aunt Edith, as she is known, is 88 years young, with short, light hair and big eyeglasses. Her husband of 63 years, Lonzo Medlin, died last year. She lives on their 200-acre ranch near Haslet-Roanoke Road in what she calls "a real country home."

On Saturday, I was honored to escort the last Medlin to the Trophy Club festival named in her family's honor. For the pie contest, Aunt Edith had baked her specialty – a caramel nut pie.

"I'm not expecting any prize," she said. "And to tell you the truth, I'm not pleased with this pie."

She asked me to carry the pie to the car. "You be careful with that," she ordered.

I gently placed the pie in the car. She climbed in the passenger seat before I could run back and open the door for her.

"I'm just an old country woman, and I'm used to waiting on myself," she said.

On the short drive to Trophy Club, she told me how she and Lonzo moved to their ranch in 1951.

"Oh, I've seen lots of changes," she said. "I almost get lost myself. In the early 1950s, this was all cotton land." Glancing at the Alliance warehouses, she said, "This is unreal! This is unreal!"

Lonzo Medlin was a great-grandson of one of the original Medlins, who first arrived in these parts from Missouri in 1844 in a wagon train of 16 families, all related by blood or marriage, according to Roanoke historian Frank Leon Fanning. The next year, 12 families arrived, and 15 more arrived two years after that.

Now, 153 years later, Aunt Edith is still doing some things the old-fashioned way. She told me that she had chopped the pecans for her pie by hand.

"By hand?" I asked in amazement.

"I've got a good board, and I've got a good chopping knife," she said. "I came up the hard way, sir. We worked hard, and we saved. Yes, we saved. When my husband made a dollar, they always said that he put 90 cents of it away."

We entered Trophy Club, and she said she remembered how it

was once "nothing but timber."

Most of her family is buried in the town's historical Medlin Cemetery.

"I come to the cemetery pretty often," she said. "When they were all living, we had some good times."

The parade that day honoring her family was great fun. She said she rode in an "open roadster." I laughed and said I had never heard anyone call a convertible by that name.

We parked in Harmony Park, and Aunt Edith jumped out of the car.

Trophy Club Mayor Jim Carter and Doyle Krauss, husband of Trophy Club Women's Club President Donna Krauss, were the other pie-contest judges. We had the wonderful job of sampling 17 pies, including Aunt Edith's caramel nut specialty.

The top layer was thick, fluffy meringue, and the middle layer was tasty caramel. The bottom was covered with finely chopped nuts.

Alas, Aunt Edith placed seventh. The competition was keen. Judy Helenberger's apple crumb pie won, but Aunt Edith wasn't concerned.

"I enjoyed it," she said. "There were some good pies. I appreciated them honoring the Medlin name. I'm proud to know that we are part of the settlement of this part of the world."

The old country woman stopped herself and quickly apologized: "I don't want to be haughty," she said.

Haughty? Aunt Edith Medlin? No way. She's a local treasure who doesn't act like it.

October 21, 1997

Chapter Eight
Mom

"The mother's heart is the child's schoolroom."

— Henry Ward Beecher

Thanks, Mom, for your love and nurturing

Dave's mom

Dear Mom,

I'm so scared this is the last Mother's Day card I'll ever get to send you. I don't want to waste it.

Who knows if the experimental drugs you were taking will work? Dad says we need a miracle. So I pray every night. We need you.

My little brother is getting married in a few weeks. He so badly wants you to see him as a husband, not just as a son.

And my father, your devoted husband with whom you'll celebrate 39 years of marriage Saturday, takes such tender care of you, and you love him all the more. The disease ravaging your body tears at his spirit, too.

I can't imagine your pain, your heartbreak, your worries about the unknown. All I can do is wish you a happy Mother's Day. And maybe a little more.

On your special day, I can thank you for everything you did for me. Too often, we never get to thank our loved ones.

Mom, I always wanted to say thank you for . . .

The way you stood patiently outside my kindergarten classroom. You knew I was scared to leave your side.

Being tolerant of my obstinate behavior.

Teaching me that when I didn't do right, I should make up the wrong.

Introducing me to the fine arts, good books, film and theater.

Showing me how to make – and keep – good friends.

Teaching me to see the world as half full instead of half empty.

Not censoring my reading as a teen-ager.

Letting me grow my hair long, even though it looked stupid.

Forcing me to write thank-you notes.

Insisting that I get some religious training.

Sending me to private school because we were scared of the city high school. And for paying the steep tuition, even though it meant you and Dad couldn't take vacations.

Taking me to the awe-inspiring 1964-65 World's Fair.

Helping me buy my first car.

Baking chocolate cakes. Cooking my favorite swordfish dinners. Spoiling me with your specialty, chopped liver (which tastes a hundred times better than it sounds).

Visiting me in lonely Florida my first job away from home. Remember how we collected seashells and filled that glass lamp? (When I broke it last year, I didn't have the heart to tell you…)

Mom, thanks for giving me money to start off my marriage. Both times.

Thanks for accepting my new wife and children into your life.

You made me believe in myself.

And you loved me from my first day through all eternity.

Happy Mother's Day.

With love,

Your son.

May 14, 1995

Seeing Mom through her friend's eyes

NEW YORK – Maybe because I'm her son, my mother never struck me as very funny. Certainly not hysterically funny. Never the life of the party.

But the young woman who brought a wonderful gift to my mother's hospital room spoke those very words. My mother, the woman told me, is very funny. The life of the party.

My mother? I guessed I missed the party.

From the moment Carol Branch walked through the door of Room 1647 at New York University Medical Center on Friday afternoon, I began to see a side of Mom that I didn't know.

"I love your mother," Carol said to me as Mom lay in a nearby bed, recovering from radiation for a brain tumor. Carol wore gold hoop earrings and stylish black glasses. The 28-year-old office secretary visits my mother in the hospital every day on her way from work to her home in Harlem.

"I wanted to get her something different," Carol said. "Something special."

Because Mom is too weak, Dad opened the box. The gift was a brass music box with a Star of David on the lid. Dad lifted the lid and music began to play:

Sunrise, sunset
Sunrise, sunset
Swiftly fly the years
One season following another
Laden with happiness and tears

My mother and her young friend had worked together at Smith Barney brokerage house. I asked Carol why she visits every day.

"It doesn't matter if her eyes are closed," she said. "I just want to see her."

We went to a waiting area to talk.

"I can't say she feels like a mother to me," Carol explained. "It's more than that. It feels like she's closer to me.

"It's not a family sort of feeling. It goes beyond that. For me to put it in words, I can't say. All I can say is I love her. I love her for who she is and what she is and why. She's the sweetest person I ever met.

"When I first took the job," she continued, "everything was so quiet. But day by day, I just started talking to Denise. She's so funny. And every day we laughed. On the boss' dictation tape, you could hear our laughter in the background. I wish I still had those tapes.

"When she left to get her treatment, the days she was gone, it was so quiet. It wasn't the same. I couldn't wait for her to come back. I can't explain it. She's just a treasure."

I told her she was explaining it fine.

"Whenever something happened, we would just look at each other and click, and we were thinking the same thing," Carol said. "When you find friendships on a job, it's very unique."

The other younger women in the office, she said, didn't talk much to my mother. But somehow Carol and Denise, through their laughter, overcame differences in age, race, religion and background. Differences not so great.

"On my 28th birthday, we had all different kinds of people at a restaurant," Carol said. "She was the life of the party. Everybody talked about her afterward. She made my birthday party one of the best I ever had. She pulled everyone together. Even the waiters were hysterical.

"A lot of people don't know that side to her," she said. "I think that's a great injustice. In our past, we must have been sisters, because it's that powerful."

Carol and I walked back to Room 1647, where she pointed to the Star of David on the music box.

"It means hope and inspiration," my mother's young friend said, "getting close to God. That's very important to me."

After my father and I left the hospital that night, Carol stayed and sat at the foot of my mother's bed. Mom's eyes were closed, but it didn't matter. Carol just wanted to see her.

It's a side of my mother that I didn't know A great injustice. Now corrected. Two sisters in a powerful friendship. Laden with happiness and tears.

November 26, 2003

Life: Priceless piece of the big puzzle

NEW YORK – My kid brother and I had a talk about death. A subject we never discussed before. Seven years older, I felt a duty to provide him with some answers. But what I said surprised me.

Told him my belief that nobody ever really dies.

Something is eternal.

I learned that in my favorite play, *Our Town*.

"Everybody knows in their bones that *something* is eternal, and that something has to do with human beings," says one of the characters. "All the greatest people ever lived have been telling us that for 5,000 years, and yet you'd be surprised how people are always losing it. There's something way deep down that's eternal about every human being."

I *want* to believe that now. I *need* to believe that. How can somebody die if *something* about them will always be eternal?

Each day is so precious to my mother and father. Mom is recovering from radiation for a brain tumor, and my father keeps telling me his only prayer: "I just want a few more months with her."

I pulled out a calculator and figured that Mom and Dad have enjoyed 14,442 days and nights together in their 39 years of marriage. So many pieces making up the puzzle of life. And now each piece is as priceless to them as the love they share.

But what surprised me about my talk with my brother was how ardently I believe that death isn't really the end. Our parents never taught us that.

My teacher is an old worn copy of *Our Town*, a play I first read in junior high school. My copy of Thornton Wilder's 1937 masterpiece is an essential of my life.

The odd thing is, I have never seen the play performed in a theater. I've only read it. But now, more than ever, I needed to remind myself of the play's message. So the other night, I left Mom's hospital room and went to see an off-off-Broadway theater group perform *Our Town*.

In the play, people in the little town of Grover's Corners live their lives as pleasantly and as meaningfully as they can. And when they die, they go to a hilltop cemetery outside town.

In the final act, Emily, a mother who dies during childbirth, takes her place in the cemetery and begins to see life on earth in a new way.

"Live people don't understand, do they?" she asks. "They're sort of shut up in little boxes, aren't they? . . . I never realized before how troubled and how . . . in the dark live people are."

For her final wish, Emily is granted a trip back in time to watch her 12th birthday. But when she sees how people take life for granted, she is so pained she asks to return to her place on the hilltop.

"Oh, earth you're too wonderful for anybody to realize you," Emily says. "Do any human beings ever realize life while they live it? – every, every minute?"

"The saints and poets, maybe," somebody tells her. "They do some."

At the play's climax, the bitter town drunk angrily explains to Emily:

"Yes, now you know. Now you know! That's what it was to be alive. To move about in a cloud of ignorance; to go up and down trampling on the feelings of those . . . of those about you. To spend and waste time as though you had a million years. To be always at the mercy of one self-centered passion or another. Now you know – that's the happy existence you wanted to go back to. Ignorance and blindness."

Seeing my mother fight for her life, listening to my father's only prayer, thinking about the words I used talking to my brother, I am reminded that there is something else to consider besides the spiritual eternity of every human being.

Each and every day we have on this earth is so very, very precious. It's a priceless piece of a big puzzle. With no time to waste.

Sometimes in a life of ignorance and blindness, I too easily forget this.

December 3, 1995

Mom called – it was time to say goodbye

My mother passed away yesterday morning.

Dad called to tell me.

Mom had trouble breathing, he said. She lay down in bed, her head on the pillow. Her eyes were open, but her head dropped to the side. She took her last breath.

Denise B. Lieber died peacefully at home in New York City, the way she wanted. She was 62.

At least we got to say goodbye on the phone.

Saturday afternoon, when I called home, she insisted on talking to me.

In a weak, whispery voice, she seemed to be tying up loose ends.

She told me how grateful she was for her two best friends, Roberta and Marian. These friends of 50 years stayed by her side.

She told how her miracle doctor, James Speyer, had visited her at home that day. She couldn't believe it! Can you imagine? A house call from the doctor who treated her cancer. She thanked him as best she could.

"I told him, 'You made me live for seven years,' " Mom said. "He did the best he could do. He can't do any more."

She turned her attention to me.

"I'm sorry," she said. "I really am."

"What for?" I asked.

"I wanted to see your baby and Bennett's baby."

There's no expected baby in either my family or my brother's, but I knew what she meant.

"You don't have anything to apologize for," I told her.

Then she talked about my father.

"I'm worried about Dad," she said. "He's so absent-minded."

I told her not to worry. Without her, he'd learn to cope. I promised to keep an eye on him. Maybe get him to move to Texas. Become a cowboy.

"Don't let him sell the apartment," she continued.

OK, I promised.

She was tiring.

"Can I say goodbye now?" she asked.

I wasn't sure if she meant the phone call or forever.

"Yes."

"I love you," she said.

"I love you, too," I said.

"Goodbye."

I hung up the phone and picked up a writing pad. I wanted to write down her words. Something told me they were her last to me.

But I couldn't write. My body was shaking and teardrops fell on the paper. I couldn't hold the pen.

My wife and children weren't home, so I was alone. I wrote "alone" on the pad. Then I heard a bell jingle. I glanced up to see the new cat in our family looking at me. The bell on her collar jingled again.

I felt empty. Almost like hunger pangs. I went to the kitchen and fixed a bowl of cornflakes. Ate it, but didn't feel any better. Ate another bowl. Felt bloated, but still empty.

It's funny the way little thoughts pass through your head.

At sleep-away camp as a little boy, I missed my mother so much, I joined the "Homesick Club" for teary-eyed campers. I feel like calling a meeting today.

Whenever I got in trouble, my mother would shake her finger at me and say: "You are such a stinker!"

At my brother's wedding last year, she literally rose from her death bed for the event. In the weeks before, she was so sick she couldn't walk. But as the wedding day approached, Mom rallied and surprised everyone.

At the reception, she got out of her wheelchair and walked slowly to the stage. In her lavender dress, she took the microphone. Mom looked so beautiful.

In a quivering voice, she said, "Thank the good Lord I made it today. I can't be happier."

She even danced that night.

Through all the days and nights of pain, she never complained. Never mouthed words of bitterness about her fate.

"You don't know the half of it" was her worst protest about her illness.

She always apologized to the nurses for causing them trouble. She gave them bags of candy as thank-you gifts.

My mother cared more about others than about herself. Her caring was her medicine.

Last week, she pleaded to my father, "Let me go." Her pain, she told him, made life "not worth living."

Her love for my father, for her family and friends gave her reasons to live as long as she did.

If she cared enough to live for us, we have to care enough to let her go.

We must accept it so she can rest in peace.

Mom, I'll always love you.

January 9, 1996

Trip home puts past in perspective

*T*he week I returned to New York City to bury my mother passed in slow motion. Shrouded beneath 2 feet of snow, the impatient city had paused in midsymphony, as if to bow its head at the passing of a great woman. But when the snow began to melt and get shoveled aside, the old city of my youth wasn't buried that deep.

It doesn't matter if your hometown is New York or Oshkosh or Amarillo. Sometimes when you've been away for a while and you must go back, the old neighborhood feels both different and the same. People move away, but memories are rooted forever.

This journey was a ride on a train going backward. Dragging me until my children, always at my side, reminded me what is important. Which way the train is supposed to go.

One day, as my parents' small apartment was overrun with an unending blur of condolence-sending friends, I told my daughter and son to put on their hats, coats and boots for a snowy walking tour of my old town.

How could I explain Manhattan life to Desiree and Jonathan?

How could I tell them about those days in the early 1960s when I caught the tail end of the old New York?

It was almost an innocent New York. If you can imagine such a contradiction. A place where they could post signs on Broadway saying "President Kennedy will be here at 11:32 a.m." and on the next block "President Kennedy will be here at 11:33 a.m." Adding a minute all the way up Broadway.

And the president passed by in an open convertible on schedule, just a few feet from where I stood gawking with my mother.

How could I tell them everything?

My children and I began our trip near Times Square, but when I looked up for the Camel sign with the guy blowing perfectly round puffs of steam, I couldn't find it. I knew this wouldn't be easy.

In my New York, bus drivers still made change, little boys like me could ride the subways alone, and the only measurement you needed to know was that 20 blocks equaled a mile.

There was no Trump Tower. George Steinbrenner was a businessman in Cleveland. The Mets were lovable losers.

Listen to me. I sound like an old fogy.

My barber's name was Jimmy. Once a month, he gave me a haircut, a pompadour and a lollipop.

Dr. Smith made house calls when I got sick. A bagel cost 8 cents, and a slice of pizza was 15 cents.

I'm not sure if my kids were interested. They were too busy walking in the snow. But I went on, anyway.

The Empire State Building was the tallest building in the world. Ever hear of a double feature? You saw two movies *and cartoons* for the price of one. Once I saw Jack Dempsey, the great boxer, standing in the window of his Broadway restaurant.

Did my kids care that one time I crossed Broadway with Bobby Kennedy after a campaign rally? Or what about the old F.W. Woolworth store that offered a game of chance? Pop a balloon and find out if your banana split costs a penny or a dollar.

At Lincoln Center, my children and I stepped inside the Metropolitan Opera House to get warm. This was no coincidence. For two years, as a pre-pubescent boy, I was a soprano in the children's chorus.

In the gift shop, I found a libretto for *Carmen* and turned to my old part. I sang the French words softly, but Desiree and Jonathan were not impressed.

We went next door to the music library, where I found a recording of *Carmen* on a record album, now an antique. I placed it on a turntable, another antique, and through headphones, the children listened to my old part.

"YOU didn't do that!" Jonathan said with certainty. "You can't sing that high!"

"Once I was young, too." (Did I just say that?)

Outside, I taught these Sunbelt children how to make snowballs. We had our first snow fight. It was high drama.

The walk in the snow up Broadway was comforting for the children and me. Desiree and Jonathan had lost *their* grandmother. They had cried, too.

When we finally headed back to the place we now call home, the place where the West begins, I no longer felt like I was traveling backward. For the first time, though, I felt very old.

January 21, 1996

Paying tribute to a mother who encouraged her son

*T*he billboard outside Richland Hills Church of Christ last week caught my eye: "All that I am, and all that I hope to be, I owe to my mother." – Abe Lincoln.

My mother is gone from this Earth but not from my heart. Not, especially, from my writer's heart.

She always supported my career. She subscribed to the newspapers where I worked, faithfully read my articles and called me with praise. When she died, my father found boxes filled with yellowing stories in her closet.

Then last year, my father told me that he had found an old audiotape he wanted me to hear. The tape captured the most important conversation I ever had with my mother.

Apparently, their telephone answering machine had recorded the conversation, and they saved it.

The conversation was in 1993 after *Star-Telegram* editors hired me as a columnist.

The first thing I did was call Mom, who was dying from cancer.

Here, according to the tape, was the talk I had with my mother:

Mom, I began.

What?

I just wanted to thank you.

For what?

For helping me get my job – because it really wasn't official until now.

What do you mean? So what do you mean I helped you?

Well, I can't think of anybody in the world who did more than you!

And Dad did. That's what you wrote on his card that was so beautiful.

Well, you, too. I mean, you were always …

I didn't do anything.

You were always backing me and, uh, and when I went to Florida for my first job and I didn't have any money and I didn't have anything. I was just like totally lost. And because of your foresight and Dad's, there was money left over in my account that you could send me to use to buy a car. You set me up with a $50-a-month payment.

Yeah, well that's what . . .

You worked me in, you know, nice and smooth. And then you come down and we hang out on the beach and we . . .

Now, David, don't make me cry. That's what parents are for.

Now listen. Now listen. I'm not done, OK? And then I got fired, you know. I'm really down and out.

I know.

Then I go to West Virginia and you come down there and even though I probably made a mistake – but nothing's really ever a mistake, really, in life.

You learn from everything.

And I got married which ended in divorce. And you come down there and you're playing the gracious parents. And then I go to work in Philadelphia, and I go on strike. And you're always with me the whole way.

But that's what parents are for.

Yeah, but the whole world is full of parents who don't do their jobs.

Well, I don't know about that . . .

So basically, among the many things that you are, right, which is a kind, decent, wonderful, thoughtful person – you have a lot of friends and everybody loves you – one of your legacies in life is that you had a son, and the son had a nearly impossible dream. And the odds were overwhelming.

I know.

And you gave birth to the son in the peak year of the baby boom – '57 – where there were more children born than any time in the history of the country.

Yeah, so?

So there's more competition. There's more of everything. More women in the hospital in '57 than any year in history.

I don't know that. Did you look this up in the almanac?

I'm going to do a book about it. Before I die, I'm going to write a book, and it's going to be called *1957*. And it's going to be about the peak year of the baby boomers.

And you're going to write everything you just said?

Ten years from now.

I hope to be alive to read this.

Oh, it could be a bestseller, because I'm going to wait until I really know what I'm talking about.

Are you going to say what you just said now?

It'll be much better than that.

Hmm. The only thing is . . . I don't know. I hope to live to read it.

They have a reference library in heaven. Check the book out.

OK, OK.

If I write a good book, right, and you're doing your guardian angel stuff . . .

Yeah, right. Highway to heaven.

And you'll be on assignment, and so you'll be going down and checking out other people. You'll hear it through the angel grapevine about my book.

Listen. I'm fighting. I'm fighting. I want to live to see a grandchild, already . . .

The tape ran out. My mother died less than three years later.

On this Mother's Day, I share it with you and ask you to remember the poignant words of Abe Lincoln.

Before it's too late, tell you mother – if you can – that all you are, all that you hope to be, you owe to her.

May 9, 1999

Chapter Nine

September 11

"If we hold hands from coast to coast,
And sing, sing, sing,
Let the church bells ring, ring, ring,
We'll lift each other up so high.
We'll soar like eagles in the sky.
All the nations will see how we behave.
We're the land of the free and the home of the brave!"

> — Poem by 9-year-old Rachel
> Engelland of Keller,
> written on Sept. 12, 2001

Girl offers uplifting message

*I*t is a simple, eloquent 106-word poem that sums up the thoughts of a nation.

Rachel Engelland, 9-year-old daughter of Shawn and Sandra Engelland of Keller, caused tears of sadness and pride in teachers and staff Wednesday at Shady Grove Elementary School when she took her assignment to write in her journal and created a work of art.

The teachers at Shady Grove had been careful Tuesday not to let the children learn too much about the terrorist attacks on America.

"We kept it as normal as possible," Principal Jayne Flores said.

When Rachel's mother picked her up as part of a carpool Tuesday, Rachel said, "Mommy, I heard that a couple of airplanes crashed into this building. Do you know anything about it?"

"We'll talk about it later, not when I'm carpooling," her mother answered. "I have to watch the traffic."

"Oh, OK," the girl said.

Rachel was surprised to see her father home from work. Like many others, Shawn Engelland, a NASA aerospace engineer, was released from his job early.

"We need to talk to you about something," he said when Rachel walked in. "This is really serious."

The father and mother sat Rachel and her little sister, Rebekah, down in the living room and turned on the television.

He showed them the videotape of the hijacked airplanes crashing into the innocence of Americans.

The family said a prayer, and Rachel, who began to feel sad, went out for a bicycle ride.

"I decided I needed a break," she said.

Tuesday night, she had difficulty sleeping.

"I said a prayer," she said, asking: "God, please help me through the night. Please help me calm down. And please help the people who are in trouble."

She awoke Wednesday morning and her first thought was, "Whoa, it really happened!"

She dressed in tan overalls and a rose-colored shirt and headed off to school, where she watched as the flag was lowered to half-staff.

In Rachel's class, her teacher, Paula Brownlee, talked about patriotism. The students stood and sang the national anthem. Then Brownlee asked the students to write in their journals.

Rachel wrote a poem titled, *It All Came at Such a Cost*.

The poem goes like this:

Yes, a lot of lives were lost,
It all came at such a cost.
There wasn't anything one could do,
But I hope you know I'm praying for you.
Yes, those lost were loved the most.
But if we hold hands from coast to coast,
And sing, sing, sing,
Let the church bells ring, ring, ring,
We'll lift each other up so high.
We'll soar like eagles in the sky.
All the nations will see how we behave.
We're the land of the free and the home of the brave!
The World Trade Center is gone, lives are lost.
It all came at such a cost.

When she was done, she read the poem aloud in class. Her teacher cried. Her classmates applauded. Then other teachers who were shown the poem cried, too.

"I wrote it to comfort people," the little girl said.

Please share it with your friends and loved ones.

Tell them that among some of the wisest people in our great land is a little girl from Keller, Texas, who wrote so eloquently what so many of us feel and what we all need to hear.

September 14, 2001

Dave's dad

A nightmare envelopes my father's city of dreams

After my mother died five years ago, my father's new girlfriend became that grand old lady – New York, the city of his dreams.

He loved the city, and the city loved him.

In every telephone conversation since Mom died, Dad spoke about the city's business, her wild politics, her glowing theater and music, her vaunted newspapers and the grand holiday festivals along the Hudson River, which he never missed.

But last week, after runaway planes smashed into the twin towers, I reached him by telephone. I had been trying for hours.

"How are you doing?" he asked, as always.

"Good," I replied, unthinkingly.

"I'm glad you're doing good," he snapped with that legendary New York sarcasm that doesn't hurt if you know it's coming. "The country is not doing good. The city is not doing good."

Neither, of course, was my father.

His best girl was covered in a smoky shroud of dust and death. The city, his city, will never be the same, and neither will he.

He had arrived in New York in 1958, when I was 1, straight from his hometown in North Carolina, where he and I were born. Without a blink, he exchanged Dixie for downtown, grits for greasy pizza. He and Mom moved to a two-bedroom apartment on 78th Street, where he still lives today, and the West Side of Manhattan became his haven and his hope.

Our neighborhood was nothing special, a little old and beat up. But the streets were safe, and manners were more common than muggings. Without the slightest fear, my parents allowed me to play outside. By the time I was 8, I was permitted to walk down Broadway by myself to buy a quart of milk or fetch a late newspaper for Dad with the closing stock prices.

When the great blackout of 1965 hit about supper time, my father was stuck in the subway. He found his way to the street, where he walked among fellow New Yorkers through the darkness block after block. When he finally returned home, my family, waiting worried by candlelight, let out a rousing cheer.

During my teen-age years, the city of his dreams grew worn and sad. Heroin junkies flooded the streets, along with the homeless and the insane. The year I graduated from high school, 1975, I left the city and never went back. My father thought I was crazy.

After that, as the city bounced from the brink of bankruptcy, his conversations about her became one long brag. Gentrification changed the neighborhood as yuppies bought old brownstones nearby and restored them to Victorian grandeur.

The block association used money from fund-raisers to plant trees, and later, to add little fences to protect tree roots from neighborhood dogs that could find no other greenery.

His city also made him paper rich. Our little two-bedroom apartment, purchased for the price of a car today, was soon worth more than $500,000. As real estate values soared almost as high as the World Trade Center towers, his spirits soared, too.

My father bragged on that World Trade Center. He saw it for what it was, a center of finance and commerce like nothing built before.

Several weeks ago, my wife went to see him before a business conference in New York. She asked him to show her the sights.

"Have you ever been to the World Trade Center?" he asked Karen.

"No," she said.

He acted as if she hadn't said that. "Well, surely, you've seen the twin towers," he said.

"No, really, I haven't."

"I just can't believe you haven't seen them," he said.

He fixed that quickly. The towers were the first stop on a walking tour that lasted all weekend. Together, the two strolled beneath the proud towers through the posh underground mall. Karen remembers the gleaming marble walls and the polished brass banisters. She also remembers how the complex proudly flew all the flags of the world.

That was his last visit, and maybe the last time that his best girl will ever offer an innocence that, even by New York standards, was purer than not.

Tuesday morning began like every other morning of his life since 1958. He listened to the latest news in the daily life of his best girl on radio station WINS, which reminds that it is all news, all the time.

Suddenly, a woman on a cellphone was patched through, talking on the radio about an airplane punching the great tower in the sky. My father rushed to the television and watched in horror as the first events of the worst day in the city's life began to unfold.

He was by himself. Just him and his city. It was the worst day for him since my mother died.

That afternoon, he went to see for himself. He picked up his little radio, still tuned to all news, all the time, and took a lonely walk down 78th Street to the Hudson River, where this time, there was no holiday festival.

He joined others at the end of a long pier jutting onto the Hudson. Together, everyone stood and looked southward toward the end of the borough at the thick, black smoke that filled the great sky.

No one in my family died that day. But you don't really have to be a victim to feel the pain.

"I'm taking this loss personally," my dad said in one of our many conversations last week. "I live here. But all Americans are taking this loss personally. It's not just an attack on New York City. It's an attack on the United States.

"My city is bleeding. My country is bleeding. But New York and America are not going to bleed forever. Ours is a tough town. But it's going to take a long time."

Without prodding, he professed his passion.

"I can't tell you how much I love this city," he said. "The city is made up of people from everywhere. There's kindness in the city. There's charity in the city. There's love in the city."

He is 79 years old, and the city of his dreams, down but not out, is the reason why he lives for another day.

September 16, 2001

Bids fly high for U.S. flag

All week long, there were questions without answers about whether to have the celebrity roast of Southlake Mayor Rick Stacy to benefit the Carroll Education Foundation.

It is hard to laugh when you are crying for your country.

But something happened at that event Saturday night, something unexpected and extraordinary that, in retrospect, erased doubts about whether to go ahead with the event four days after last week's tragedies.

I'm not talking about jokes made at Stacy's expense, which were funny and plentiful. Or about the mayor's wonderful willingness to subject himself to the abuse of his roasters to benefit Carroll district teachers, who need money to pay for educational projects not covered in the school budget.

I'm not even talking about the $100,000 raised for the foundation during the five-hour benefit.

What I want to tell you about is this: Amid hundreds of auction items, there was one item for sale that aroused great passions in the audience of mostly Southlake residents.

It was an American flag flown over the U.S. Capitol.

A week ago, an auction item such as a U.S. or a Texas flag flown over the national or state capitols would not be considered unusual. Indeed, at first, this particular flag donated by U.S. Rep. Kay Granger, R-Fort Worth, was not even slated for the live auction. The flag was listed in the previously printed program as Item No. 630.

When foundation organizers decided to conduct the event Saturday, they added a few touches, including a speech by outgoing Chairman Jack Milner. He said that after "a lot of thought," organizers decided that canceling the event "would give the terrorists one more victory."

Instead, organizers donated $5,000 from their proceeds to the American Red Cross and also moved Granger's donated flag from its place as Item No. 630 to the climactic offering in the auction.

Until that flag was displayed before the audience, the auction had been a bit sluggish. Bids on other items had jumped by $100 increments. One of the highest prices came for a cute golden retriever puppy, which sold for $2,400.

But when Stacy, who was also auctioneer, brought out the flag and announced that it had flown atop the U.S. Capitol, everyone perked up. As the large flag was unfurled, the Lee Greenwood song *God Bless the U.S.A.* played on the speaker:

I'm proud to be an American
Where at least I know I'm free.
And I won't forget the men who died
Who gave that right to me.

Stacy began to speak, but he stopped for a moment. His eyes welled with tears, and the Army veteran choked back emotions. Then he called out, "Who gives $100?"

Dozens of hands shot up across the ballroom.

Suddenly, the whole room was energized. The bidding became fast and ferocious. Bids did not jump by $100. No, bids vaulted in $1,000 increments.

"Five thousand!" Stacy cried.

"Six thousand!"

"Seven thousand!"

Many in the room began to applaud. I felt goose bumps. But the bidding wasn't done.

Larry Marshall, owner of Cotton Patch Café Restaurants and a Carroll school supporter, was one of the bidders.

"I kind of felt an overwhelming sense of a need to do something," he said later. "Whatever I could. I guess just the emotions of the moment got to me. I got caught up in the spirit."

As did everyone else.

"Eight thousand!" Stacy shouted.

"Nine thousand!"

"Ten thousand!"

Southlake resident Lee Roy Hess, owner of Prestige Gunite, a Fort Worth-based commercial pool contractor, raised his hand with the final bid.

"Eleven thousand!" Stacy roared triumphantly.

With the Lee Greenwood song turned up, everyone stood for a loud and long ovation.

Foundation officials said later that the $11,000 for the flag, plus the foundation's pledge of $5,000, will be sent to the American Red Cross to help pay for disaster recovery.

"I was surprised, encouraged and renewed by that showing in our own community," foundation Chairman Brian Stebbins said.

The large flag was neatly packed in a box and handed to Hess, who gave it to his wife, Colleen, for safekeeping.

"America is a great country," Lee Roy Hess told me later. "I don't know what to say. It's just great. This is special."

It really is. God bless America.

September 17, 2001

North Richland Hills firefighter grieves alongside brethren

Dan Gannon

*F*or 22 years, North Richland Hills firefighter Dan Gannon has answered the call. He has saved burning houses, raced into flaming buildings in search of victims and once brought an infant back to life after she stopped breathing.

Generations of Birdville school district children know him as "Dan Dan the fireman," who lectures about fire safety.

But there was one call that got to him. One call that nothing in two decades of public service could prepare him for.

The call came from his firefighting buddies in New York, firefighters who grew up with Dan on Long Island when they started as volunteers fresh out of high school. These lifelong buddies, tough guys who thought they had seen it all, were in tears after the Sept. 11 attacks on the World Trade Center towers.

"We need guys to come up here and go to these funerals," one buddy told Dan. "Will you be able to come up here for us?"

"I'll see if I can get enough time off," Dan answered.

That's how the hand of fate reached down to North Richland Hills and pulled Dan Dan the fireman away from Fire Station No. 2 on Rufe Snow Drive.

Dan and his wife, Anne, arrived in Texas in 1979 so she could keep her job with American Airlines. Dan was hired by North Richland Hills. Meanwhile, his old buddies took jobs with the Fire Department of New York.

Last week, Dan took time off and flew to New York for the five saddest days of his life.

He visited the World Trade Center site and attended three firefighters' funerals.

"One part of me really didn't want to go, but we've got a saying in the fire service that you've got to do the right thing," he said. "And the right thing was for me to be with my friends."

That first night in New York, Dan sat with his best buddy, Nick Dolce, who works in Queens with Ladder Co. 163, which lost three men Sept. 11.

Over a couple of beers in Nick's living room, he told Dan how he spent three days at the World Trade Center digging with his hands, crying and looking for old friends in the rubble.

"In the 30 years I've known him, it was the most emotionally draining conversation we ever had," Dan said. Nick cried. Dan cried. The crying didn't stop for three hours.

The next day, another buddy, Nick D'Alessandro, said, "Come on, Danny. You need to come downtown and see this so you can tell your guys back home in Texas what it looks like."

Before Dan stepped on a city bus to ride with New York firefighters to the World Trade Center site, they lent him firefighters gear. When the North Richland Hills firefighter put on a helmet that stated FDNY, he felt, more than ever, a part of the firefighters brotherhood.

When Dan arrived in lower Manhattan, he couldn't believe what he saw. It looked like the movies you saw of England or other parts of Europe during World War II after bombing raids. Maybe even worse.

"The devastation was so overpowering," he said. "I had known that the rubble was 10 stories high. But I didn't know the hole between the two towers was 7 stories deep. There was still red hot steel.

"Once I kind of got over the devastation, I realized that I was smelling something that I had smelled before. It was the smell of death. Decaying bodies. It's a very unique smell. It's a smell you don't forget."

Dan spent three hours there, talking to firefighters, watching them work, thinking over and over, "All those firemen. All those lost souls."

That night, back in his hotel room, Dan couldn't sleep. He lay in bed and looked at the clock – 3:30 a.m. But he couldn't shut his eyes even though he knew that in a few hours, he was going to a funeral.

Fourth Battalion Chief Thomas D'Angelis was killed in the collapse of the first tower. Dan was asked to be part of the honor guard.

"It's a big honor," he said.

Wearing a borrowed dress uniform, Dan stood at attention on the church steps as relatives and friends of the fallen firefighter walked past him.

"It was an empty casket," Dan said. "But it didn't make any difference to anybody there."

The next day, Dan attended another funeral. And the day after, he attended still another.

"From all the guys there, all I kept hearing from them was, 'Thanks. Thanks for being here.'

"When you look at them, your heart goes out to them. You know how much they are suffering. A lot of people don't understand, but we live with each other. This is a family member you've lost, not just somebody you work with."

The trip home to Texas was lonely.

The plane was crowded, but Dan didn't notice anyone else. He thought about the previous five days, what he heard and saw, how he felt.

When he returned to the Rufe Snow Drive firehouse, he kept his promise.

He told his family – the other firefighters – everything that had happened. The North Richland Hills guys listened with quiet reverence to Dan's sad tales.

"People don't understand this job," Dan Dan the fireman said. "They see us working, and they ask if we're scared. Yeah, we're always scared. But somebody's got to do the job."

October 19, 2001

For those forgotten veterans

You are a Vietnam veteran, and you never got your due.

On this Veterans Day, it has to hurt. You look around and see the flag flying for our fighters in Afghanistan and for our nation's pride. But when you were half a world away, who flew the flag for you?

Today is your day, too. But it feels like everyone else's. It's OK for you to ask, "What about me and my guys?"

Who sang *God Bless America* or wore red, white and blue for you? The silent majority was always so silent.

In your family, war was always a matter of pride. A tradition. You heard your grandfather talk about marching in the doughboys' parades after World War I.

Your dad told you about how pretty women kissed him when he stepped off the troop ship at the end of World War II. Your uncle died. Maybe a cousin, too.

There was Korea, another win, and the Persian Gulf War, a made-for-TV spectacular that was over in a few days. Now there's Afghanistan, where the American people are ahead of their government. We want more firepower and more troops, and the politicians have to catch up. The opposite of the way it was for you.

And what about you? You started out with dreams of duty, honor and valor. You were fresh meat in the Nam.

You were in-country. Jumping in with both boots on your first night patrols. Learning to sleep with your eyes open. Avoiding friendly fire not so friendly.

It was the longest year of your life. Carrying your grenades, your banana clips, your C-rations and your best friend, the M-16.

This was no John Wayne fantasy with a happy ending. There was all that bull about hearts and minds. Yeah, you fought with your heart, while we were home protesting and losing the war with our minds.

That war made you old, turned your skin pale and killed off your smile.

They called you a grunt. What a perfect name. You knew you really were the bottom of the barrel.

The college boys back home were growing their hair and getting their degrees so decades later they could pretend they were experts on wars they only read about in books. Nobody ever asked for your opinion. But you were the expert.

You wore your poncho on rainy night patrols. Used your helmet for a pillow. Swiped ants off the back of your neck. Checked the malaria pills in your pocket.

"Go take the hill!" the brass said.

Charlie's coming. It's an ambush, a firefight, a skirmish. Pretty words for slaughter.

You still can't forget the smell of napalm, even though you try.

You see the Viet Cong shooting at you from their dank spider holes.

You feel the puddle water around your ankles in those dark, wet tunnels through which you crawled with only a flashlight and a pistol.

You hear the screams, the sobs, the moans . . . the silence. The horrible quiet of a deadly defeat.

Your best buddy got greased. So many bodies they couldn't be covered properly. Your tears mixed in with the jungle rain.

You were surrounded by the dead, theirs and ours. You walked through bombed-out moonscapes. The valley of the shadow of death.

There was no light at the end of this tunnel. You had to destroy the village in order to save it. Those dominoes fell.

But if you never hear the words "lock and load" and "fire in the hole" again, that's OK.

You made it. You survived. But your war wasn't over. There was no parade for you.

Back home, some jerk saw you in uniform and spit on you. Welcome home, killer.

All you got were discharge papers and a pain in your heart that never goes away. Nobody wanted to hear your stories. Nobody does today.

Agent Orange. Delayed stress syndrome. "He's crazy, man. He's a Vietnam vet!"

So now you get a big black wall with more than 58,000 names. An ode to those left behind. The good dying young.

Defeat is a horrible idea, a concept we ignore. Nobody calls you a member of "the greatest generation."

Even today, all these years later, we still see right through you as you wear your baseball cap that says, "I'm a Vietnam veteran."

All we see is that last helicopter leaving the roof of the U.S. Embassy in Saigon.

More than 30 years ago, you were slogging through rice paddies, but we never took hold and helped you win.

You can't win a war without support and admiration for those who do the dirty work. You grunts really weren't the bottom of the barrel.

Years passed, and we never said thank you. Still haven't. Never. Never ever.

So take this as a small one. Too little, too late. But here it is for you anyway. On your holiday, Veterans Day.

Thank you, hero.

November 11, 2001

Explaining an empty sky to a little boy

Playing ball

Although I grew up in New York City, I have raised my little Texas boy to be as Texan as a Texan can be.

He has visited the Alamo, knows the story about what happened there and doesn't like the ending. At 5 years old, he is already on his third pair of cowboy boots. He attends the Fort Worth Stock Show every year and knows how to fling a rope almost like a real rancher. Of course, we named him Austin.

But the time had finally come, on the occasion of my father's 80th birthday last week, to take my little Texas boy on his first visit to the place of my past. I wanted to show him the equivalent of the family farm – actually only a small apartment on Manhattan's Upper West Side. He needed to see how his daddy's upbringing was so different from his own Texas life on a visit he would never forget.

Before the visit, I told him that one thing he would not see in New York was the big Texas sky.

"How come, Daddy?" he asked.

"Because there are so many tall buildings everywhere you can only see a little piece of the sky, not like here, where the big sky is everywhere."

Later, I realized this was something of a lie. There was one place in Manhattan where we did see the big sky. It was at our new national shrine, the place where life and death collided on a terrible day last September. The place they now call Ground Zero.

"Why do they call it Ground Zero, Daddy?"

"Because there's nothing there, like a zero."

But of course, that is not really true either. Everything is there in that giant hole and all that is around it.

There is the world's cleanest construction site, or maybe it is a destruction site.

Not a speck of dust remains because each speck is actually something more. There is that flag flying proud at the edge of the site, as inspiring as the flag that once flew for Francis Scott Key.

There is the inexplicable crucifix of steel girders that remains, a reminder of God's tenderness amid this horrific act of evil.

And there are the hundreds of people lined up along the fence, each alone with his or her thoughts about what all this means.

On the morning of my father's 80th birthday, our three generations – my father, my little Texas boy and me – stood peering through the fence at this sacred land.

I looked up and saw that there really is a big Texas sky in New York, but that it is in a place where it was never meant to be.

And as I gazed upward, my own thoughts about what it all meant took me back to what my son and I did an hour before our visit to Ground Zero.

We were inside the little apartment when I grabbed a pink bouncy ball from my suitcase and said, "Austin, let's go downstairs." We took the elevator down – of course, he had to push the button – and emerged on the street that had served as the concrete playground of my childhood. There, on West 78th Street, I introduced my little Texas boy, who only knows the grassy back yards and lush playgrounds of Texas, to the games of my childhood.

The tool of these games is the pink ball known as the Spalding High-Bounce ball, but called by street kids everywhere "the Spaldeen." It's the true city ball because of the way it bounces beautifully off the pavement.

I showed my little Texas boy how to bounce it off the tall steps of a brownstone and catch it on the ricochet. It didn't take him long to master it.

"Nice play, right Dad?" he asked, as he caught one and then another. "You like that, Dad?"

I felt a lump in my throat and then began to recite the long history of the game on this very block.

"There were boys that played here 60 years ago, even before I was born," I began. "Their names were Eddie, Bobby, Maury, Dickie, Bernie, Joel, Barry and Ralph. They played in the 1940s during World War II with this same kind of ball, in the very place where you are standing."

"How do you know them, Daddy?"

I explained that I didn't, but I had read about them in a book called *The Block*, written by one of them, Ralph Schoenstein, who had his memoir published in 1960. One of the boys even lived in the same apartment where I grew up.

It was one of the great pieces of luck in my life that such a precious book exists, so I could understand that my world had once belonged to others.

"Twenty-five years later," I told my little Texas boy, "those guys were gone and they were replaced by my friends. There was Alberto and his kid brother Carlos, Miriam, Charles, Lesley, Jay, Harold and his sister Laurie, and me. We played the games with the same kind of ball."

I told him how we used to hit the ball and how a long hit was considered a three-sewer home run.

"What's a sewer, Daddy?"

"It's where the dirty water goes, underneath that manhole cover there. See, that was home plate, and that one was second base, and the third one was center field."

"What about the cars, Daddy?"

"Well, when they came, we just got out of the way."

"Do the boys still live there?"

"No, they grew up and moved away, just like I did. But now you are here and playing the same games here in the 21st century."

"What's a 21st century?"

"It's this year, 2002, more than 60 years after those boys played here. Isn't that something, Austin?"

"Yes," he said, as he continued bouncing the ball against the steps. My father came downstairs and saw what he was doing.

"Don't throw it there!" he shouted. Maybe he was afraid my little Texas boy would break a window.

"Don't worry, Austin," I whispered. For 60 years or more, the parents of this street had been telling us to stop, but you know, of course, that we never did.

And so an hour or two later, I was looking up at that big Texas sky above Ground Zero and thought about this.

Bouncy ball games were not what I expected to be thinking about at Ground Zero.

But like roping in Texas, or lobster-catching in Maine or basketball in Indiana, these geographic idiosyncrasies represent the beloved traditions of our America.

Life is not a straight line with no beginning and no ending. Now that I have played street ball with my little Texas boy, a life-affirming act for me, I have all the proof I need that the circle of American life remains unbroken.

July 28, 2002

Chapter Ten
The Yankee Cowboy

*"No matter how much I may exaggerate it,
it must have a certain amount of truth."*

— Will Rogers

Lone Star crusader has lonely battle

The Yankee Cowboy

My guest today is J.R. Lieber, the Yankee Cowboy everybody loves to hate. J.R., why does everybody hate you?

Howdy, pal. Let me start by saying that, among Texans, hating Yankees is the last acceptable form of bigotry. I'm leading a civil rights crusade to expose this injustice.

How's your crusade going?

Not so hot. I started a group called Y.A.N.K.S., which stands for You Are Not Kind Southerners. But we have no members.

Why not?

It's probably my strong personality. I act like I know everything. Even other transplanted Yankees don't like me.

What are you trying to accomplish?

We'd like to educate Texans about Yankee greatness. But for some reason, they're not interested.

Why do we need to know?

Somebody needs to teach Texans how to drive, how to talk and how to behave. Life has changed since the Alamo days.

And don't you think Texans know this?

Come on, pal. Look around. When was the last time you saw a Texan act rude? Where I come from, rude is a good thing. At least you know where you stand with the other guy.

How do you stand with Texans?

Oh, they treat me great. Always polite and friendly to my face. But nobody could be that wonderful. I know what they're thinking. They hate me.

What's wrong with the way Texans drive?

Don't get me started! What is it about car horns that Texans don't understand?

You mean Texans should toot their car horns more often?

Why do you think the car manufacturers put the horn so close to your fingertips? They want you to beep.

This lack of beeping bothers you?

Bothers me terribly.

What else annoys you?

Big hair. At ballgames, I always end up sitting behind a woman with big hair. I say, "Excuse me, big-haired Texas lady, but I can't see through your bleached coloring! Giddyap!"

What's their reaction?

Well, let's just say things got rougher after the concealed handgun law went into effect.

What else bothers you?

Mrs. Baird's bagels.

Did you ever try one?

No need. Nobody named Baird could ever make a bagel.

Speaking of names, why is yours J.R.?

I changed it after moving here. J.R. Ewing is my hero. He's the real thing. Did you see the *Dallas* reunion movie on television?

Missed it.

Well, J.R. said, "Some days you're the windshield. And some days you're the bug." Isn't that a great philosophy?

Which are you?

Texas is the windshield, and I'm the bug.

J.R., I notice you're wearing Justin cowboy boots, a bolo tie and a Resistol cowboy hat.

I'm making a statement.

Which is?

Even though I look like a Texan on the outside, I'm different on the inside. And one day, after a period of mutual respect and admiration, our children can all be the same.

How will that happen?

We're marrying your daughters.

Do you ever plan on returning to your homeland?

Can't afford it. The quality of life here is too good. And I still can't get over the free parking.

But I thought you said . . .

Hey, nobody said a civil rights leader has to be destitute. I gotta eat. Especially if it's barbecue.

November 19, 1996

Rodeo-speak leaves Yankee fit to be tied

Yankee Cowboy talks too fast.

When he speaks to cattlemen at the Stock Show, they don't understand a word he says.

"Boy, you talk as fast as a New York minute," one told him.

"Faster than a prairie fire with a tail wind," another said.

"As quick as the snap of a bull whip," said a third.

What's a New York minute? A tail wind in a prairie fire? A bull whip? Yankee Cowboy can't understand Texas-talk.

But Yankee Cowboy loves to listen to Bob Tallman. The words fluttering out of the Stock Show Rodeo announcer's mouth beneath his Marlboro-man mustache possess their own Western majesty. This Shakespearian cowboy speaks with a rhythm and dignity that inspires the Yankee Cowboy everybody loves to hate.

When a rider falls badly from a bucking bronco, for instance, Tallman puts a positive spin on the mishap. We Yankees are not so optimistic in our choice of words. Besides talking too fast, ours is a different language representing a contrasting culture.

As a public service to Yankee transplants, Yankee Cowboy is pleased to translate some classic Tallmanisms that you hear at the Stock Show into Yankee-speak:

He's human. He's a good-for-nothing loser.

Ain't it great to be above ground? At least the chump didn't fall flat on his face.

Let 'er rip, potato chip. Hit the street, you piece of meat.

Maybe you can make him feel a little better. Hey dirtbag, my grandmother can do better than you.

Are you watchin' some great bull ridin' or what, folks? Yo, what you see is what you get. Don't even think about a refund.

You don't have to be from Texas to be a world champion. Yeah, but if you can make it in New York, you can make it anywhere.

Keep yer butt in the saddle. Stand up and you're dead.

It broke an egg in him. His guts are splattered across the sidewalk.

You'll find a pretty girl, fall in love, move to Texas and the rest is history. Her father is rich. He'll let you take over the family business. Her face doesn't scare little children. I think I'm in love.

If you wear a white hat and ride a white horse, you gotta be a good guy. Everybody's a stinkin' jerk. And no stupid hat is gonna change that.

He's sittin' on that bull tighter than two coats of paint. A woman could be in labor and he still wouldn't give her his seat on the bus.

When the rest of the country is in the ditch, Texas makes the water flow through. For cryin' out loud, don't tell me another water main broke in Midtown.

Texans don't know quit. Walk away, fool, 'cause then there's more for me.

January 30, 1998

More than seven wonders for non-Texas visitor

*T*he Yankee Cowboy everybody loves to hate is confused. OK, what else is new? But the Stock Show raises more questions than it answers:

What do lighted plastic-sword souvenirs have to do with a rodeo?

If goat milk is so good, why don't more people drink it?

Do you have to wear a mustache to be considered a real cowboy?

If "eating gravel" refers to a cowboy being thrown from a bucking bronco or wild bull, and the rodeo arena has a dirt floor, wouldn't "eating dirt" be more accurate?

Is the proper pronunciation ROW-dee-oh or row-DAY-oh?

If the "road to college starts in the calf scramble," as the Stock Show program asserts, why bother going to classes?

Where do cutting horses keep their scissors?

Is there a rule that everyone attending the Stock Show must drive a vehicle that gets less than 10 miles per gallon?

Why do they call one of the exhibits a milking parlor if milk isn't served?

A brochure promoting "the strategic dewormer" brags that "We can deworm our cattle without touching them." What's wrong with touching cattle?

If a bull is considered an honorable and strong creature, how come when you say "bull," it means you don't believe something?

If spit cups are considered a necessity, how come jeans don't have a special pocket for them?

Shouldn't the breed of chicken called the "opposite sex frizzle" be appearing at a strip joint instead of the Stock Show?

Were Rhode Island Red chickens blacklisted in the 1950s?

Why does the Yankee Cowboy love the feel of sawdust beneath his sneakers?

With all the music played at the Stock Show, how come so little of it is rock 'n' roll?

If the Stock Show is about promoting beef, why is the most popular concession the one that sells cinnamon rolls?

If the Stock Show is about promoting beef, why is one of the biggest crowds in the Amon G. Carter Jr. Exhibits Hall gathered around a product called "the Saladmaster"?

Why do people call them "corny dogs" when they are spelled corn dogs?

Why does the Internal Revenue Service have an exhibit booth?

If you were a bull rider, would you ride a bull named Wipeout?

Isn't the phrase "fighting bull" redundant?

What's so funny about a rodeo clown running from an angry bull trying to knock the clown unconscious?

Why can't bareback riders afford to buy saddles?

Why don't calves in the calf scramble protest their working conditions and form a union?

When you hit a pinto horse from behind, does the gas tank explode?

Why does everybody hate the Yankee Cowboy?

February 4, 1998

Original Lieber-man feeling left out of party

Campaign button

(Note: In 2000, J.R. Lieber, the Yankee Cowboy everybody loves to hate, launched a year-long campaign to run for vice president as part of the George W. Bush-Yankee Cowboy ticket. It seemed like a stupid idea, but then something happened during the real campaign that made this prank a little too life-like.)

Many of you – no, all of you – laughed at the idea of a short, nerdy Jewish guy from the Northeast running for vice president of the United States.

Well, the joke is on you!

J.R. Lieber, the Yankee Cowboy everybody loves to hate, announced his candidacy for vice president in December. He campaigned long and hard, from the working-class neighborhoods of Colleyville, up to Oklahoma, over to Washington, D.C., and back.

He had a message. He had a Web site. He had a campaign button.

Now, Vice President Al Gore picks a Connecticut Yankee in King Al's Court as his running mate, another J. Lieber-man.

And everyone is all gaga.

They love this other guy. But we all know that U.S. Sen. Joseph Lieberman is the second-string short, nerdy Jewish guy from the Northeast.

Candidate interview

The news media keeps saying the other Lieber-man is the first of his kind.

Ha! Readers of this column know better.

This is a blatant attempt to deceive the American people.

Another example of Gore's transparent wimpiness.

Let's recap:

After a slow start, Yankee Cowboy's campaign earns respect.

Yankee Cowboy sells buttons by the bushel and attracts Web site hits by the hundreds.

Yankee Cowboy gets newspaper endorsement. ("We don't usually endorse candidates for political office at *The Justin Whistler*, but in the case of J.R. Lieber, we are willing to make an exception," an editorial stated. "J.R. Lieber would be an ideal candidate.")

Wherever Gore goes, people tell him, "Get that Lieber-man guy."

Focus groups say, "We like the short, nerdy Jewish guy from the Northeast. That . . . that Lieber-man."

Then, George W. Bush, Yankee Cowboy's mentor (another Northeasterner who moved to Texas and found acceptance), does the worst thing imaginable.

He picks a guy from Dallas as his running mate.

Dallas! Ugh!

So, there's an opening.

And what does Gore do?

The alpha male panics (again).

He picks the wrong J. Lieber-man.

Don't you see it?

This week, when the other Lieber-man makes his acceptance speech at the Democratic National Convention, this second-stringer will not address the issues that are important to J.R. and his supporters:

Scary: at the Pentagon

Where is "Texas friendly" when it comes to Yankees?

Why is hating Yankees not considered a hate crime under Texas law?

And most important, how come there are no real delicatessens in Hurst-Euless-Bedford?

J.R. Lieber is furious at this sudden turn of events. He is as mad as Tipper Gore on a bad hair day.

At 7 p.m. tomorrow, Yankee Cowboy will address the Northeast Tarrant Democratic Club at UAW Local 218 headquarters.

J.R. is going to give those Northeast Tarrant Democrats (all four of them) a ripping speech that would make even the Rev. Jesse Jackson cover his ears.

Yankee Cowboy vows to take his campaign the distance. From the hills of Haslet to the bar ditches of Bedford, he has not yet begun to flight, uh, fight.

It's time for a new party – The Liebertarian Party.

There are plenty of buttons left. We'll just pretend that Dubya's picture ain't on 'em.

Go, J.R. Lieber-man, go. The *real* short, nerdy Jewish guy from the Northeast. Beware of imposters.

August 13, 2000

Yankee realizes he's become a cowboy

*T*he other night I looked in the mirror and didn't recognize myself.

What I saw was a middle-aged man with graying hair wearing a beautiful brown cowboy hat, a ranch shirt, worn black cowboy boots, and jeans with a belt buckle the size of a tree stump.

Who is that man staring back at me in the mirror? And how did those boots get so worn?

When I moved here almost 10 years ago, I didn't know whether chicken-fried steak was chicken or steak. I didn't know who won or lost at the Alamo. The only thing I knew about horses was that you don't want to stand behind one.

I turned away from the mirror and looked around. Nearby, I saw a woman wearing a black cowboy hat and a suede cowboy outfit. I saw her son, a little boy wearing his own cowboy hat, ranch shirt, jeans and cowboy boots, answering to the name of Austin and sharing my last name.

Who were *these* people? How did I get tied in with them?

Doug Newton, real cowboy

The doorbell rang, and three more cowboy types stood at the front door. The tall man was Doug Newton, owner of Rocky Top Ranch in Keller. His wife, Vivian, and their grandson, Dakota Wing, accompanied him. Their giant white diesel truck was parked in the driveway.

Who were these people? I felt like Rip Van Winkle just waking up from a long sleep. Obviously, I am no longer the person I was when I moved here 10 years ago. On this Saturday evening, we were all going to the Ranch Rodeo on opening night at the Southwestern Exposition and Livestock Show and Rodeo. I did not think this was strange.

I guess I am like Eliza Doolittle from *My Fair Lady*. All you folks have taught me how to talk and behave these past 10 years. I take my blue jeans (I used to call them dungarees) to the dry cleaners and no longer believe that to be a complete waste of money. I wear a cowboy hat in public and no longer feel as if people are looking at me, asking, "Why is that stupid Yankee trying to dress like us?"

I now believe that the term *y'all* is one of the finest words in the English language, even if it is not recognized by the know-it-alls. I even say it on occasion, y'all.

Sometimes in the middle of the night, I wake up and think, "Boy, my life would have been easier if my daddy and mommy were Texans. If my birth name were Buster instead of Dave, I wouldn't have to prove myself every day." But now I realize this is God's test. There is nothing wrong with having to prove yourself.

I believe that I must be some kind of affirmative action case, placed here to prove that a New Yorker can come to Texas and not get killed. My kid brother came here once a few years ago. He lasted three days and hasn't been back since.

Think how easy it is to be born here, go to high school here, make a lot of friends and spend the rest of your life here. Where is the challenge in that?

Now imagine that the only person who wore a hat back home where you grew up was the congresswoman. That's how it was for me. My former congresswoman, Bella Abzug, was one of the best-known liberals. She also was the only person in my neighborhood who wore a big, black hat. They used to say that hat was Bella's trademark. I mean, hat-wearing was so rare, it was considered a personality quirk.

Bella would have lasted two minutes in Texas politics. Her hat, though, would have done very well.

We jumped into the Newtons' diesel truck and headed to the Stockyards for a restaurant that, as part of my ever-growing confidence, I had selected. Los Vaqueros is a fine Tex-Mex place. "Good choice," Doug said.

At Los Vaqueros, I knew exactly what to order – the dinner combo, which consists of a meat taco, guacamole, a crispy-fried tortilla topped with chili con queso, an enchilada and a tamale with chile con carne. It took me 10 years to figure all that stuff out. But I finally got it. Do you think Bella Abzug ever ordered a meal like that?

I also know the secret to ordering good margaritas. All you have to tell the waiter is, "Top shelf all around."

The margaritas came and the woman in the suede cowboy outfit, my wife, began bragging on me. I heard her tell Doug, "The last two times I've seen him on a horse, he looked good."

Doug whispered something that I couldn't hear, and they both laughed. But I didn't care. Ten years in Texas and I am no longer sensitive about my roots. Laugh all you want, y'all.

I've come so far. We entered the Will Rogers Memorial Coliseum for the rodeo, and Doug said: "You got that smell? You got that aroma? That's when you know you're in heaven."

It was a smell of sawdust mixed with cow droppings and horse dung. But you know what? I breathed deeply, and I didn't gag. I've come so far.

That night, we watched cowboys rope animals, cut horses and ride broncs. I did not think any of that was unusual. These cowboys came from places with names like Tongue River and Wagon Creek, and I didn't think that was weird either.

Don't let me paint too impressive a picture. I still have a ways to go. For instance, during the rodeo, things got so exciting when some of the Tongue River boys were riding that I stood to watch. When I sat down, it was too late. I had sat on my beautiful brown cowboy hat.

Doug laughed so hard that folks turned around to see what the fuss was about. But I knew how to pop that hat back up, and now you can't even tell. I wonder if Bella Abzug ever sat on her hat.

Yes, I can surprise you. Did you know, for instance, that this Sunday is a state holiday? It is recognized as Confederate Heroes Day in Texas. Now isn't it interesting that I knew that, and you probably didn't?

With all this progress I have made, though, I'm still not sure that I will celebrate.

January 14, 2003

Proud to fall in with this tough crowd

*T*he woman at the desk in the back office at the Will Rogers Memorial Coliseum watched the Tuff Hedeman Championship Challenge bull-riding events a week ago on a small television. She was keeping official score of what was happening in the big arena.

She turned to me and said consolingly, "Ninety-nine percent of the time when you see a man injured in the arena, it's not as bad as it looks."

I said, "In a crazy way, this is an honor."

"It really is," she said.

I looked at my watch and saw there were 15 minutes to go. Pam Minick walked in and handed me a release form to sign. The print was very small.

"What does it say?" I asked her.

"It just says if you get hurt, we own you," she said.

Nine years ago, I rode a 1,300-pound bull at a church rodeo in Azle, fell hard and hurt myself. I swore I'd never do it again. But a few weeks ago, Pam, the marketing director for Billy Bob's Texas, called and asked if I wanted to ride in the Celebrity Butt Bustin' competition at the Tuff Hedeman event, which is part of the Professional Bull Riders circuit. She told me it was a benefit for St. Jude Children's Research Hospital in Memphis, Tenn.

Minick – who lives in Roanoke, is a former Miss Rodeo America and is an inductee in the National Cowgirl Museum and Hall of Fame – is not the kind of person to whom you say no.

A man walked into the office, and Pam said, "I have another victim, uh, excuse me, another volunteer." The man was a TV producer for the bull-riding competition. Pam recruited him and a half-dozen others to compete in the celebrity event.

"In all the years we've been doing it, nobody has ridden for eight seconds," she said. "So whomever rides the longest will win."

On the little television in that back office, we watched as a pro rider fell off and hit his head on the arena floor.

"Is he OK?" somebody asked.

The woman who was scoring replied, "Somebody said he's all right and he just got knocked out a little bit."

"How did Tuff Hedeman get his nickname?" I asked the woman.

"When he was little, he slammed his finger in a car door and didn't cry," she said. Tuff went on to become four-time world champion before he retired to produce his own events.

Out in the arena, I found a familiar face, Brett Hoffman, the *Star-Telegram* rodeo writer. I told him I was about to compete in a steer-riding event.

"What *exactly* is a steer?" I asked.

"It's a bull that's been castrated," Brett said. "Takes some of the fire out of him."

"How much fire?"

"Well, they're usually leaner and not as bulky. It'll be more about balance than strength. He'll be wiry and fast. Good luck."

Pam gathered all the victims, uh, excuse me, volunteers, in the arena hallway. She introduced us to someone by saying, "This is Ty Murray. He's a seven-time world champion."

Ty looked at my leopard-skin jacket that I wear when I appear at charity events as my alter ego, the Yankee Cowboy everybody loves to hate.

"What's this here?" he asked.

"My lucky jacket."

"Put it on," he said. "Get ready."

Ty asked each of us who was going to win. I replied, "I am!" The rest mumbled about how they would try, how they would do their best, how they didn't know for sure.

Ty pointed at me and told everyone, "This guy here is the only one who says he's going to win."

"What's your one major piece of advice?" Pam asked him.

Ty said, "Keep your eyes shut until you feel your head hit the ground."

Everyone laughed – nervously.

"Nice meeting you guys," Ty said. "Good luck."

"That's Jewel's boyfriend," whispered my wife, who was watching nearby.

Just then, a bull rider stepped out of the arena tunnel and walked past us. There was a welt the size of an ice cube on his forehead and a big, bloody cut on his face.

"I think I'm going to get sick," my wife said.

Dave winning the celebrity ride

Pam introduced me to Dave Samsel, a pro on the tour who has career earnings of a half-million dollars. Dave took me into the locker room and fitted me with chaps, a protective vest and a glove. He also gave me advice: tuck my chin against my chest, extend my free arm for balance, squeeze my legs hard.

Behind the arena chute, many of the pro riders looked at me in my silly leopard-skin jacket.

One said, "I won't even ask."

After Pam introduced us to the crowd, Dave put me on a steer and wrapped the rope tightly around my gloved hand.

"Are you ready?" somebody asked.

"Let's get it over with," I said.

The chute door swung open. My steer took off jumping and bumping. Soon, we were almost in the center of the arena. I felt like I stayed on forever. Or at least a few seconds.

Finally, I began falling. I couldn't stop and wound up facedown in the dirt. I heard cheers, stood up and walked back to the chute. It was a long, wonderful walk.

I looked up at the scoreboard, which read: "LEADER ... DAVE LIEBER."

The next competitor, from an area radio station, took off on his steer, but fell off close to the chute.

Sitting atop the rail, I watched as the same happened to the next, and the one after that, and all the others. My name stayed on the leader board. Nobody hung on as long as I did.

Tuff walked over and handed me a pair of spurs with a silver inscription that said: "Tuff Hedeman 2003 Championship Challenge."

"You're the champ," he said.

"It's an honor," I heard myself reply.

"I'm proud of you," Pam said.

Later, when I sought out Brett for his critique, he said: "Well, you rock, buddy! Whoever thought a guy from New York could ride a bull?"

March 16, 2003

Chapter Eleven
Texas Politicians

*"I remember Sen. Ed Muskie the night he won his last
election back in 1976. He'd had some vodka, which I
sensed he'd drunk fast – like a Russian against the winter.
He said: 'The only reason to be in politics is to be out
there all alone and then be proven right.'
That goes for good columnists, too."*

— Chris Matthews in his final
column, Sept. 1, 2002

Governor's doing all the right things

Dave meets George: one pol he likes

*T*he governor of the great state of Texas posed poolside last week in Grapevine for the grip and grins. That's the Grand Old Party tradition of rewarding big contributors with photographs of their 30-second handshakes with political distinction.

George W. Bush grew up watching his father grip and grin into the night. And like the old man, the son of the president is good at the little things. Very good. The line at Austin Ranch snaked up the steps Thursday, but the rookie governor stayed riveted on his task – a warm, personal hello for everyone.

Big boy, he said, *good to see you again.*

Whatcha been doing?

I'm awright. I'm awright.

Gov. Bush is still in the first year of his first elected office. Hard to believe. His performance during his first legislative session was flawless. His administration is scandal-free. And unlike his new Republican counterparts in New York and Pennsylvania, his public image hasn't taken a hit.

"Just wait," he says, knowing a honeymoon doesn't last forever.

Good to see you, man. How ya doing?

You bet!

Yeah, this is neat.

Bush flew into Grapevine for State Sen. Jane Nelson's fund-raiser, her "5th Annual 40th Birthday Party & Re-election Kickoff." The governor said it was the perfect way to begin a series of political trips around the state.

"I've been so focused on policy," he said in a brief interview. "This is a fairly mercurial business. You lose focus and purpose if you don't stay riveted on doing a good job as governor.

"I love everything about being governor. This job has exceeded my expectations."

It's a pleasure.

See you, sir.

Thanks. It's nice to meet you, too.

When was the last time a politician promised a four-point plan – and delivered?

Blessed with luck and an ably led Legislature (credit Senate President Bob Bullock and House Speaker Pete Laney), the Bush-led government shows that the lost art of governance really isn't lost.

Bush signed into law big changes in education, juvenile justice, welfare and legal torts. He kept his campaign promises.

And don't forget he was elected last year on a positive campaign. Something the experts said couldn't be done.

You've lost a lot of weight. You look great. You really do.

I saw your boy.

You bet. You need to let me know.

How are all those towheaded kids of yours?

Bush started his grip and grins 10 minutes before the scheduled time. When was the last time a politician was early?

"He's *always* on time or early," spokesman Ray Sullivan emphasized.

Bush writes thank-you notes. Just like his father. Little things that mean a lot.

"I was raised right," he said.

In his speech to about 900 people at the Grapevine dude ranch, Bush praised Sen. Nelson, talked proudly of his first-year accomplishments and spoke of his newest challenge.

The rookie governor wants to replace property taxes as the chief funding method for Texas schools.

And he doesn't want to do it with a state income tax.

"I don't have a solution to present to you," he said. "But if one comes up, and it's revenue neutral, fair and not an income tax, I'll call for its support."

A new legislative panel has begun searching for alternatives.

"This is a big item," the governor promised.

Politics is about little things like small talk and big things like the art of governance. Obviously skilled at both, the new governor of the great state of Texas is proving he's no Shrub. And he's not some jerk, either. No, this rookie is a comer.

October 15, 1995

Officials' dinner perk going stale

*T*he note was posted outside Bedford City Hall:

Notice is hereby given that the City Council of the city of Bedford will meet in open session for dinner at 6 p.m. on Feb. 8, 1994 at Tony's Café Italiano.

Two weeks later, a similar note said that the council and top city staff would meet at Don Pablo's.

Tuesday, the council convened at the Black-Eyed Pea.

Bedford's council – and also the Bedford Planning & Zoning Commission – have dined at restaurants during the first scheduled portion of their public meetings for as long as former Mayor L. Don Dodson can remember. And he was first elected in 1972.

"In our charter, it says the mayor and the council work for free," Dodson explains. "And that's a little reward for their time."

Other towns in Northeast Tarrant County feed their council members before nightly meetings, too. In Colleyville, Hurst, Haltom City, Keller, North Richland Hills, Southlake and Euless, councils eat take-out or catered dinners in City Hall meeting rooms.

A few towns, including Haslet, Watauga and Richland Hills, don't serve dinner.

"I don't want to be stingy," Richland Hills Mayor C.F. Kelley explains, "but I think we go to City Hall for a different purpose than to feed ourselves. But to each his own. We just don't feel it's necessary in our community."

Some cities pay their council members to attend meetings. Bedford does not. But Bedford is the only Northeast Tarrant city that begins its biweekly meeting night in a public restaurant.

The bills for the past 30 days – three council dinners and two P&Z dinners — totals $389, city records show. That would make it about $4,700 a year.

It's not the money as much as the perception. Why should elected officials get to eat out at taxpayers' expense when the rest of us don't?

Sure, the meetings are open to the public and are legally posted in case city business is discussed there. But outsiders are rare. Mayor Rick Barton says he cannot remember any residents attending in the two years he's been mayor.

Three months ago, Barton suggested ending the practice.

"It adds an additional hour of meeting time, and I was missing events that my children were attending," Barton said.

But nobody else on the six-member council agreed, he said. So the dinners continue.

The Feb. 8 council dinner at Tony's Café Italiano cost $87.73. The bill for the Feb. 22 dinner at Don Pablo's was $94.66. On Tuesday, the council spent $57 at the Black-Eyed Pea.

Below are explanations offered by council and city staff about this perk. To see *exactly* how tax dollars are spent, their entrees from the past month are listed, too:

City Manager Jim Walker (baked tortellini, Three Amigos, absent from Tuesday's dinner): "It's more of a fellowship thing. Break bread and relax. It allows a little bonding rather than be thrust in this business environment. Maybe we haven't seen each other in two weeks."

Barton (chicken carciofo, fiesta salad, Caesar salad with char-broiled chicken): "The dinner provides a setting that enables the council to prepare for the beginning of our evening together. ... Could you sit around a [City Hall] workroom and have people watch you eat while you're trying to conduct a work session? I would not be comfortable doing that."

Councilman Leahmon Chambers (veal picatta, El Presidente, chicken-fried steak): "We've always patronized our restaurants here in the city, and this is one small way that we can pay our restaurants back for appreciation of being in our city."

Councilman Ron Epps (chicken Murphy, grilled chicken parilla): "As far as catering in, I personally don't like to sit and try and eat and talk with papers all over the table."

Councilman Steve Kennedy (veal, house salad with tortilla soup, meatloaf): "I don't think it's necessary. We need to spend more time going over city business, extending the work session afterward and just bringing in sandwiches. However, I'm still new on council and this is apparently a tradition."

Councilman Nelson Moore (fiesta salad, veggie plate): "Instead of running home, they can come by and relax a little and have something to eat. It makes it a little more convenient."

Councilman Charles Orean (veal marsala, enchilada-taco combination): "I don't believe I'm benefiting from the dinner since I'm not a member of 'the group.' There is no fellowship going on in that area. Certainly, we go through congeniality, asking how things are going and so forth. Some issues come up, but right now it's fairly minimal."

Councilwoman Melinda Watts Smith (cheese enchiladas, Caesar salad with charbroiled chicken): "When you're asking someone to be away from their family at home for an entire evening to do city business, then they should at least be fed."

Assistant City Manager Bob Miller (beef enchiladas, chicken-fried steak): "Some of them come right from work to the city. So from that perspective, they are getting a good meal before going to work. And this past Tuesday, they worked until 11:30 p.m."

Assistant City Manager Nancy Moffat (chicken parmigiana, Diego's Especial): "We think of food as somewhat of a leisure activity, so it bridges the gap from having to work all day and then switch gears into council."

Meanwhile, Mr. and Mrs. Bedford, average taxpayers, work hard, pay taxes, support their city. Yet they don't get to eat out – free – twice a month in restaurants.

Yes, it's a good thing that council members contribute their time to serve their community. But eliminating this perk would serve to remind public officials that they are no better than the rest of us.

March 13, 1994

Postscript: Shortly after this column appeared, the city of Bedford discontinued the practice.

Hurst officials take freebies at Texas Stadium

Hurst Mayor Bill Souder and his wife, Dodie, arrived at 10 a.m. last Sunday in the parking lot at Hurst City Hall. They met Mayor Pro Tem Charles Swearengen and his wife, Gwendolyn, who were also waiting.

Minutes later, a white van pulled up, and everybody got in. The van was driven by Doug Rivers, general manager of Trinity Waste Services, Hurst's waste disposal company, which also collects trash for nearly every greater Northeast Tarrant County community.

Hurst's top two elected officials and their wives were Trinity's guests that day at Texas Stadium in Irving. Trinity treated them to lunch at the Stadium Club. Then Rivers led them to the company's luxury suite upstairs, where they watched the Dallas Cowboys beat the Arizona Cardinals.

In Hurst, there is no law or rule that prohibits public officials from being guests of city vendors at ballgames.

The invitation, which was sent to Hurst City Council members, came as the council has begun rewriting its code of conduct for elected officials to address land ownership, acceptance of gifts, business interests and conflicts of interest.

If, say, a $25 limit is placed on future gifts, council members could no longer be guests of city contract holders at Cowboys games.

As the two senior members of the Hurst council, Souder and Swearengen have 37 years of tenure between them.

Two other councilmen, Henry Wilson and Richard Ward, said they did not attend the game for ethical reasons.

Wilson said, "I thanked Doug Rivers and told him that as we're re-evaluating our code of conduct, it didn't seem appropriate at this point in time to accept the invitation."

Ward said, "I chose not to go because we are in the middle of developing an ethics policy, and I thought it best to turn this invitation down."

The only thing that matters to me here is my informal little Wimpy rule, which I named after J. Wellington Wimpy, the character in *Popeye* who says, "I will gladly pay you Tuesday for a hamburger I eat today."

Before the May election, I polled every Northeast Tarrant County candidate running for mayor, city council and school board and asked whether they would pledge to voluntarily abide by the Wimpy rule during their next term of office.

The Wimpy rule states: *Do you pledge to refrain from accepting any gifts from any vendors, contractors or anyone else for whom you might vote or decide issues that can advance their business, careers, etc.?*

Souder was one of 69 area candidates who agreed to the pledge, and the results of my Wimpy survey were printed in this space before the election.

At the time of his pledge, Souder was being challenged by another councilman for the mayor's job that he has had for 20 years. The challenger hammered at ethics, making it his central campaign theme. Souder won that election.

Last week, when I talked to Souder about Sunday's football game, he told me that he never understood the Wimpy rule and did not feel bound by it.

"I didn't know what you were talking about," he said about the pledge question.

Swearengen was never polled about the Wimpy rule because he was not a candidate this year.

The letter sent by Trinity this month to council members at the Hurst City Hall stated, "You and a guest are invited to attend the Cowboys vs. Arizona Cardinals game on Sunday, Oct. 22, 2000. We plan to leave the Hurst City Hall parking lot at 10 a.m. and have lunch at the Stadium Club prior to kickoff. Please RSVP to myself. . . .

"Sincerely, Doug Rivers, General Manager."

Rivers told me that, although he invites city councils to the luxury suite, he never invites members of a council the same year that their city trash contract faces renewal.

"I don't want any conflict of interest accusations, of course," he said.

The Hurst contract does not expire until 2004.

"There is no intended purpose other than to let them know who we are," Rivers said about his invitation to the luxury suite. "It's marketing. If there are any service issues, they'll know who to contact."

Souder's explanation about why he attended the game – not his actual attendance at the game – earns him the 2000 Wimpy Award for Most Outstanding Performance by Someone Who Originally Took the Wimpy Pledge.

Here is some of what Souder told me:

"I went as Bill Souder. I didn't go as mayor. I didn't go as a representative of the city."

"I wasn't invited as the mayor. I was invited as Bill Souder."

"Any time I go to any of these events, I'm not going as the mayor of Hurst. I'm going because of my personal desire, and with my wife."

"I don't accept those invitations as mayor. Unless it's official. Going to a ballgame is not official for anything."

Swearengen, not eligible for the Wimpy Award, said he attended because he wanted to negotiate with Trinity officials about whether his model airplane club could fly its planes above the lake near Trinity's old landfill off Airport Freeway.

"I didn't go as a representative of the city at all," he said.

Souder and Swearengen said they did not remember receiving an invitation in their City Hall mail, similar to the one received by other council members.

"I don't think I got one," Souder said.

"If I did, I don't remember it," Swearengen said.

Swearengen said he was invited by Souder's wife, Dodie, who works for U.S. Rep Kay Granger. Dodie Souder cleared up the matter: "It was a joint letter to both of us," she said, referring to her husband, the mayor of Hurst who is our 2000 Wimpy Award winner.

October 29, 2000

Postscript: Dave continued to write about the perks offered by Trinity to various city officials, and by 2002, several cities had begun to seek trash bids for city contracts. Because of the bidding process, cities and their residential and business customers began saving millions of dollars.

Mayor must mend diploma deception

*F*or nearly 40 years, Charles Scoma convinced others that he was a college man with a master's degree. It wasn't true.

Yet, as the North Richland Hills mayor prepares to announce his candidacy for state representative, his story has unraveled.

The unraveling began when *Star-Telegram* reporter John Kirsch performed the most basic chore of journalism. He checked Scoma's resume and learned that Scoma's claims about earning a bachelor's degree from the University of North Texas in Denton and a graduate degree from the University of Rome were false. Scoma attended both universities, but he did not obtain diplomas.

Scoma made these claims in biographical information that he provided to the League of Women Voters when he ran for office and also on his biography posted on the North Richland Hills Web site, Kirsch reported.

Scoma explained that he had almost earned the degrees, but technicalities prevented completion of his studies.

If it had ended there with an apology by Scoma and a promise to make amends, I could leave it at that. But I have uncovered other situations where Scoma perpetuated misinformation. And Scoma's response since Kirsch's Oct. 2 story has made his situation worse. In an interview with me last week, it became painfully obvious that Scoma doesn't believe that he misled voters.

"I'm saying I earned a degree," he told me. "You can call it word-smithing if you want. I accomplished the course work necessary. Technically, I was not able to receive the diploma."

Scoma's responses in recent weeks to questions about his claims provide a sad example of the adage that when you are in a hole, stop digging.

Scoma keeps digging and digging, and the dirt he has flung threatens to bury him.

It is sad because Scoma could have been a worthy candidate in his challenge against State Rep. Bill Carter, a Republican who represents District 91. While Scoma served as a Birdville school board member, the district improved into one of the state's best. As mayor, he has done the job.

But Scoma has shown that he is not ready for prime time at the state Capitol. If voters were to send Scoma to Austin, his legislator colleagues and the state news media would slaughter him with jokes behind his back. His issues would get lost in the laughter.

In Kirsch's report, Scoma explained the misinformation on the city Web site by saying the Webmaster "obviously interpreted" his statement that he had studied at the University of North Texas (then called North Texas State College) and the University of Rome to mean that he had actually earned two degrees.

After this statement was published, I interviewed former city Webmaster Christine Johnson, who told me: "I didn't change anything. I just took what they had and put straight on what they gave me word-for-word."

Scoma said he never checked his Web page until after Kirsch pointed out inaccuracies. At that point, Scoma requested that the information be deleted. But it had appeared on the site for three years. If Scoma were anything less than the highly organized and thorough individual that his former school board colleagues and current City Council members describe him to be, I would believe it.

Last week, I found an archived videotape at Citicable North

Richland Hills showing the 1996 Richland High School graduation ceremony when Scoma was school board president. At that ceremony, he wore the school colors of the University of Rome on the hood of his commencement gown. Only graduates are entitled to wear the colors.

"The colors we wore were based on the college or university we attended and the degrees we received," said former Trustee Calvin White, who is now Haltom City mayor.

Yet another example of Scoma's attempt to mislead the public can be found in the book *The History of North Richland Hills*. In Scoma's biography on page 232, it states that Scoma "received his master's of business administration from the University of Rome, Italy. He earned his bachelor's degree in business and economics from the University of North Texas."

Members of the city historical committee, which produced the book, told me that they took this statement word-for-word from materials provided by Scoma.

During our interview last week, Scoma said that he had apologized for his errors and that he still intends to run for state representative.

"I don't know what else I can do," he said. "Do I need to cut off an arm?"

No, Mr. Mayor, you don't have to do that. You simply have to make amends.

I suggest that you return to the University of North Texas and make up the 12 hours that you need to earn your bachelor's degree. I also suggest that you defer your campaign for at least two years, giving yourself time to finish your education and show voters that you are making amends.

Scoma likes the first suggestion, but not the second.

"You raise a very thought-provoking option," he told me last week. "I have considered going back. The reason I have not is, again, I felt I had the education, and did the diploma really matter that much over and above what I had learned?"

A little later, he said, "I can assure you that within the next week or two weeks, I am going to go back to North Texas and talk to them about what I need to do to compete those last few hours."

As we neared the end of our talk, I noticed that Scoma was wearing a University of North Texas ring. When I asked about it, he explained that he had earned the right to wear it because he attended the school. I argued otherwise, saying that the ring was a symbol of graduation.

"I'll tell you what I'm going to do," he said. "I'm going to take it off." He slipped off the ring and placed it in his jacket pocket. He promised not to wear it again until he earns his diploma.

Perhaps that moment marked the beginning of Scoma's actual understanding of the seriousness of his offense.

I wish the mayor well in his quest to make things right and earn his diploma 40 years later. But still, I implore him not to run for state representative until he earns the right to place that college ring back on his finger.

October 28, 2001

Postscript: Scoma kept his promise and returned to college. He did not run for state representative, and when his term as mayor ended, he left public life. In August 2003, he graduated from Dallas Baptist University.

Haltom municipal judge taking ethics to the edge

Mary Osman, the victim

When a constable visited the home of Mary Osman a year ago to serve her grandson James with a court summons, he offered some advice: "Be sure to go get you a good family attorney."

With the hearing 10 days away, Osman, an 80-year-old widow who has lived in the same Haltom City house since 1952, embarked on a search that led her to the Bedford law office of Haltom City Municipal Judge Jack Byno.

"I figured him being a judge – I heard something about how he got stuff done," she said. "I thought he might be able to help me out."

Unlike the case reported here two weeks ago involving another former client of the Byno & Byno law firm who successfully sued Laura Byno, Jack's wife and partner, for legal malpractice, Jack Byno was directly involved in the Osman case.

Jack Byno has said he intends to run for Tarrant County Criminal Court in 2002 against 25-year incumbent Billy Mills, who was the top-rated county criminal court judge in this year's Tarrant County Bar Association survey.

Last week, I hand-delivered to Jack and Laura Byno's Bedford firm a letter detailing the story related to the Osmans along with a request for an interview. A legal assistant who declined to give her name for publication telephoned later to say that both had declined.

"If they [former clients] want to provide anything to you, that's between you and them," the legal assistant said.

The Haltom City widow said she knew only one lawyer – the one who wrote her last will and testament 20 years before. But he was on vacation. She tried a lawyer whom her daughter had met on a cruise, but he was busy, too. So she found an old magnet on her refrigerator that Jack Byno had dropped off when he was campaigning door-to-door in 1999 for Haltom City judge.

Osman said, "I thought, 'Well, I'll call Judge Byno at his Bedford office and ask if he knows of a good family attorney.' I called his office. They said, 'Yes, he's here, and you can see him today.' "

She and her grandson met with Jack Byno at his Bedford office. After talking with him, they decided to hire him to represent James in his legal fight against the mother of James' daughter.

"We thought he was representing us," Mary Osman said. "James signed a paper, and he said, 'I'll need a thousand-dollar retainer fee now.' He said, 'When we get through, if there's any left, we'll pay you back.' "

Osman said she wrote the check. "After he got everything down and took the check, he said, 'Now you know that I'm a judge and I have work to do, and I may not be able to do this.' " He said his wife would be the primary lawyer.

Osman said she responded, "I hope she will defend us." According to Osman, Byno replied, "She is reliable."

Mary and James Osman contend that Laura Byno went on to commit numerous gaffes in the case, including lack of preparation, lack of consultation with her client and a lack of defense at one key hearing. After Mary Osman paid nearly $4,000 in fees for what she felt was little in return, she complained.

Laura Byno's response was to file a court motion to withdraw as the lawyer in the case. The Osmans are still billed for nearly $500 each month in owed fees, plus interest. Mary Osman said she didn't want to pay any more.

She said, "I thought Mr. Byno would have been a good attorney, and I thought he was going to be our attorney. That's what I thought. And then the bomb was dropped that she was going to take it."

Byno's legal assistant said, "Mary Osman wasn't our client. Her grandson was."

It's not uncommon for lawyers to pass off clients to other lawyers in their firm. The Code of Judicial Conduct prohibits a judge from lending "the prestige of judicial office to advance the private interests of the judge or others."

Former Texas Supreme Court Justice Bob Gammage, who testified as an expert witness against Laura Byno in her malpractice trial, told me that Mary Osman and her grandson could have withdrawn at any time. But Gammage questioned Jack Byno's delay in informing that he would not be the primary lawyer until after the contract was signed.

"If it doesn't cross the [ethical] line, it's right on it," Gammage said. "I think it's inappropriate. My personal opinion as an ethicist is he should have advised them before they signed the contract."

Mary and James Osman also told me that when they visited Jack Byno the first time, he handed them a business card that listed his occupation as both a Haltom City judge and a lawyer in private practice. Municipal judges are allowed to maintain a legal practice, but they must not mix the two.

Byno's legal assistant said, "Mr. Byno can represent people who live in Haltom City so long as it does not interfere with his duties as a judge. When he was campaigning, he wasn't a judge at the time."

When I visited Byno's office last week, I saw two sets of business cards on display side by side in the lobby – one was his Haltom City judge's card, and the other was his law firm card. (From another source, however, I obtained a copy of the single card in which both jobs are listed.)

In either case, lawyers and judges say, the cards and their presentation appear to be a violation of the judicial code, which prohibits a judge from "business dealings that ... exploit his or her judicial position."

Ethics expert Gammage said, "It's inappropriate. No lawyer who holds any kind of office of public trust should parlay that as far as his law practice is concerned."

North Richland Hills Municipal Judge Ray Oujesky said, "If you were to walk into my law office, you would not find a business card for me as North Richland Hills judge. What I do in my law office and what I do as municipal judge are two different things."

Haltom City Mayor Calvin White said the city has no legal authority to supervise Byno.

"Our responsibility was to make a decision on whether we hire him or not as a municipal judge," White said. "Any charges of misconduct cannot be addressed by the mayor or council. There is a process of judicial review."

Haltom City Councilman "Big" John Williams voted against the recent appointment of Byno, who is known as "Max" Jack because of his tough sentencing practices.

"You should be held accountable for the same things that you hold other people accountable for," Williams said.

Otherwise, I will add, your court is a travesty and your judge is a hypocrite in robes, which is the case now in Haltom City.

September 2, 2001

Postscript: Byno lost his race for county criminal judge. After that, in early 2003, Byno was accused of sentencing women to jail based on the size of their breasts. He denied the charge, but the accusation against him was part of a wider scandal at the Haltom City Jail in which former women inmates accused an ex-jailer of sexual abuse. Byno subsequently resigned as Haltom City Municipal Judge and retired from public life.

Politician promotes open, responsive government

Until this week, I never met a politician who improved my life, both professionally and personally. Most politicians, I believe, enter public life for the right reasons but lose sight of their original goals.

A few years ago, there was one Texan who ran for public office based on a few promises about some issues that were near to my heart. But I didn't believe him or his promises, and I didn't vote for him.

Now, four years later, I am amazed to see that not only did Texas Attorney General John Cornyn keep those important promises, but because he did, my working life and my family life are better for it.

This week, Cornyn visited Southlake for a Republican fund-raiser at Timarron County Club. He is running against former Dallas Mayor Ron Kirk, a Democrat, for the U.S. Senate seat being vacated by Phil Gramm, R-Texas. Cornyn is no fiery orator, and he is easy to overlook, as I did four years ago. But I won't make that mistake again.

As a devoted advocate of open government, I want to tell you that I have never seen a politician who did more for openness than Cornyn has in his four years as attorney general. He worked tirelessly to open Texas government at all levels to public scrutiny, often angering public officials who had supported him.

Compared with his Democratic predecessor, Dan Morales, Cornyn's office doubled the number of open-records opinions issued to governments and citizens when open-government conflicts arose. Cornyn also created a telephone hotline on which his employees answer open-records questions from elected officials, the media and the public. Last year, Cornyn won the James Madison Award from the Freedom of Information Foundation of Texas for his achievements.

The other reason Cornyn has affected my life – the personal reason – is because when he took office, the biological father of my two stepchildren was more than $20,000 behind in child support. When my wife and I tried to call the attorney general's office for help during the previous Democratic administration, we could never get through. There was always a busy signal.

Cornyn reorganized the state collection system and beefed up law enforcement. Soon after, the overdue monthly support checks, funneled through his Austin office, began arriving regularly in our mailbox. They have not stopped, and, you know, I see this as nothing short of a miracle.

At the Southlake fund-raiser this week, I waited to talk to Cornyn outside to ask how he had accomplished these achievements. So much of our political debate is about fluff words and broken promises.

My questions to Cornyn were: How did you keep your promises? What motivated you to do so? By recognizing and understanding the good that could be accomplished in public life, maybe others can do more good.

Cornyn told me the most important thing he could do as a state official was help those "who are not able to protect themselves." He was referring to the 1.2 million Texas children who are owed child support. Making sure they got their money, he said, was "my highest priority."

"It was just an enormous, convoluted bureaucracy that wasn't working," he said. "People weren't held accountable." I told him about the busy signals, and he replied, "At the basic level, you expect government to at least answer the phone."

He hired new managers to run his child-support division and re-created the system. Employment records were checked and when a deadbeat parent was found in a job, his office sent an administrative order by overnight mail to the employer ordering that the parent's wages be garnisheed and sent to his office.

In the 15 years before he took office, the attorney general's office collected $4.5 billion in child support. By the end of this month – after nearly four years as attorney general – Cornyn's office will have collected another $4.5 billion.

"It really has been sort of a mission," he told me. He often meets parents like me who say thanks. "That's the reason I do what I do," he said.

His appreciation for open government began, he said, when he was a college student studying journalism. But when he found out how much a cub reporter earned, he said, he decided to go into real estate. Eventually, he became a lawyer and rose to Justice on the Texas Supreme Court.

"To me, saying the power of government is in the hands of the people is the conservative principle," he said. "But the only way we know what the government is doing on our behalf is if we have access to the meetings and the papers that reflected how those decisions are made. So to the extent that people consider themselves conservatives and they have not been supporters of open government, they have been missing the boat.

"It's not just for the newspapers and the broadcasters," he continued. "It's really for the public generally – to make sure they retain that power. I expect that if I do something bad or something I shouldn't do, the press is going to call me on it. More power to 'em. I shouldn't be doing bad stuff.

"But to me, open government is a no-brainer. It's something I'd like to carry with me to Washington. It seems like they could use a dose of sunshine up there."

Amen. Thank you, Attorney General Cornyn, for keeping your promises.

August 16, 2002

Postscript: Cornyn was subsequently elected as the junior U.S. senator representing the state of Texas.

Stereotypes are hard to overcome – just ask the governor

The first time I met Gov. Rick Perry, at a campaign rally in Southlake seven weeks ago, we had a pleasant conversation, but he said something that surprised me. We were standing in the third-floor hallway of Southlake Town Hall when I introduced myself.

"Hi, Governor Perry," I said.

"Hi," he replied.

"My name is Dave Lieber, and I'm a columnist for the *Star-Telegram*."

He asked, "Is that L-E-I-B-E-R?"

"No sir," I said. "That's L-I-E-B-E-R."

Then he said, "Did you ever live in Israel?"

In my life, I have never been asked that question. The governor is either an incredible mind reader or he looked at me, learned how to spell my name and quickly tagged me as Jewish, which I happen to be.

I say he might be a mind reader because I was holding an envelope that contained a 2-year-old column I had written about being Jewish in Texas. But he didn't know that yet.

I had wanted to share this column – "Bible Belt can sometimes feel too tight for comfort" – with the governor because of an incident that occurred a year ago at Palestine Middle School in East

Texas. Perry had prayed publicly at a mandatory school assembly, and afterward, when he was criticized for his apparent violation of the U.S. Supreme Court ruling against organized prayer in public schools, he said he didn't agree with the court ruling.

Many don't agree with that ruling. But as the state's highest elected leader, Perry, I would have thought, had a responsibility to lead by example. Instead, at the time, he said, "Why can't we say a prayer at a football game or at a patriotic event like we held in Palestine? I just don't understand." He said the Sept. 11 terrorist attacks make public prayers more appropriate and necessary.

I wanted to share my column with Perry to help him understand a different view. The column was my favorite, and my favorite experience in Texas – not because of what I wrote, but because of the extraordinary reaction from readers. I heard from dozens, and hardly anyone had a negative word. It was not what I expected.

A North Richland Hills woman wrote me, "I am embarrassed to say that I had never thought of what my Jewish, or for that matter, any other non-Christian brothers might be feeling when the words 'in Jesus' name' are used. I do believe in school prayers, but I see your point. Tolerance of each others' beliefs is the only way the human race is to survive, and I thank you for opening my eyes."

A Fort Worth woman wrote: "Having lived in North Texas my entire life I never had the exposure to other religions until I was an adult and felt comfortable asking questions of close friends. ... I looked at prayer as a positive thing to bring people together, but now I realize it can be hurtful to people not of the same religion. Your column made me feel your pain and realize that what we need to unite on is a common respect for all people as human beings."

Because the governor had said, "I just don't understand," I wanted to show him a different side. I didn't expect to change his mind.

But after he asked, "Did you ever live in Israel?" my mind flashed to an image of a black person standing in front of him and the governor asking, "Did you ever live in Africa?" But I remembered that I was there for a reason.

"No, sir," I said. "I haven't lived in Israel. But it's funny that you mention that because I have an envelope here for you that has an old column I wrote after the U.S. Supreme Court ruling about organized prayers at public school events. It's about being Jewish in

Texas, and I thought maybe you'd enjoy it."

"Oh, I would," he said. "Thank you very much. I'll read it."

We were walking down the stairs and I said, "Because you know, governor, you and I really come from different worlds."

"We really do!" he said. "We really do!"

Then he started to talk about the Israeli air force pilots he met while he was in the Air Force. "I just always admired those guys," he said.

He talked about how he once led a trade mission to Israel. "It's just the most incredible place," he said. And he spoke about President Bush's strong support for Israel, which, he said, surprised many American Jews. "He never projected that support before," the governor said about his predecessor. "He did some really positive things for them."

We shook hands, and I said, "Please read my column and let me know what you think."

"I will," he said.

Weeks went by, and I didn't hear from the governor. But I talked to a communications professor at University of Texas at Arlington about the governor's question about my living in Israel.

Alex Mwakikoti told me that the governor had stereotyped me. "Because of stereotypes we have, we don't understand much about others," he said. "We use preconceived ideas of what we have from others, and then we use that with everyone else we meet. That type of stereotyping is really dangerous, especially when you are dealing with individuals who are in leadership positions. Leadership ought to learn about other cultures, so they don't make those kinds of mistakes."

Last week, I caught up with the governor again before he made a speech at Texas Motor Speedway. He remembered me.

"Did you ever get to read that column?" I asked.

"Yes."

"What did you think?"

He answered, "I don't necessarily agree with you that [public prayer] is a slap in the face to individuals of the Jewish faith. I'm a big fan of us talking about our faiths openly." He said that talking about our religion publicly was more important after Sept. 11.

"I'm a Christian," he said. "I have a very biblical connection with Israel. The Israelis are God's chosen people. My political support of Israel is because of my Christian beliefs. I don't have a problem with a rabbi coming to schools, the Legislature, or, for that matter, a Christian preacher coming and saying a prayer. I think that is good for America to get back and grasp our values."

I said, "Governor, you know it means a lot to me that you read it, and I appreciate it. One more quick question. When we met for the first time and I introduced myself to you and you asked about my name and how to spell it, you said, 'Did you ever live in Israel?' I was a little taken aback by that. It was like, maybe you saw me just as a Jewish guy standing in front of you."

The governor's voice became higher pitched when he quickly said, "No."

He changed the subject and asked if I had heard about a young Jewish man from Dallas who had died last month fighting for the Israeli army. I told him I hadn't.

"Anyway," he said, as he walked away to give his speech.

Later, I talked to the communications professor about the encounter.

Mwakikoti said, "I tend to forgive a lot of individuals who I believe don't understand what they are talking about. I try to call to their attention what they are doing wrong, just as you did. They don't want to be found in that situation again with someone else. But not everyone will accept what you are calling to their attention to correct."

Candidates running for office are carefully protected in a campaign bubble. Sometimes, only the briefest of encounters can illuminate a candidate's personality or beliefs. In this instance, I only wish that the governor of Texas could have looked at me in a different way the first time we met.

October 6, 2002

Postscript: A month later, Gov. Rick Perry, who was serving out President Bush's unexpired term, was elected governor.

Nothing fond about farewell to Armey

A congressman from our area, House Majority Leader Dick Armey, R-Flower Mound, is a tacky man. In less than three months, he will be out of office, and we will no longer have to listen to his stupid comments.

His son, Scott Armey, who could not win the House seat even

though he shares his daddy's name, will still be a federal employee, thanks to political patronage. But neither father nor son will be an elected official, and for that, we should say a small prayer of thanks.

What motivates my call for prayer? Dick Armey's latest stunt. Still fuming over a series that *The Dallas Morning News* published on the eve of his son's loss in the Republican primary in April, Armey tried to pull an unbelievable power play this month. He attempted to insert language into a military appropriations bill that would have forced the *Morning News'* parent company, Belo, to sell one of its three media properties in the region. His Belo-related amendment alluded to, but did not name, these Belo properties: WFAA/Channel 8, the *Morning News* and the *Denton Record-Chronicle.*

Armey's amendment stated that any media company that owns a network-affiliated TV station; a newspaper with a Sunday circulation of at least 750,000 that doesn't have a competitor with a Sunday circulation exceeding 350,000; and a second daily newspaper with a Sunday circulation of 25,000 or less – all in the same market – would have to divest the smallest property.

That type of vague language is how lawmakers have historically inserted last-minute amendments that aid cronies or target enemies. Therefore, in celebration of Armey's pending retirement, I suggest that the following amendments – based on incidents culled from his career – be inserted into bills:

- **The Mispronounced Name Amendment:** Applies to any congressional leader who in 1995 referred to an openly gay congressman with a term that rhymes with rag. The leader shall be forced to wear, for an entire year, a rainbow-colored tie with the words "Ask me what my first name is."

- **The Fool-Me-Twice-Shame-on-You Amendment:** Applies to any congressional leader who apologized for the above incident and then in 2000 made another derogatory joke about the same congressman. The leader shall be forced to do aerobic exercises with Richard Simmons on live television.

- **The Failed Coup Amendment:** Pertains to any top House leader who tried to orchestrate the ouster in 1997 of his boss, then-House Speaker Newt Gingrich, and, when asked about it later, did not tell the truth about his role. The leader shall be forced to tell the story of George

Washington and the cherry tree to every first-grader in Flower Mound.

- **The Thanks for the Memories Amendment:** Applies to any congressional leader who spread a false report on the House floor that comedian Bob Hope had died. The leader should be forced to serve as an unpaid intern for Sen. Hillary Rodham Clinton, D-N.Y., for no less than one year.

- **The False Pretenses Fund-raiser:** Relates to any congressional leader who had a fund-raiser for his re-election campaign on Dec. 6 with Vice President Dick Cheney in Dallas, then announced six days later that he had no intention of running again. The leader shall repay, with interest, the more than $400,000 his campaign received from contributors.

- **The Misleading Signs Amendment:** Pertains to any congressional leader whose son has lost a primary to replace him in Congress. If supporters put up signs stating "Support the Armey Flat Tax" to confuse voters into thinking that the father was running for re-election, the congressional leader shall remove the nails from each stake using his front teeth.

- **The Father-Son Nepotism Amendment:** Relates to any congressman who helped get his son a job as the regional administrator for the General Services Administration in a city whose name is Fort Worth. If the father and son said afterward that the son got the plum patronage job on his own merits, then the congressional leader shall be forced to tell the story of George Washington and the cherry tree to every second-grader in Flower Mound.

You get the idea. Dick Armey's career has been one long comic routine of cheap tricks, half-truths and foolish remarks. In a few months, the area will start fresh with a new congressman who can restore dignity to the office as the people's representative.

Good riddance.

October 15, 2002

Chapter Twelve

The Writer's Life

"The only people you write about are rich businessmen, politicians and yourself. You are two-faced and a glorified gossip columnist."

— One of Dave's
disgruntled readers

Note: Not long after Dave moved to Texas, he wrote this column.

Tale touches on triumphs, tears in Texas

You don't know who I am.

After writing 100 columns for the *Star-Telegram*, I realize there comes a time when a man's gotta do what a man's gotta do: Fess up.

So here's my tale:

I am a third-generation Texan.

I married a girl from Lubbock.

I am the father of three children: Travis, Bowie and Susannah, named after Alamo heroes.

And here's my deepest, darkest secret: I am an Aggie.

I grew up in the house my grandfather built. It's on Elm Street in Keller. An old wooden-frame house Granddaddy put up after he arrived here in 1906 from Tennessee.

He had a horse called Buck, which he kept in a shed about 20 feet behind the house. Every morning, he rode two miles west to the family farm, where he grew corn, wheat and cotton. He also grew a little sorghum cane for homemade syrup.

My grandmother, meanwhile, ran the mercantile on Main Street where she sold cloth and sewing needs. Folks said she had the best variety of buttons in the county.

My daddy was born in 1922 in the front bedroom of the Elm Street house. Dr. Reed, who lived over on Price Street, took care of the birthing. Daddy was baptized in the Mount Gilead Baptist Church. He attended the Keller School, which had grades 1-12 in the same building.

The family was hard-hit during the Great Depression – but so was everybody else.

Daddy used to laugh and say, "We didn't know when the Depression began, but we didn't know when it ended, either. Life was still just as hard." The mercantile went under. So my people made it through by farming. (And Grandma had enough buttons left to keep the family buttoned up for years to come.)

World War II took Daddy away from Keller for the first time. But not far. Just to Fort Worth. The Army said he couldn't serve – so he got a job at the Bomber Plant. He built airplanes that dropped bombs. Everyone was very proud.

He met my mama there. She worked on another assembly line. A mutual friend introduced them during break at the water fountain. For their first date, they went to a movie at the Hollywood on Seventh Street. Afterward, they went to the Pig Stand at North Side for soda pop. Following a proper courtship of two years, they were married.

After the war, Daddy worked for Armour & Co. His job was to knock the cattle in the head with a hammer after they came up the ramp and entered the building on the top floor. Daddy never talked much about work.

Mama set up housekeeping in a little house next to Granddaddy's in Keller. There were three kids. Jim Bob, Betsy and me. I was born in 1957 in Harris Methodist Hospital. Not long after, Granddaddy died, so we moved into the big house with Grandma.

I was just a quiet country kid. I spent a lot of time at the Keller Library, housed in the old telephone building, reading Louis L'Amour books. I was best known for being the smallest tackle who ever played at Keller High School. They called me "Wart Hog."

I met Cheryl, my future wife, in college. We both studied agricultural journalism at Aggieland. But she quit ag journalism to become a teacher back home in Lubbock. I stuck with newspapering.

My first job was at the *Lubbock Avalanche-Journal*. I was a livestock reporter. That left my nights free. Me and the schoolmarm hitched up. Honeymooned in San Antonio. Decided then to name our children after the Alamo heroes.

I came home for a job at the *Star-Telegram* in 1983. We bought a house in Grapevine, a 2-story deal my daddy and granddaddy would have liked. The place has a squeaky screen door, a big front porch and a rock fireplace. Cheryl and I spent many hours and piles of money fixing it up.

Our kids are doing well, I think. They're too young for gangs or drugs or even dating. They spend a lot of time playing in organized T-ball leagues and also some soccer.

I teach a Sunday school class. Belong to the Rotary. And keep a small boat for fishing at Lake Grapevine.

Cheryl is still a teacher, but she asked me not to mention the school. She likes it here fine, but she jokes that she misses all the wind in Lubbock.

Oh, I forgot to tell you: My dog's name is Buck – after my grand-daddy's horse. And I reckon that about covers it, except for one more thing.

April Fools'.

From a New York boy who can't change his past but sure took great pleasure in pretending.

April 1, 1994

Columnist's death spurs smile, sorrow

*T*hat summer in Atlanta 16 years ago, on my very first newspaper job, I discovered the South and hush puppies and Southern belles and okra and pickup trucks and fried catfish.

I also discovered the works of a great Southern writer who explained it all to me: Lewis Grizzard.

The only thing southern in my hometown, New York City, was the South Bronx. The newspapers there didn't carry Grizzard's syndicated column. But reading him for the first time in *The Atlanta Constitution* made me laugh. Out loud. And when you move to a new region, you need to laugh. Get comfortable. Understand your surroundings.

I never met Grizzard (pronounced Gri-ZARD). He worked in the *Constitution's* eighth-floor newsroom; I was a college-intern reporter down on the sixth floor, at the old *Atlanta Journal*. But late one night, after a few beers left me feeling bold, I waited for the security guard to pass on his rounds, then sneaked into Grizzard's office.

Didn't touch anything. Just stood and looked at his big, messy desk. Tried to absorb some of the energy in that room. Wondered how one writer could make so many people laugh.

Monday's front-page news that Grizzard had died over the week-end of heart failure hit me hard. He was 47.

I knew he was sick. His recent columns told of his hospital stays, his heart operations and his loss of appetite (which he conquered by eating barbecued pork, but only from his boyhood barbecue joint in rural Georgia).

And last Thanksgiving, his dog Catfish, a black Lab, died of a weak heart. Up and died, Grizzard wrote. "My own heart, or what-ever's left of it, is breaking," he added ominously.

Monday, I sat at my desk and thought of Grizzard. Of his influence. Couldn't work. Needed to do something to honor him. But what?

I looked up above my desk and saw, "The 1994 Lewis Grizzard Wall Calendar & Guide to Political Incorrectness." I forgot it was hanging there. Filled with sayings and dates important to Grizzard: like Garth Brooks' birthday (Feb. 2); Elvis International Tribute Week (Aug. 7-15); and Sherman Occupies Atlanta (Sept. 2).

Just sat there and looked at that calendar. Thought about Grizzard and his dog Catfish. How both up and died.

One thought led to another. Grizzard loved adventures. Loved to travel the rural backwoods.

I'd heard about a catfish place just over the Texas line in Oklahoma, called McGehee's Catfish Restaurant. Located in the Red River Valley, it offers all you can eat and is a favorite of pilots because of its great landing strip. It sounded like a Lewis Grizzard-type place.

On a whim, I asked the transportation reporter at the *Star-Telegram*, G. Chambers Williams III, if we could ride up there together.

Williams owns a plane. Actually, he owns two. He keeps one near his house, the other near our office. (He takes his job as a transportation writer seriously.)

So that afternoon, the two of us played hooky from work. Climbed into his single-engine Piper Cherokee, the one near the office.

Williams flew us north, past Denton, over farmland and cattle ranches to a muddy bend of the Red River at the Texas border. We landed on the little grass strip beside the restaurant.

Williams is a Grizzard fan, too. Turns out that in 1980, Williams was editor of the Troy, Ala., newspaper when Grizzard came to town for a college speech. Williams chauffeured him around, and after his speech, Grizzard wanted to go out partying. So they went. Drank long-neck beers, of course.

"That night," Williams told me, "Grizzard said the doctor told him if he quit smoking, quit drinking and quit carousing every night, he'd live a whole lot longer.

"And Grizzard said he asked his doctor, 'Why would I want to?'"

The meal was wonderful. Grizzard would have loved the thin menu ("Catfish Dinner – All You Can Eat – No Doggie Bags, Please") and the worn red carpet and the way the place filled up so quickly with fried-catfish devotees. I'm sure he would have enjoyed the juicy entrée, the first-rate cole slaw and the crispy hush puppies.

On the flight home, Williams told me how he left Alabama and became editor at six daily and weekly newspapers. At each one, he bought Grizzard's syndicated column and watched circulation increase. "People loved him," he said.

The sun slipped behind the horizon, and I pulled out my Grizzard calendar. "To all you virgins," he wrote for August, "thanks for nothing." I laughed and put the calendar away. It was getting dark. And one of my heroes up and died. And now this silly calendar won't let me forget. Every single day for the rest of the year. It's just too sad.

March 23, 1994

A day reserved
for honoring columnists

I always wanted to be a newspaper columnist. As a struggling young reporter, I stuck to my belief that if I thought like one, I could be one.

So several years ago, I joined a group called the National Society of Newspaper Columnists, composed of writers from American newspapers big and small who meet at an annual convention.

Ernie Pyle

As the only noncolumnist in the ranks, I contacted the president, *Kansas City Star* columnist Bill Tammeus, and volunteered for active duty.

"I'd like to get involved in something that represents my future," I wrote with steadfast optimism. "What ya got?"

He wrote back, "I have a half-baked idea that there ought to be a National Columnists Day – to be proclaimed and celebrated far and wide with hangings in effigy and whatnot.

"Would you be willing to do a little research and recommend some dates?" he asked. "Like the birthday of some great columnist or other? This may go nowhere, but I think it might be kind of fun."

An easy question for me.

Ernie Pyle.

Pyle's on-the-road dispatches, six columns a week, offered Americans a folksy escape from the pains of the Great Depression. And his landmark in-the-trenches World War II columns transmitted the fears and emotions of the average GI Joe back home in a way no other medium could compare. He was the most widely read newspaperman in the world.

But at the height of his popularity, Pyle died in a way almost impossible to imagine by today's celebrity-writer standards: He was shot in the head by a Japanese sniper near the front lines.

The date was April 18, 1945.

At the columnist convention last year in Florida, my first as an official member of the column-writing corps, my peers listened patiently as I explained why April 18 should be designated National Columnists Day.

In a vote afterward, they approved the idea. As Tammeus later wrote, "It's to give columnists one free column idea a year."

Several weeks ago, I traveled to Pyle's former home in Albuquerque, N.M., to learn more about him. The white cottage, mostly unchanged from Pyle's time, is now a public library.

After five years on the road, Pyle and his wife, Jerry, built the house in 1940. "Definite walls in a definite place that we could feel were ours," he wrote. "The house will be here for us to come back to."

The library contains scrapbooks, Pyle's worn felt hat and some personal letters. Here's one he wrote to his wife:

"I'm on another invasion. I never intended to but I feel I must cover the Marines, and the only way to do it honestly is to go with them."

In Pyle's old back yard, a stone monument shows the chiseled words of his most famous column: "In this war I have known a lot of officers who were loved and respected by the soldiers under them. But never have I crossed the trail of any man as beloved as Captain Henry T. Waskow of Belton, Texas."

Pyle died 50 years ago Tuesday. How fitting to mark it as National Columnists Day.

So remember Ernie Pyle. And toast your favorite columnists.

You can even hang me in effigy. I wouldn't mind. In fact, I'd be honored.

April 16, 1995

Tune in tomorrow and see columnist fall into video stardom

*T*his is a good news, bad news story.

The good news is that I'll be on national television tomorrow night.

The bad news is that I'll be on *America's Funniest Home Videos*, which is scheduled to show a clip of my fall off the stage at Keller High School. I fell 8 feet into the orchestra pit in front of hundreds of people.

I've purposely never written about this story. I always told myself, "I'll write about this when it gets shown on national television."

Never thinking it would.

The night of the fall, I was master of ceremonies at the Keller High student talent show. I wore a tuxedo. I was excited and honored because it was the first time the school's $6 million fine arts theater would be used to showcase the school's talented students.

From backstage, I announced into the microphone, "The show is about to begin." There were cheers. I said, "It's Feb. 26, 1998. It's 7 o'clock. History is about to be made at Keller High School."

More cheers. The curtain opened, and I stepped out.

I walked onstage – blinded by the spotlights. I kept walking, thinking the front of the stage was a lot longer than it was. On the fifth step, I felt nothing beneath me.

The 8-foot drop felt like it happened in slow motion. Fortunately, the pit was empty. I landed on my feet.

From above, I could hear pandemonium.

"This is so embarrassing," I remember thinking. "I have to go back up there and pretend this was planned."

And that's exactly what I did.

I ran up the stairs to the stage. People in the audience were standing and screaming in horror. Parents were running to the front to see whether I was OK.

I smiled, waved my arms to show I was fine and ad-libbed. "When I say, 'We're about to make history,' we're about to make history! It was all planned. I was here yesterday practicing. Did I do a good job?"

There were scattered cheers.

I continued, "I saw dads coming down, running, saying, 'He's hurt! He's hurt!' Wanna see me do it again?"

There were a few more half-hearted cheers.

Then I introduced the first act, a rock band appropriately called Turmoil, and walked backstage.

The only pain I felt was in my right heel, which was bruised from the fall. I resolved not to limp the rest of the evening. I asked Chi Chi King, the school choir director and the show producer, for an aspirin.

"I fell off the stage," I told her. She had missed the action and thought I was kidding.

"No way, Dave," she replied. "I'm really busy. Don't joke with me. It's not funny."

Helen Lewis, the school drama teacher, told her I wasn't joking.

I don't remember the rest of the show, except that I was determined not to let it be known that my fall was an accident.

Rick Thomsen, a Keller parent who videotaped my fall while he waited for his son to perform in the talent show, told me this week, "We went home that night, and I kept saying to my wife, 'Do you think that was planned or did he really fall?'

"You didn't appear hurt," he said. "I thought it was planned. A fall like that, I couldn't imagine anyone just bouncing back."

Josh Freedberg, the TV show's video screener, told me, "When we find the good ones like that, it kind of makes it worth it. We've never gotten a clip like that before. Accidents like that tend to be funny things and make the show. Anything like people falling into a ditch."

Until now, most people who saw it will tell you they believe that the fall had been rehearsed.

OK, the ruse is over. Now you know the real story behind the clip to be shown during the show at 7 p.m. tomorrow on WFAA/Channel 8.

The producers call the segment "Man Walking Off Front of Stage."

I call it the most humiliating thing that ever happened to me.

December 11, 1998

An apology simply won't be enough for this mistake

*T*he 650 students at Spring Garden Elementary in Bedford celebrated Citizenship Day yesterday in a poignant ceremony around the flagpole. Almost everything went perfectly.

The Harwood Junior High School Band showed up to play *This Is My Country* and *America the Beautiful.*

Girl Scout Troop 1332 faithfully raised the flags.

The Spring Garden choir sang delightfully, and event organizer Ulana Strutz, a third-grade teacher, delivered a talk on *The Meaning of Citizenship.*

There was one problem. A certain newspaper columnist who was listed on the program as giving a talk titled "Why I'm Proud To Be an American" did not bother to show at the 8:30 a.m. ceremony.

I overslept.

When I awoke and checked my daily schedule, I let out a howl that unnerved even my howling Psycho Dog. I quickly called the school to apologize, but there was a noticeable – and well-deserved – chill in the voice of the office staff member who answered the telephone.

In record time, I showered and dressed and drove to the school, where I presented myself in the main office as "the bad boy who has come to apologize to the principal."

An unsmiling Principal Bill Barnes led me to his office. He didn't ask me to sit down.

I told him I was mortified and embarrassed, and that in 20 years as a newspaperman visiting schools, this had never happened before.

He showed me the Citizenship Day program and told me how well the event turned out.

Except for one missing element.

He said parents were displeased at my nonappearance. He said my failure had not gone unnoticed by Hurst-Euless-Bedford school district Superintendent Ron Caloss, who was in attendance, and by teachers, by staff, by Girl Scouts, by the school choir, by the junior high band and by the other students.

Strutz, who had contacted me about the event numerous times, arrived in the office. She, too, was not smiling.

I repeated my apology to her and described my acute embarrassment.

I told her it was important for me to deal with my mistake and to try to make amends. I told the principal and the teacher that I will donate 20 hours of service to the school to make up for my failure to appear for the speech.

I offered to conduct my reading-and-writing seminars for third-, fourth- and fifth-graders during the next several months.

They said they would take my offer under advisement.

I immediately sent Superintendent Caloss an apology letter: "I am ashamed because speaking to our children is the most important thing a newspaperman can do."

What particularly irks me about my failure yesterday is that our nation is going through a troubled time because of our top elected leader's failure to keep his commitments.

That helped me to admit my mistake and to offer to make up for it.

It's important as American citizens these days to make sure that we do not act like our president.

I publicly apologize to the members of the Spring Garden Elementary School community and look forward to my opportunity to make amends. I hope they can forgive me.

September 18, 1998

For shame on the rush to judgment

My most exciting moment of 1996 took place on an Atlanta street corner during the Summer Olympics. Looking back now, I can only remember how it led to my most disgraceful moment of the past year.

I hadn't planned on telling anybody this little story. But with Michael Irvin about to become a sympathetic character because of his Richard Jewell-like treatment by the police and the news media, it's probably something I should get off my chest.

The exciting moment took place at 4:30 p.m. Tuesday, July 30. I was walking down Peachtree Street when a car pulled up to the curb and somebody tossed out a bundle of newspapers. A woman picked up the bundle and began hawking the papers outside.

"Extra!" she shouted. "Extra!"

I looked at the headline of *The Atlanta Journal*, coincidentally the newspaper that hired me for my first job almost 20 years ago.

"FBI suspects 'hero' guard may have planted bomb," the headline said.

I read the story. Twice. My knees started to shake, adrenalin began pumping and I felt like I was at the flash point of history. The biggest story ever.

That morning, I had watched Jewell, the security guard who discovered the knapsack with the bomb that exploded at Centennial Park, interviewed on a TV show. I knew what he looked like. I decided to go find him.

The radio plugged into my ear reported that Jewell had told reporters outside his apartment that he was leaving to go to work as a security guard at the AT&T pavilion. I walked over as fast as possible.

I kept circling the building, expecting Jewell to show up for his shift. When he didn't, I noticed other reporters hovering around an AT&T spokesman.

The spokesman was telling the reporters that he didn't know anything yet and there was no information to release. After the reporters left, I worked him a little harder.

"Come on," I snapped. "How could you not know about this guy? You don't even know if he's coming to work? He's the prime suspect?"

The flack said he hadn't seen the story and didn't know of any proof against Jewell.

Then I said something I'll regret for the rest of my life.

I said, "Richard Jewell coming to work here now would be like Lee Harvey Oswald going back to work at the Texas School Book Depository."

The flack looked horrified at my glib remark.

Certainly, I had come on too strong. A couple of days later, feeling repentant, I visited the media encampment outside Jewell's apartment complex. I counted 40 press people and nine video cameras – including cameras from NBC, ABC, CBS and CNN – on a continuous stakeout.

An official-looking man stepped before the microphones for an announcement.

He said his name was Allan Furhman, and he was the property manager. He wanted everybody to move off the property.

"Is that Furhman with an 'h'?" one reporter yelled.

The cameras were trained on Furhman with an "h" and they followed as the reporters moved their lawn chairs and thick novels off the apartment complex property where Jewell lived. All this action came in time for the noon news.

I followed Furhman down the street and asked what he thought of this zoo.

"It's overwhelming for these residents," he said. "You can't park. You can't drive around. You can't do anything."

The property manager said that if Jewell were found guilty, "then maybe the press will be viewed as a positive influence."

"But if the press takes a hit from this, maybe it will be done a little differently next time."

Well, the next time is here.

And what, if anything, have we learned from the Richard Jewell embarrassment?

If Michael Irvin is innocent of these latest accusations, what have we done to him?

And what have we done to ourselves?

January 3, 1997

Postscript: The allegations against Irvin, the former Dallas Cowboys wide receiver, were later proven false.

Turtle's tale a crushing, telling tragedy

One morning this week, a turtle tried to cross the road in Keller.

It was a long, hazardous trip for the turtle. One after another, cars and trucks slowed and swerved.

Green and almost a foot long, the turtle was almost halfway across the road – just shy of the double yellow line. I nearly hit it as I was driving along Johnson Road – in a big hurry to avoid a storm coming in from the north. I passed over the turtle safely and noticed in the rearview mirror that other drivers behind me were slowing and swerving, too.

There was something poetic about this little creature causing us humans to alter our ways. So I made a U-turn.

I wanted to witness and then write a story celebrating the turtle's triumph. I wanted to record that drivers on this particular morning had been careful and considerate.

Maybe a good Samaritan would come along and move the turtle. If that happened, I'd ask him or her the regular interviewer's questions: *Why did you stop? Where were you going? How did you feel?*

In journalism schools and newsrooms, they teach us writers not to shape the stories ourselves. Don't get personally involved. Let events unfold around you.

So I stopped at the side of the road near the turtle crossing and began taking notes.

A thing of beauty. The first turtle I'd seen crossing a road. Usually, it's a skunk, an armadillo or a cow.

After each step, the turtle would stick its neck out as far as it could – as if straining to see cars coming.

Soon, the turtle had crossed the double yellow line – more than halfway home. Three vehicles approached from the west.

The first, a sport utility vehicle, slowed almost to a stop before it inched its way around the turtle, which had retreated back inside its shell.

The second, a white maintenance truck from the Keller school district, also slowed considerably before swerving around it.

But the third vehicle, well, that changed the story. This vehicle, also a Keller district maintenance truck, was so big that it took up almost the entire lane. And it had four wheels in the rear – doubling the chances *against* the little turtle.

The truck was doing fine, but at the last moment, it swerved and the front tires ran directly over the turtle. The thump that followed was gut-wrenching: the truck smashed the turtle and flipped it up in the air.

Horrified, I heard myself scream.

The turtle, its shell cracked in half, lay dead, with its legs sticking up and its tiny mouth wide open.

I followed the Keller school trucks. At the first stop sign, at Bourland Road, the driver of the first truck opened his door, leaned out and yelled back to the second driver: "DID YOU SEE THE TURTLE?"

But the second driver, the one who hit the turtle, didn't answer.

A few miles down the road, they pulled into Florence Elementary School. All three of us hopped out.

I asked the driver who hit the turtle if he had seen it.

"I thought it was just dirt," he said.

Then he went back inside his truck and rolled up his window.

The driver of the other truck, the one who missed the turtle, introduced himself as Steve Phipps, a maintenance worker.

"I saw it immediately," Phipps said. "That's why I swerved to miss."

The storm was almost overhead now. The wind was blowing leaves off trees. I returned to the spot in the road.

At first, vehicles continued to slow and swerve around the turtle mess. But then the rains came and washed it all away.

Guilt-ridden, I called the Fort Worth Zoo to ask about the Keller turtle. Dave Blody, the resident amphibian and reptile expert, told me that it was a male, probably a red-eared slider, who was crossing the road in search of a new hibernation spot.

"He was looking for greener horizons," Blody said.

Aren't we all?

There is no story of turtle triumph. Now I wish I had just picked up the little turtle and moved it along. Forget the story. Live a life. Then we both could have gone on our merry way.

October 28, 1994

Chapter Thirteen
A Magazine Story

"The degree of civilization in a society can be measured by entering its prisons."

— Feodor Dostoevski

Note: The following story appeared in The Philadelphia Inquirer's *Sunday magazine on January 6, 1985*

Growing up with Poorboy

It had been interesting for the high school boy, being pen pals with an imprisoned murderer. But a decade later, what would it be like being friends with an ex-con?

Bob Sacha

Dave and Poorboy on the magazine cover

When I was younger and felt the need to score a point in conversation, I told whomever I wanted to impress that a very good friend of mine was locked away in prison. "Yes," I would say innocently, "my friend is a murderer serving 15 years to life." Then I would watch my listener's face.

At the time, I never considered that one day, after I had become an adult, my friend could be released from his "life" sentence in prison. But it happened recently, and with some trepidation about what to expect, I went to visit him. Beneath a deep-blue sky, I drove to the Bronx one crisp Saturday last spring to celebrate the freedom of my friend. He and I had never shared a free moment together.

From the beginning, ours was a most peculiar friendship. I was a skinny, naïve Jewish kid from the Upper West Side of Manhattan whose only trouble with the law came when my mother turned me in for possession of firecrackers. He was a tough, canny convict from Harlem who was serving 15 years for killing a friend in a bar brawl that began over $2. Yet the friendship endured: He satisfied my adolescent curiosity about life inside a penitentiary; I was his link to life in the outside world. And over the years, in ways we both were unaware of, we learned much from each other, and grew.

His real name is John Reynolds, but he is nicknamed Poorboy. We met through a prisoner pen-pal program when I was 15. Eleven years later, when John became a free man, I was 26, and he was 48. Although I was happy for him, I felt reluctant to face up to the responsibility of being his friend. After his release, I delayed visiting John for several months because, I told him, I was busy settling into Philadelphia, where I had just moved to take a job at *The Inquirer*. With the job, a car and my own apartment, my career as a reporter had progressed neatly in the five years since college.

At the same time, I learned from John's letters and phone calls that he was struggling in his new life. Unlike me, he had no job, no car and no apartment. He wrote me after his release and asked whether he could borrow $200 for automobile insurance. With the insurance, he explained, he could legally drive a car. With the car, he could get a job. And with a steady paycheck, he could afford an apartment. My $200 was the key to open the door.

I wrote back that I was sorry. No money to spare.

Shortly after that, John called early one morning and told me in a dejected tone that it was a fine line between staying honest and turning to crime. He said he feared he would have to cross it to survive. I told him to be strong and promised to visit soon.

*   *   *

That brilliant spring day would be a jumble, mixing events of the day with fragments of the past. As I drove, I recalled the first time I had visited him, at a penitentiary in upstate New York. It was on a rainy day, and I had shuddered nervously as I stepped off the bus and looked through the fog at the high gray walls.

Inside, past the barred front gate, the guards frisked me, confiscated my lunch of two soggy peanut butter and jelly sandwiches, and directed me with dour looks to the visiting room. Moments later, a sturdy black man, about 6 feet tall and wearing a tan sweater and green prison pants, recognized me from a photograph and slowly walked toward me. I knew it was John because he was smiling.

Only once after that did I ever envision his freedom. In 1974, John was temporarily transferred to a Brooklyn jail for an appeal hearing. I rode the subway to see him. Inside the jail, as we talked by telephone through a glass wall, he told me he might be released. We planned our celebration. We would escort two fine ladies to a fancy dinner. Take a stroll down Broadway. Maybe go dancing. As it turned out, we didn't go anywhere together. John went back upstate to prison. I went to college.

Though we kept writing, the formal pen-pal program was canceled in 1975. The director told me there were problems. After inmates were released, they had high expectations of their pen pals. Some of the friendships ended with threats and bad feelings. None of this jibed with the man I had come to know. John was soft-spoken, sensitive, even philosophical. When he was paroled last year, one of the first things he did was write to my parents, thanking them for letting me be his friend and telling them he would call when he got back to New York. My mother dreaded that phone call. She told me she didn't want John calling. She didn't want him to come to the house. She feared he would kill our family.

Although my parents were not pleased by my decision to visit John that Saturday (my mother said it might cause a bad reaction in him), our decade-old friendship held a certain amount of sentimentality – even for them. For old times' sake, they suggested that I take him a kosher salami. I'd always taken him one in prison.

It was noon when I arrived at the quiet Bronx street where John was staying at his sister's house. With the salami tucked under my arm, I tapped lightly on the screen door. John appeared in the doorway, and we shook hands. He looked smaller than I remembered.

"How you been doing?" he asked. "How's your family?"

Good, I replied, as I handed him the salami. A big smile spread across his face.

"You don't forget!" he said.

"The salami was my parents' idea."

He was sorry he could not call them, he said softly. "What really held me back was when you told me it might upset your mother. I didn't want to do that."

He looked hurt. His smile was gone now.

*   *   *

June 29, 1973. Dear David: I am in the hope that you haven't forgotten who I am, since it has been over a year since you sent in the form for correspondence and visits with me.

I have recently been transferred here to Green Haven Correctional Facility, and believe it or not, I just found out that I could write to you, and the only thing I can say is the circumstances was beyond my control. Therefore, I am in hope that you are still there and willing to write to me.

I am thirty seven years of age, six feet, two hundred pounds, was married with three children, but am now divorced. My children are two boys and a girl, age 10, 13 and 15. They are living with my ex-wife their Mother in Baltimore, Md. Prior to my confinement, I lived in Brooklyn and worked as an 'A' plumber.

I was arrested in August of 1968 on a charge of assault that subsequently became manslaughter, and still later it became murder for which I was convicted by a jury's verdict and sentenced to a term of 15 years to life. I have been through all the courts without any action and now I am about to start all over again, but this time I will have a little help.

Well, this is about the best I can do for an introduction so in the event that I have left something out, please feel free to ask anything you might think of, okay, and hope to hear from you soon so take care.

Peace, John Reynolds, 19195

*   *   *

It was after midnight on Aug. 14, 1968, when the events that led to the murder began. According to testimony, John Reynolds stopped off on his way home for a nightcap at Roy's Palace Bar & Grill on Broadway and Myrtle Avenue in Brooklyn. John, then 33, walked into the dimly lighted tavern and immediately spotted 28-year-old James Edward Davis, who owed him $2. John reminded Davis of this and asked Davis to buy him a drink in return.

"No, I don't have any money," Davis said.

John asked again. Davis repeated his answer. When John asked a third time, Davis slid off the bar stool, removed his shirt and said: "If you want to fight, come on outside."

"No," John replied. "I don't want to fight. I have a sore arm."

John walked away. After a few minutes, he returned and told Davis, "OK, sucker, you can keep the $2."

"I told you to let me alone," Davis said. "Don't bother me." Again, he asked John whether he wanted to fight.

"No, I told you I have a sore arm."

"Which one?" Davis asked.

"My right arm."

Davis put his own right arm in his back pocket. Then he punched

John with his left hand. The two men tied up and fell to the floor, where they were separated.

John left the bar, but he returned 20 minutes later. He asked the barmaid for a rum and Coke.

"Are you paying?" she demanded. "I'm not serving you if you aren't paying."

"Give me a drink."

"Do you have any money?"

John paid her for his drink and took it to the men's room, where Davis and others were playing a game of craps. Tension flickered between John and Davis. The two men left the restroom and moved to the rear of the bar, near the pool table.

Davis lifted a wooden chair over his head. "OK, if you want me, come and get me," he said.

"Why do you want to fight with me?" John shouted. "Don't hit me with that chair!"

John took a step toward Davis. Davis threw a chair at him. Then Davis tripped and fell beside the pool table. John fell on top of him and pulled out a 7-inch knife. He made a punching motion toward Davis' stomach, stabbing him once in the abdomen. Then he stabbed Davis in the right armpit and once more in the back.

With the knife in his hand, John ran outside. He sought refuge down the street at a place called the Oasis Bar. A policeman found him at the Oasis several minutes later.

"He came at me with a chair, and I stabbed him," John explained.

Davis was carried out to the sidewalk and taken to the hospital. He died four hours later.

John was arrested for assault. The charge was later changed to manslaughter, and bail was set at $50,000, which he could not pay. Later, John was shocked to find that a grand jury had upgraded the charge again. One year later, he was tried for murder.

On May 14, 1969, a jury of 12 men returned to a Kings County courtroom in Brooklyn after a four-day trial. The foreman asked the judge whether they could take one more look at the 7-inch knife. Shortly after that, the jury announced its verdict. John Reynolds was found guilty of murder. Soon after, he went to Sing Sing. He was later transferred to the state prison at Attica, and then, in 1973, to Green Haven, which is where I first met him.

Sept. 19, 1973. I am up in the morning about 6 a.m., get myself together and the doors open at 7:30 a.m. We then go to eat, back to the cell and then to work, stop at 11 a.m., eat and go back to work at 1 p.m. Stop at 3 p.m. and go to the yard until 5 p.m., during which time if you want you can go and eat the last time for the day. But at 5, you go to the cell until the next morning.

I just changed jobs and now make 25 cents per day so you can see I will get rich by 2319.

* * *

I did not learn the details of John's crime until long after we became pen pals. Only when he felt sure that our friendship would survive did he mail me his well-thumbed copy of the 350-page trial transcript. Reading it, I learned how he killed James Edward Davis.

To me, John was no murderer. He didn't look like a killer in the photograph he had sent me – just a troubled man with eyebrows that peaked with worry. He played the flute ("the only thing that is helping me do this time"), offered to ghostwrite my adolescent love letters and asked me to pray for his appeal.

My letters to him were filled with questions. What was his job? (It changed often.) Were our letters censored? (They were.) Was he guilty or innocent? (He avoided a direct answer.) What did he think of President Nixon and Watergate? ("If he can say to hell with the court, then why can't I and the other prisoners?")

We had little in common. His main concern was something I took for granted – freedom. My life revolved around the high school track team and Friday night dances. I was at the stage where I rehearsed my telephone conversations with girls before calling them. Normally, I did not spend time with known criminals.

My interest in prisons began in 1971 when 11 guards and 32 inmates were killed in the uprising at the Attica Correctional Facility, a maximum-security prison in upstate New York. That incident played a part in the development of my emerging social consciousness.

But the event that truly sparked my interest came at a high school assembly when I was a ninth-grader. The guest speaker was Fran

O'Leary, a tough-talking 34-year-old ex-convict with short hair and a nasty temperament. She shocked me with her stories about life in and out of prison. She has been convicted of prostitution, armed robbery and forgery. Prison was rough, she said, but getting out was even rougher. Dumb things almost got her sent back. Once in a crowded department store, she found she had forgotten what it was like to be pushed and shoved by others without fighting back. She even began plotting ways to return to prison, where she felt more comfortable.

Instead, though, she joined the Fortune Society, a group of New York ex-convicts who helped prepare prisoners for their release and provided emotional support afterward. The Fortune Society borrowed its slogan from Russian novelist Feodor Dostoevski, who once wrote: "The degree of civilization in a society can be measured by entering its prisons." The society's philosophy was that prisons should provide rehabilitation as well as punishment, that they should serve as schools for social and vocational skills rather than simply as warehouses for caged animals.

This made sense to me. Hoping to learn more, I joined the group and signed up for its pen-pal program. Because I was a minor, I had to pester my mother into signing the permission slip for correspondence with an inmate. "Why can't you write to a Vietnamese orphan instead?" she pleaded.

By the time John's first letter arrived a year later, I had read books on penology, the study of prisons. To impress my new friend, I mailed him a 40-page term paper I wrote for my 10th-grade social studies class titled, "The Prison Reform Movement in the United States, 1865-1915." It was a big hit with John and his friends. "We all agree that you will make a good research lawyer," he wrote.

Another time, I sent him a carton of cigarettes and one of my first published articles from the high school newspaper. The headline was "Prison Reform."

"It is a sad but important fact that 80 percent of all major crimes are committed by ex-convicts," I wrote. "Prison does not do its job. Upon leaving a prison, the ex-con lacks a skill, and therefore to support himself, he turns to the only thing he knows – crime."

*   *   *

I visited John only eight times after we became friends during the final decade of his confinement. The visits themselves were warm and rewarding. John was always glad to see me. But what got to me was the strain of the bus trips. I would stuff my knapsack with two salamis for John and a book and arrive at the Port Authority bus terminal in New York one hour before the public bus was scheduled to leave for Green Haven Correctional Facility in rural Dutchess County. Any later than that and I had to stand for the 2½-hour ride.

On one trip, when I was 16, I took the last seat, and the bus continued to fill up with women – the wives and girlfriends of men inside "the Haven" – and their children. Life was obviously difficult for them. They apparently were too poor to own cars, and the bus company never provided enough buses for everyone to have a seat. The women on my bus began to complain to the driver about the lack of seats.

"If you have any complaints, you can take them to the boss," he replied with a sneer. "I only drive." The women complained even louder.

Unfortunately, our driver did not know his way to the prison. He was supposed to follow another bus, but the driver of that bus went too fast, and our man lost him. We circled Yonkers Raceway twice looking for the lead bus, but it was long gone. The women quickly realized this mishap would cut into the allotted time with their men. Their clamor grew into a bitter roar.

Sitting on my armrest, a woman with long false eyelashes shouted at the driver: "You can't trust whitey!" The harried driver made the mistake of yelling back. I was frightened. I felt trapped inside a crowded madhouse with no escape – surrounded by angry, screaming people, and at the mercy of a befuddled man.

Then it hit me: This was what their men felt inside prison every day, every hour and every minute. I buried myself in the book and pretended it wasn't happening.

*   *   *

April 14, 1974. I am in the hope that you arrived home safe. I wish there was words that I could use to express my satisfaction for your coming to see me and whether you believe it or not, I learned a little something from you today and I am looking forward to our next visit because Dave you are out of sight and I love you.

*   *   *

I expected John to be jubilant about his release, but instead he just seemed weary. We were sitting on the sofa in his sister's living room. He wore silver-framed sunglasses, although we were inside, and smoked a cigarette. The mood was serene. Through the white-lace curtains hanging over the window, we could see tree branches swaying softly in the wind.

He showed me his newly acquired trappings of freedom. There was his new driver's license, which he earned after passing the driving test on his second attempt. And he had a readmittance card to Plumbers Local 1, his trade union before he was sent to prison. He worked as a free-lance plumber now, and because he was starting from scratch, his rates were much lower than those of the licensed plumbers in the area. "I don't have no overhead," he explained. "I don't have nothing."

The day before, he had finished work on a house, his first big job since his release several months before. He worked with another plumber. "He doesn't know about me," John said. "One day, I walked past his shop, saw his sign and went in. I asked, 'Could you use a mechanic?' He said, 'What do you do?' I said, 'Everything.'

"He pays me by the work. The guy gave me $60 for the day. It's not big pay, but it keeps me from asking people for bus fare or for a pack of cigarettes."

Returning to work after 15 years was harder than John had imagined. He held out his hands to show fresh cuts and scrapes. "It's hell, man. The pipes are different from when I went in. Where there were cast-iron pipes before, there is plastic now. Before, the pipes were joined with lead, but today they've got a washer."

His lack of steady work bothered him. "It seems like nobody cares," he said. "One time, I asked to sit down with the parole officers and talk, to get some direction. But they were too busy."

I wanted to cheer him up. We had been friends for a decade but had never shared drinks together. So I asked John whether he had any beer. He walked into the kitchen, and I followed. A pork leg cooked in a pot of boiling water on the stove. The kosher salami sat on a nearby counter. John pulled two beers from the refrigerator and handed one to me. We tapped the bottles together.

A Magazine Story | **267**

"Here's to freedom," I said.

"Thanks," he said, and lifted the bottle.

Again, the recollections of the letters and prison visits came rushing back.

*   *   *

Jan. 19, 1975. Dave, I got the decision from the court and lost, but one thing must be considered and that is I got a decision, something which my lawyer did not get on direct appeal. So now I believe I will really be able to get some relief in the higher court.

Dave, I have to stop. Tell you why later — something up.

John Reynolds, 19195

*   *   *

None of my other friends wrote such dramatic letters. But none of them lived in a 7-by-10-foot cinderblock room painted pink. I never saw John's cell, but he told me it contained an army cot, a toilet, a closet, a desk, two throw rugs, family photographs on the walls and a flute, which he called "my confidante."

He knew I yearned for letters filled with tales resembling *The Birdman of Alcatraz*, one of my favorite movies. Sometimes I think he teased me with nuggets. "How is it going? Fine, I hope," he once wrote. "As for myself, I am still hanging in, trying to find a way out. Otherwise, nothing new has happened that I can talk about in this letter."

Trouble in his life was not infrequent. In 1974, he wrote: "I don't think I told you but I had a fight and got kicked off my job. I could have used the money but this was one of those suckers that liked to tell on people. I think I did a right nice job on him because he don't have too much mouth lately."

In 1975: "Some strange things have been happening. Matter of fact, I am uptight at this very moment and under the circumstances you could say it is impossible to express myself to you as it is in a letter."

In 1977: "There has been a lot happening since I last wrote to you. A few officers were arrested for bringing in drugs. And a couple of dudes was killed for having too much mouth. Matter of fact, the joint is still upside down."

His letters stopped in the summer of 1978. When one finally arrived in the fall, it explained his absence: "During the first of August, an informer came to me and told me I was going to be set up, and would you believe I was. They came up with some smoke and $50 cash and gave me 60 days in lockup, 60 days lost time and 60 days loss of privileges. . . .

"I am now a grandfather. My daughter had a son on the fifth of October last. No, she is not married. She hasn't brought him up here yet but I anticipate she will in the foreseeable future."

After that, when I did not hear from him for several months, I feared the worst. I felt a responsibility toward him. I could feel him watching me grow up. His own son, a year younger than me, went to prison at age 16 for armed robbery. One time, he announced his informal adoption of my younger brother and me by writing: "Oh! I forgot to tell you that when I show a picture of you and your brother, and am asked who you are, I say my sons because the two of you are the fruit of a father's eye and I am sure your father is proud of the both of you. And I hope he don't mind my saying that."

*　　*　　*

March 4, 1974. Hi there: I received your letter and was happy to hear from you. And believe it or not, I have been thinking about you all week, and I guess it was because I talked to my son who is about your age. This was the first time in six years, so I guess you can understand I do feel good under the circumstances. Since my birthday is the 16th of this month, I feel the talk with him was a good present.

*　　*　　*

I drank just a sip of my toast-to-freedom beer in the time John finished his. He grabbed his trench coat, and we headed out the door into the bright afternoon sun for a drive through the neighborhood. I asked him to tell me about his last day in prison.

"I stayed up late the last night," John began. "I was in a cubicle just big enough for a bed. It was 2 a.m. when I went to sleep. I waited, so when I went to bed, I knew I'd be tired.

"At exactly 7 a.m., I woke up. I just laid there and looked up at the ceiling. Then I brushed my teeth, washed up and took a shower. I came back and packed my stuff in a pillowcase – a transistor radio, work pants and a work shirt.

"Now, the wait is on. About 9 a.m., they called for everybody being paroled. They took me to the 'dress-out room,' where I left all my bedding and state clothes. There I got my going-home clothes. They gave me a cocoa-brown three-piece suit.

"I took the state clothes off, threw them in the corner and put on my new clothes – a brown shirt, new brown shoes and the suit. It fit beautiful. I felt good. After I buttoned that vest up, I had a gold chain and put it on. I felt like a million dollars.

"When I got to the door, I wondered why they're holding me so long. They took me back upstairs to pick up my money. The state gives you $40 – no matter how long you've been there.

"Then a lady said, 'Your sister's downstairs waiting for you.' I came down and went into the captain's office. He gave me my release papers, and I walked out. My sister was there with one of her girlfriends. We went to the bank where I cashed the check."

"What did you do next?"

John smiled at my question "That girlfriend of my sister – a West Indian girl – we went to bed."

"Was it your first time in 15 years?" I asked.

John paused for a long time, as if he were rewinding the years 1968 to 1983 through his memory tape.

"Yeah," he finally replied, "that's what it was."

*　*　*

Dec. 21, 1975. You know for the longest time I have been waiting for you to tell me that you had a nice girl for me but it looks like you don't think that the old boy could use one. Now if you happen to run up on one, send her to me and I will handle it from there. I don't give a damn who, what or where she come from as long as she is a girl, age 18 and up. Now can you handle that, and hurry up because I am in need. HELP HELP. From top Pop? John Reynolds, the Poorboy.

*　*　*

During one prison visit, I asked John how he stayed sane. We sat in the corner of the large prison visiting room with several dozen other inmates and their guests, under the gaze of uniformed guards.

"The challenge of this here joint" prevented him from going crazy, he replied. "Not to let it break me. Not to lose my sense of reasoning. That's what keeps me going."

"To put the whole thing in a nutshell, I think this place can make a person realize what's happening in his life. Listening to silence. Being alone. Eighteen hundred men confined together, and there's a time when we are not allowed to open our mouths."

We were in the far corner, near a soda machine, an obscure spot I had picked while waiting for John, because it seemed removed from the crowd of men in green pants with their families. Several feet to my right, a man with a handlebar mustache sat in a chair. He looked very animated. A woman sat on his lap, facing him with her back toward me. Whenever I looked over at them, the man stared at me so coldly, I averted my eyes as fast as humanly possible.

I tried not to look, but it was difficult. His hands were up her dress. Her head dipped to one side. The couple rocked back and forth, ever so slightly. They were making love.

Every time I peeked, the man shot me a laser-like glare. But John pretended he didn't see.

*   *   *

April 30, 1975. Let me give you my good news. My ex-wife and my kids came up from Baltimore to see me, and man, they were out of sight. And last night I received my first letter from her since I have been away. I also received a letter from the Appellate Division that tells me that a pre-hearing will be held on my case.

*   *   *

From studying John's case, I learned he never saw his court-appointed lawyer before his indictment. Never informed that he could present his side to the grand jury, John was surprised when he found himself charged with murder. He thought he had been held for manslaughter, as indeed he initially had been. Furthermore, because of undisputed evidence that John was not the aggressor in the murder, he turned down an offer by the prosecutors to avoid trial by pleading guilty to a reduced homicide charge – a bad move in retrospect. "Offered seven years," John wrote in his diary. "Went in and told judge of innocence. Judge stated it was either a case of self-defense or murder."

So I sought out lawyers for help.

I contacted William J. vanden Heuvel, a New York politician who met John on a prison visit and gave him hope that there was merit to his appeal argument. "I have to ask a favor of you," I asked him. "Through the Democratic club in my neighborhood, I campaigned for you for district attorney last year. So I guess I do not feel as uneasy as I should about my request. All I would like to know is – Does this man have a case? Was he treated as unfairly as he claims? As a 16-year-old, I do not have the knowledge of law to judge for myself." Vanden Heuvel wrote back that he believed John had a weak argument.

I talked to a Manhattan assistant district attorney who handled inmate appeals. I was his child's baby sitter. He told me that John had a strong case but that he would need a very good lawyer.

I telephoned John's lawyer. The lawyer was very short with me. "I've been ready for trial," he said. Only one thing held him back: "Get me the names of some witnesses."

And I visited a veteran lawyer on my street who was best known for his unsuccessful attempts to be elected state judge. With little patience, he read John's appeal brief and told me that my friend was a mere jailhouse lawyer hustling me to help obtain his release. "Stay away from him," the lawyer chided. "That man is nothing but trouble. Does your mother know you are doing this?"

Eventually, I realized I was never going to get John released.

I also decided I no longer wanted to be a lawyer.

*   *   *

Aug. 21, 1976. Did I tell you my son got a 10-year sentence? I am trying my damndest to guide him through, so far so good. I just got a letter from my ex-wife telling that she has fell in love with me all over again. I really don't know what brought all of this about but I am going along with the program because I have nothing else to do.

*   *   *

Poorboy owned a reputation as the best woodcarver in the penitentiary. Perhaps, he thought, he could win my parents' approval with a gift. So he spent weeks carving a piano-shaped jewelry box for my mother. At first, she told me she did not want any gifts because she suspected some ulterior motive on his part. Besides, how pretty could a present made in prison be?

One day the piano box arrived. The sides were intricately carved to look like leaves. There were black and white keys and tiny foot pedals painted gold. The inside contained green felt and an ice cream stick to prop up the lid. Only a sensitive person could create something that lovely. My mother placed it prominently in the living room and showed it to her friends. Still, she maintained, her feelings toward John had not changed. She wanted nothing to do with a convict. But she thanked him in a way that warmed his heart. She sent him homemade fudge.

*　*　*

July 3, 1976. Dave, I am sure you have been wondering why I haven't written to you, and I wanted so badly to write but between problems and waiting to hear something on this clemency, I really can't get my mind on anything. The grapevine had it that I would get word by the Bicentennial, but nothing has come up as of yet. So I guess this 4th of July will be like the others.

*　*　*

We drove around aimlessly until late afternoon, when I pulled my car into a large fenced-in parking lot next to a one-story white building. Facing west, John and I could watch the setting sun sink behind the squat structure. I asked John to tell me about a subject he would never talk about while in prison.

Attica.

The word is synonymous with the bloodiest prison conflict in American history. John was one of 1,280 men who camped out in the D Yard of Attica those four tense days in September 1971. The rebellion ended with a brief but violent attack by armed corrections guards and troopers against the inmates who had seized 50 hostages and threatened to kill them.

Now, the parking lot where we sat seemed to become the Attica yard. "It's about the same size," John said as he looked around. "Yeah, it's the exact same size."

John was not a leader in the rebellion, he told me, but he spent the four days about five feet from the circle of hostages.

When the attack on the rebels began, "you heard this big motor and looked in front of you and saw a helicopter rising up," he said, looking at the building in front of us.

"As it came across the wall, troopers were jumping off and shooting. When the first trooper came down in that yard, two people I knew moved in on him. One guy had a baseball bat and bashed this bird's brains out to take the rifle away from him. But by the time they got to the rifle, they were dead. I stood there and watched as other officers hit them with rifle butts.

"In the meantime, as I turned and talked to another dude standing right next to me, a corrections officer on this roof killed him with a shot.

"As the guys over here," he said, pointing to his right, "were knocking off this trooper, the guy over there," pointing to his left, "was getting shot by a corrections officer. The guy fell, and then he just laid there. He just laid there."

"That close to you?" I asked. John nodded, then stopped for a moment before continuing. By now, the sun had slipped behind the building.

"It was right then that I decided I really had a little discipline about myself. I didn't panic. I didn't run. I just came to the conclusion that when my time comes, it comes. It ain't my time. And there is nothing to worry about."

He paused, and I thought about how his sense of fatalism might sustain him now.

"I ain't going back," he said of prison.

I looked at him, but he was no longer looking at me. He was staring through the car window at the white building beyond.

"Ain't going back," he said firmly. "Ain't left nothing in there."

*   *   *

Jan. 18, 1977. I didn't get the clemency, but I still have my case in the courts and the legislature has a few things that will be very helpful to me if passed. So again I find myself saying patience will get me out. Otherwise, things are about the same. I am broke and can't get my hands on anything. But you know me, up today and down tomorrow.

*   *   *

In prison, inmates assume roles to help them cope. There is the trusty who works for the administration, the rat who provides information, the politician who manipulates to get what he wants, the gorilla who forcibly takes what he wants, the wolf who is a bully, the fag who usually was gay before prison, the punk who becomes gay inside, the hipster who tries to be like everyone else, the tough who sells forbidden goods and the real man or right guy who is the favorite of everyone because of his wisdom and leadership.

Poorboy was a hustler and a trusty, but also a right guy. He was a juggler who, in his words, "could take nothing and make something." He could obtain food, clothing, carpentry materials, a pound of lamb meat, a gram of cocaine, anything anybody wanted.

Proof that John was a trusty and a right guy came in a 1983 parole report written by a psychiatric social worker: "He has conducted himself admirably. He works in a trusted position in the 'front office' and is respected by inmates and staff alike. Currently, he is an inmate/counselor in our Behavioral Intervention Program. He has much wisdom and experience to share with our young residents who are having adjustment problems, and he is most effective in communicating with them."

Once, I asked John what he talked about with the young inmates, and I could tell from his explanation what a deep lesson he had learned. "Our motto is, 'Con in reverse,' " he said of the group. "Let's say, the man tells you to sweep the floor over there. So you get the mop and the bucket and ask him if he wants you to mop it, too. You see? You give a little bit more. It's like the Scripture says: If a man smacks you in your cheek, you should look the other way."

*   *   *

Aug. 19, 1981. Last Sunday morning a fellow picked another up by the arm and leg and beat his head against the side of the building. This morning a dude got completely broke up with a baseball bat. The afternoon was completed with a dude just getting plain beat up. Tell me, did you hear about the female officer getting knocked off here in Green Haven? . . . I'm well Dave, still working at the courts with two years, 8 days to release if not before.

*   *   *

The talk of Attica carried us into dinnertime. John wanted Chinese food, so we drove to Chinatown, where I knew of a spicy Szechuan place on East Broadway. "One thing I always thought about doing was going to a Chinese restaurant," he said happily, "and here I am."

He asked me to order for him. I selected fried dumplings, shredded beef, the chicken and shrimp combination and two Tsingtao beers. I taught him to eat with chopsticks.

After dinner, we walked up Mulberry Street against a stiff evening wind. I asked whether he wanted to go to a popular coffee shop in Little Italy for dessert. He said no. "Having a lot of people around bugs me."

We continued walking, and in the afterglow of a pleasant dinner, he began to dream. "By the end of this year, I want an apartment," he said. "By the end of next year, I can get my own car."

We returned to the dark street where I had parked my car, and I began the drive back to the Bronx.

"We didn't do anything unusual today," John said, "but the whole day was unusual. You dig what I mean? I appreciate you being my friend. I've watched you for a long, long time. We're opposites. You're white, formally educated and well-off. But you know what? I think I've learned a lot from you today in the way you do things, in the way you handle me and our situation. It's beautiful."

Now, I felt good. My worries about the visit had been for nothing. I had taken good care of him, and the day was a success. But I had no idea of the role reversal about to take place.

I got lost driving through the Bronx. I pulled over by a pay phone so John could call his sister for directions and I could check the map in the trunk of my car. As he stepped up to the phone, I walked to the rear of my car. But I could not open the trunk lid. The lock was jammed. Someone had smashed it while we were eating. "What am I going to do?" I asked, moaning as if it were the end of the world.

"At this point, we can't open it, so be cool," John said.

I didn't respond. Seeing this, he shouted at me.

"Hey, partner?"

"Yeah?"

"Be cool!"

But I was losing it. My brows knitted as I tried to figure out a way to get into the trunk. I mentally listed the possible stolen items: a briefcase, a favorite pair of shoes and a pair of trousers. I sighed deeply. John was watching me.

"I think you're panicking," he said. "If the stuff is gone, what are you going to do?"

I did not answer.

"I asked you a question. What are you going to do?"

"Nothing."

"You parked your car in a very, very dark spot, right? This is reality. This is what happens."

But I could not get my mind off my shoes, my trousers, and my briefcase.

"Dave, don't let me down! You're giving me the strength to go on. They're beating me out here, and you call me one thousand times to check on me. So to be concerned about that trunk is out of order."

I did not speak the rest of the way back. When we finally arrived at his sister's house, John got his toolbox. While he held a flashlight so I could see, I nervously fumbled with a wrench to unscrew the back seat. My heart raced as I yanked the seat out and crawled through the rear to check whether my possessions had been stolen.

Nothing was missing. I turned to face John.

"So now you panicked for nothing, right?"

"Right," I said sheepishly, feeling incredibly stupid.

"We were in a situation where either way, you couldn't do anything about it," he analyzed. "It's like the Attica thing. Hear? I learned I had discipline."

His message was clear: Sure, I may be formally educated and well-off compared with him, but I was not disciplined. From that moment on, I knew John must be looking at me in a different way.

*   *   *

Feb. 3, 1984. I'm in good health, and that is just about it. I was led to believe one thing before I got out, and once out, nothing was like what I was told. I have had no money, no job and no one seems to give any help. I'm free and yet not free.

*   *   *

Back inside the Bronx house, the smell of boiled pig's leg lingered in the air. We sat in the living room and put our feet up on the coffee table. It was almost midnight, and the room was lit by a single bulb. John still wore his sunglasses.

"I've grown. I really have in all ways," he told me. "I realize that I'm human, you know, and I do care about people."

I asked him whether he felt he had been rehabilitated. For some reason, the question irked him and triggered a scowl. He stood up quickly, grabbed my coat and held it out for me.

"Let's go," he said.

"Where are we going?" I wondered whether I was about to get thrown out.

"By the time I get to the car, I'll have it figured out," he said. He walked upstairs and told his sister he was leaving. Then we went outside and got into the car. But we just sat in front of the house.

"What's the matter?"

"I keep telling you," he said. "I want my own."

"Your own place?"

"My own everything! And I just don't feel comfortable. I want so much to say, 'Take off your shoes, get comfortable.' But I can't do that. It ain't my place." He began to feel sorry for himself. "I'm out here, struggling for something, anything."

Suddenly, he realized it was after midnight and now Easter.

"I'm going to go to church in the morning," he said quietly. "I'm going to wash up, change my clothes and go to church. I haven't gone since I've been out. Tomorrow is a new beginning.

"Dave, I'm going to close out the night for you. Thank you, man. Be cool, you hear?"

We parted with a handshake. Then he turned around and walked off into the dark toward his sister's house. I watched him, ready in case he turned around for a final wave. I thought he might need some reassurance, but I realized later that I did. John never looked back.

EPILOGUE

On the autumn anniversary of John's first year of freedom, I returned to New York for a small celebration. My gifts to John included a large kosher salami decorated with a lighted candle. John still had his good spirits and his will to survive. "I'm not going to give up," he told me. "Next year, I'm going to be doing better than I am this year, you know?"

After one year outside, John had a full-time job with a small plumbing company. He also had his own apartment, although it was unfurnished. And he had a stomach ulcer that came, he said, from the difficulties of his first year of readjustment to the outside world. Some day soon, I hope John will get permission from his parole officer to visit me here in Philadelphia.

NOTE FROM THE AUTHOR

This book reflects a lifetime of learning about the craft of column writing – with the assistance and support of many people, too many to list here. It all began when I was a young boy growing up on the Upper West Side of Manhattan and my father would send me out before dinner to buy the late edition of the *New York Post* containing the closing stock prices. I waited at the corner of 79th Street and Broadway for the *Post* truck to make its way north. The driver tossed out a bundle, and Joe the newsstand guy gave me the first copy off the top. I'd read it on the way home.

As I walked along Broadway, columnist Pete Hamill made me laugh or cry, sometimes both, with that day's column. Because this was the era of Vietnam and Watergate, I often felt great outrage at the subjects about which he wrote. I found it incredible that for 15 cents, you could feel that kind of emotion from reading words on a newspaper page. By age 14, I decided I wanted to be a columnist like him. But it was a dream that took decades to come true.

After Hamill, I discovered the works of Jimmy Breslin, who, in my mind, is the greatest columnist in the history of the world. From Breslin, whom I have never met, I learned almost everything I know about storytelling. The rest came from reading and studying the lifetime works of Ernie Pyle, F. Scott Fitzerald, Lewis Grizzard, Gay Talese and Tom Wolfe.

Although they wanted me to become a lawyer, my parents, Stanley and Denise Lieber, supported me in my dream to become a newspaperman. Later, my in-laws, John and Joan Pasciutti, proved to be wonderful supporters, too. They have been like a second set of parents.

My four years at the University of Pennsylvania working on the student newspaper, the *Daily Pennsylvanian*, was my true training ground. Subsequent work at the *Charleston Gazette* in West Virginia and *The Philadelphia Inquirer*, where I spent 10 years, prepared me for that glorious day in 1993 when I learned I would finally become a metro columnist.

At the *Star-Telegram*, I partnered with the greatest editor of my life, Lois Norder, who edited most of the pieces in this book. She taught me so much about writing and life that I can't begin to list all these lessons. I admire her skills, intelligence, courage, integrity and work ethic. Also at the *Star-Telegram*, I thank former editor Mike Blackman, who brought me to Texas; Jim Witt, the *Star-Telegram's* gutsy executive editor, who has always supported me in the crunch; Wes Turner, the publisher, who despite an advertising background ended up being one hell of a journalist; Kelley Pledger, the *Star-Telegram/Northeast Tarrant* marketing director who helped me with so many creative projects; the *Star-Telegram* copy desk, whose members copy-edited these columns and served me well all these years; copy editor Anita Robeson, who has helped me with all my books; and the *Star-Telegram* photo staff, whose members took several of the photographs in this book.

My friend, Jim Boughton, the greatest computer guru I know, has willingly spent his time partnering with me on many groundbreaking projects. In appreciation of his teaching, we have bestowed upon him the title of Director of New Media Convergence for Yankee Cowboy Publishing, which produced this book.

My friends at the National Society of Newspaper Columnists, where I have served in leadership positions for many years, must be thanked, too. This is a group devoted to excellence in column writing. For more about them, visit their Web site, www.columnists.com, ably maintained by Boughton.

Finally, this book could not have been done without assistance from designer Janet Long; Vicki Maloney, who is always there; Joyce Roach, my Texas mama; Christopher Cleveland, who gave me confidence; and Gerald and Deanna Luke, who taught me about the book business.

Of course, my family, whose lives are thoroughly documented in this book and who lost their privacy for the sake of my storytelling, must be acknowledged here. One can only imagine how difficult it is to be married to or be the child of a newspaper columnist, especially one such as me who spends so much time upstairs in his home office. Much thanks and love to Karen, Desiree, Jonathan and Austin for their patience, support and understanding. And thanks for the vacuuming, dusting, lawn mowing, weed trimming, flower planting, car washing, laundry and all the other chores that they have done for me so I could be upstairs working on my many projects.

I love you, and thank you for loving me.

A final note of appreciation to Sadie the Psycho Dog, who actually wasn't crazy at all. She didn't live to see this book finished, but that's OK. Because it's my book, she would not have cared anyway.

Dave Lieber
Fort Worth, Texas

ABOUT THE AUTHOR

Dave and his Psycho Dog

Dave Lieber is a senior columnist for the *Fort Worth Star-Telegram*. Since 1993, his general interest column has appeared three times a week on the cover of the Northeast Tarrant County news section.

He's a member of the *Star-Telegram/Northeast* editorial board. He also co-writes a four-panel comic satirizing suburban life that appears every Monday on the metro page. The cartoons were also published in book collections, *I Knew Rufe Snow Before He Was A Road* and *Give Us A Big Hug*.

Dave was America's first regular video columnist, with his innovation appearing, for several years, on the Web. The video column was cited for its pioneering role in American online journalism by *Editor and Publisher* magazine, *The American Newspaper Columnist* by Sam Riley and *You Can Write a Column* by Monica McCabe Cardoza.

Dave is co-founder of Summer Santa Inc., the largest children's charity in Northeast Tarrant County. Created under the auspices of the *Star-Telegram/Northeast*, Summer Santa distributes thousands of new toys to needy area children, sends hundreds of children to summer camp, buys back-to-school clothing and school supplies for dozens more and offers free medical checkups for children who otherwise could not afford to see a doctor. The program also funds after-school programs and a youth league. His annual Yankee Cowboy Celebrity Miniature Golf/Bowling Tournament is a major fund-raiser for the program. Summer Santa is run entirely by volunteers with no office expense or paid staff. Visit www.summersanta.org for more information.

Since 1995, Dave has been secretary for the 400-member National Society of Newspaper Columnists (www.columnists.com). For six years, he edited the society's newsletter, *The Columnist*.

Dave won the 1995 National Society of Newspaper Columnists Best General Interest Column award, was named Best Local

Columnist by *Fort Worth Weekly*, won the Dallas/Fort Worth Association of Black Communicators Award for Best Commentary, was named the *Star-Telegram's* Community Service Volunteer of the Year in 2000 and was the 2002 winner of the Will Rogers Humanitarian Award from the National Society of Newspaper Columnists.

The Will Rogers Humanitarian Award is given to the U.S. newspaper columnist "whose work best exemplifies the high ideals of the beloved philosopher-humorist who used his public forum for the benefit of his fellow human beings." Will Rogers Museums director Michelle Lefebvre-Carter commented that Lieber's work is "a reflection of the Will Rogers humanitarian spirit. Especially today, excellence in newspaper reporting and solid thinking and writing among columnists are vitally important for our democracy."